THE TWO TRADITIONS OF MEDITATION IN ANCIENT INDIA

The Two Traditions of Meditation in Ancient India

JOHANNES BRONKHORST

MOTILAL BANARSIDASS PUBLISHERS
PRIVATE LIMITED • DELHI

First Edition: Delhi, 1993
Reprint: Delhi, 2000

ISBN: 81-208-1114-3 (Cloth)
ISBN: 81-208-1643-9 (Paper)

Also available at:

MOTILAL BANARSIDASS

236, 9th Main III Block, Jayanagar, Bangalore 560 011
41 U.A. Bungalow Road, Jawahar Nagar, Delhi 110 007
8 Mahalaxmi Chamber, Warden Road, Mumbai 400 026
120 Royapettah High Road, Mylapore, Chennai 600 004
Sanas Plaza, 1302 Baji Rao Road, Pune 411 002
8 Camac Street, Calcutta 700 017
Ashok Rajpath, Patna 800 004
Chowk, Varanasi 221 001

Printed in India
BY JAINENDRA PRAKASH JAIN AT SHRI JAINENDRA PRESS,
A-45 NARAINA, PHASE-I, NEW DELHI 110 028
AND PUBLISHED BY NARENDRA PRAKASH JAIN FOR
MOTILAL BANARSIDASS PUBLISHERS PRIVATE LIMITED,
BUNGALOW ROAD, DELHI 110 007

Table of contents

Preface to the second edition vii

Acknowledgements to the first edition xv

Introduction xvii

Part I: Two traditions of meditation

ch. 1: The ascetic practices of the Bodhisattva 1

ch. 2: Further Buddhist criticism of alternative practices 26

Part II: The main stream

ch. 3: Early Jaina meditation 31

ch. 4: Meditation as part of asceticism in early Hindu scriptures 45

ch. 5: Theory and practice in the main stream 54

ch. 6: The influence from Buddhist meditation 68

Part III: Buddhist meditation

ch. 7: Influence on Buddhist meditation (I) 78

ch. 8: Influence on Buddhist meditation (II) 96

ch. 9: The origin of Buddhist meditation 112

ch. 10: Pratyekabuddhas, the Sutta Nipāta, and the early Saṅgha 124

Conclusion

ch. 11: The position and character of early Buddhist meditation 128

Abbreviations 129

Primary Sources 131

Modern Authors 135

Index 151

Preface to the second edition

The Two Traditions of Meditation in Ancient India has been out of print for a while. Reactions to the first edition have been varied, ranging from positive to critical. It is clear that these reactions are determined, at least to a large extent, by the positions of the scholars concerned with regard to the question of what can be expected from research into earliest Buddhism. The brief discussion that follows of some of the criticisms that have been expressed against the first edition, is therefore more than just a defence of this book; it is meant to be a contribution to a more general discussion regarding the aspirations and possibilities of scholarship in this particular field of study.

Lambert Schmithausen has recently (1990) distinguished three positions held by scholars of Buddhism with regard to the question whether and to what extent the early Buddhist texts can be regarded as faithfully preserving the doctrine of the Buddha himself at least *in essence*. They might be presented as follows : (i) stress on the fundamental homogeneity and substantial authenticity of at least a considerable part of the Nikāyic materials; (ii) scepticism with regard to the possibility of retrieving the doctrine of earliest Buddhism; (iii) cautious optimism in this respect. This book takes position (iii). This position is to be preferred to (ii) for purely methodological reasons : only those who seek may find, even if no success is guaranteed.[1]

The danger of position (i) is that it may raise a hypothesis into a principle. And once the homogeneity of the early Buddhist texts is taken as point of departure rather than as a hypothesis to be tested against the evidence, one is in the same situation as the Christian church, which managed to obstruct progress in Biblical studies for many centuries,

1. Position (ii) is essentially adopted in the review by S. Collins (1987). For a discussion of some of the points raised there, see my forthcoming review of T. E. Vetter's *The Ideas and Meditative Practices of Early Buddhism* in the *Indo-Iranian Journal*.

precisely because it insisted on the fundamental homogeneity of its scripture.[2] This parallelism becomes almost complete, once the further requirement is added that the early Buddhist texts have to be interpreted in the light of the later tradition.[3]

It would be unfair to those who uphold position (i) to put too much emphasis on the parallelism with the unfortunate history of Biblical studies. We must assume that they look upon their position as, in their eyes, the best hypothesis available, which they are ready to abandon at any time, if only good enough evidence were forthcoming. The present book concentrates on contradictions and inconsistencies. Upholders of position (i) – such as R. Gombrich (1990) – argue that some lack of homogeneity is only to be expected in the early Buddhist texts, even on the assumption that all of them go back to the Buddha himself. No far-reaching conclusions should therefore be drawn from 'inconsistencies' and 'contradictions', especially not where these latter occur in descriptions of such notoriously elusive 'things' as meditational states. Similar problems about 'contradictions' are voiced by D. S. Ruegg (1989 : 9 n.9) who, while specifically referring to the first edition of the present book, complains that the "treatment of the relevant material is not infrequently based on unexplicated or unexamined (and anything but self-evident) presuppositions about 'contradictions' in the tradition".

It seems that the main arguments of this book have escaped Gombrich and Ruegg. They may escape other readers too. For this reason these main arguments will be once more presented in this Preface, but in an abbreviated and differently arranged form. This new presentation will, I hope, show that the criticisms mentioned above are not applicable to this book. Details and references will be found in the main body of the book.

The point of departure is the undeniable fact that even the oldest Buddhist texts we have do not date back, in their present form, to the period of the Buddha. Linguistic considerations alone suffice to show that "all Buddhist texts, as they are read today, are not only heavily influenced by linguistic developments known to be much later than early days of Buddhism, but also reformulated perhaps, and certainly recast from one

2. I refer here to Gusdorf, 1988.
3. As is proposed by R. Gombrich (1988 : 21; cp. 1990 : 11-12).

language into another before they reached their present linguistic shape" (Hinüber, 1991: 184). There is therefore no guarantee whatsoever that all these texts represent the teachings of the Buddha, and it is at least conceivable that some of their contents are non-authentic.

How can we imagine non-authentic views and practices to have found their way into the canonical collections, primarily the collections of Sūtras ? This is not difficult. It is at least conceivable that in the process of collecting some texts or passages were included that contained elements that derived, ultimately, not from the teaching of the Buddha, but from other religious groups and ideals current at the time.

The preceding remarks concern *conceivable* events; no evidence has yet been presented that they actually took place. Suppose they did take place. How could we ever discover the non-authentic elements in the Buddhist texts? In general this would be difficult or even impossible. Elements that were not part of the teaching of the Buddha but were not rejected either, might find their way in – after or even before the death of the Buddha – without anyone ever noticing, least of all the modern scholar. Perhaps the only hope ever to identify non-authentic elements in the Buddhist texts is constituted by the special cases where elements which are recorded to have been rejected by the Buddha, yet found their way into the texts, and, moreover, are clearly identifiable as belonging to one or more movements other than Buddhism.

This gives us what might turn out to be an objective criterion for identifying foreign intrusions into the Buddhist texts : An element that is (i) rejected at some places in the Buddhist texts, (ii) accepted at others, and (iii) known to fit at least some non-Buddhist religious movements of the time, such an element is very likely to be a non-authentic intrusion into the Buddhist texts. As we have to work with only limited evidence, I would not know what better criterion there could be in the circumstances. Unfortunately, the importance of this criterion seems to have escaped all of my critics.

Of course, having a criterion in theory is one thing, applying it to the texts, quite another. This book tries to apply this criterion to the one aspect of Buddhism – perhaps the only one – where it seems to work: that of meditation. Much of the book is dedicated to the presentation of the meditational and ascetic practices and related ideas found in early Jainism and other non-Buddhist religious movements of early India. Since no one has criticized this presentation, whereas several scholars have expressed doubts with regard to the 'inconsistencies' and 'contradictions' in the Buddhist texts (see above), I shall concentrate on the latter. I shall briefly discuss some examples, all of them taken from the main body of the book:

1. The *Mahāparinirvāṇa Sūtra*, in its various recensions, records a discussion of the Buddha with someone called Putkasa (in Sanskrit) or Pukkusa (in Pāli). The Buddha here boasts that once, in a violent thunderstorm when lightning killed two farmers and four oxen nearby him, he did not notice it. It is known that abilities of this kind were sought after by certain non-Buddhists. Another Buddhist Sūtra (the *Indriyabhāvanā Sutta* of the Pāli canon and its parallel in Chinese translation), on the other hand, ridicules such 'cultivation of the senses' which leads to their non-functioning; the Buddha is here reported to say that if this is cultivation of the senses, the blind and deaf would be cultivators of the senses.

The passages here mentioned may not logically contradict each other, yet they come about as close to that as one could hope for in this type of texts: on one occasion the Buddha disapproves of the practice that aims at the complete suppression of all sense-activities, on another he boasts about his attainments in this direction. This situation calls for a solution. One solution would be to think that the Buddha changed his mind about this practice. A more plausible explanation is that a practice that was respected among non-Buddhists came to be ascribed to the Buddha, either before or after his death. This latter explanation implies that the practice concerned is not authentically Buddhist.

2. A Sūtra of the *Majjhima Nikāya* (the *Cūḷadukkhakkhandha Sutta*) as well as its parallels in Chinese translation describe and criticize the Jainas as practising 'annihilation of former actions by asceticism' and 'non-performing of new actions'. This can be accepted as an accurate description of the practices of the Jainas. But several other Sūtras of the Buddhist canon put almost the same words in the mouth of the Buddha, who here approves of these practices (see note 8 to chapter 2, below). Did the Buddha first hold one opinion, then to change his mind ? Or did he not

know how to describe his experiences ? Obviously it is far more plausible that, again, practices that were widely accepted outside the Buddhist fold, but not inside it, found their way in.

The argument here summarized is again presented, in a but slightly different form, by no one else than Ruegg, apparently without realizing it, in the very same book in which he dismisses my arguments. This situation is extraordinary enough to warrant quoting the passage concerned at length (Ruegg, 1989: 142-143):

> Now, in some old Buddhist canonical texts also there are in fact found certain references to the idea that liberation from Ill (*duḥkha*) results from, and consists in, the non-production of any future karman at all and from the ending, often through austerities (*tapas*), of any existing bad karman. This idea is there usually ascribed to the Nigaṇṭha Nātaputta (Nirgrantha Jñātṛputra), in other words to Mahāvīra and the Jainas. We also read that immobility of body and renunciation of speech bring Ease (*sukha*). Moreover, in a couple of Buddhist canonical texts the idea that no new karman at all should be generated, and that any existing karman should be ended, has even been connected with the Buddha himself in a sermon he once addressed to a Nirgrantha and in another one he addressed to Vappa, a disciple of the Nirgranthas.
>
> The connection of such a teaching with the Buddha himself seems nevertheless to be rare. When it does occur, it is evidently to be explained by the fact that his auditor was a Nirgrantha and that the teaching was thus intended as an introductory salvific device, a circumstance that would lend support to Kamalaśīla's statement denying that such relinquishement of all activity was the Buddha's own teaching. In the majority of other places where it has been mentioned in the Pāli canon, this doctrine has in fact been severely criticized. It is patently inconsistent with such basic principles of Buddhist doctrine as the four correct efforts (*sammāppadhāna / samyakprahāṇa*) ...

It is not a little surprising to see how Ruegg, who rejects my arguments, arrives here at my conclusions, using my arguments and basing himself on the inconsistencies whose very existence he had attributed to my ill-founded presuppositions. In the situation it is no doubt kindest to Professor Ruegg to assume that he dismissed my book without having read it.

3. The *Vitakkasanthāna Sutta* of the *Majjhima Nikāya* and its parallels in Chinese translation *recommend* the practising monk to 'restrain his thought with his mind, to coerce and torment it'. Exactly the same words are used elsewhere in the Pāli canon (in the *Mahāsaccaka Sutta, Bodhirājakumāra Sutta* and *Saṅgārava Sutta*) in order to describe the *futile* attempts of the Buddha before his enlightenment to reach liberation after the manner of the Jainas. Once again it is hard to see a better explanation than that these Jaina practices had come to be accepted by at least some Buddhists.

It would be unrealistic to expect that all 'contradictions' in the Buddhist canon are quite as explicit as the ones mentioned above. This does not however mean that they are any less real. Consider the following:

4. Four states of meditation are often enumerated in the Buddhist Sūtras in varying contexts, but almost always together. They are: 1) the Stage of Infinity of Space; 2) the Stage of Infinity of Perception; 3) the Stage of Nothingness; 4) the Stage of neither Ideation nor Non-Ideation. The texts say little by way of explanation of these stages, but the names make clear that they together form a list of graded exercises aimed at the cessation of all ideations. This aim conforms very well with the aims we have to ascribe to the early Jainas and those of similar convictions. Moreover, the Jaina scriptures describe 'reflection on infinity' as one of the accompaniments of 'pure meditation'. These stages are denounced elsewhere in the Buddhist canon, be it indirectly: The Buddha is said to have had two teachers before his enlightenment: Ārāḍa Kālāma and Udraka the son of Rāma. From the former he learned the Stage of Nothingness, from the latter the Stage of neither Ideation nor Non-

Ideation. However, the Buddha left these teachers, because he came to believe that these Stages would not lead him to his goal.

Here the question seems justified: do these stages lead to the goal or do they not ? Various answers can be imagined, such as, "they do to some extent, but not all the way", "the Buddha had second thoughts about the usefulness of these stages", etc. But I insist that there is a problem here that demands an answer, and not just a manifestation of my "unexplicated or unexamined (and anything but self-evident) presuppositions about 'contradictions' in the tradition", as Ruegg would have it. Criticism of this kind, which refuses to study arguments, is not only counter-productive, it constitutes one of the greatest enemies of scholarship which, as Gombrich rightly points out, should at least try to progress by argument. Returning to the Stage of Nothingness and the Stage of neither Ideation nor Non-Ideation, it will hardly be necessary to add that in my opinion they comply with the criterion of foreign intrusion into the Buddhist texts formulated above.

The conclusion that the above four meditational Stages were not accepted in earliest Buddhism finds support in an altogether unexpected quarter; for a detailed presentation of the argument I must refer the reader to BSOAS 48, 1985, pp. 305 f.[4] Among the early (Abhidharmic) *mātṛkās*, one seems to have been considered particularly important. It occurs a number of times in the early texts, but not always in exactly the same form; to an original enumeration of merely mental characteristics, meditational states came to be added. But initially the meditational states thus added did <u>not</u> contain the four Stages discussed above, even though these Stages, collectively known as 'the Formless States', are very prominent in the Buddhist scriptures as we have them. The most plausible explanation is again that the Formless States were not accepted during the earliest period of Buddhism.

5. The Buddhist texts are not of one mind concerning the time when liberation is reached. A great number of passages emphatically states that liberation is reached in this life, i.e., well before death. This is hardly

---

4. This article has been criticized by R. M. L. Gethin (1992: 281). Be it noted that this criticism –whatever its worth – does not affect the argument here presented.

surprising, for the Buddha himself is agreed to have passed many years teaching after his moment of liberation. Yet other passages speak about liberation as taking place at death. As in all the preceding cases, there is here a contradiction in the texts. Various solutions are conceivable, such as "the Buddha didn't know", "he expressed himself variously", "he changed his mind", "some are liberated at death, others in life", etc. Indeed, anyone with some imagination can add to this list of possibilities almost indefinitely. However, we know that among many non-Buddhists liberation took place at death, and that many Buddhist texts emphatically hold the opposite opinion. It is no doubt superfluous to add that an intrusion of foreign ideas seems to me most plausible here, too.

These examples should suffice to induce critics, at last, to read this book, rather than presenting their a priori reasons for thinking that the effort made in it cannot possibly lead anywhere. Scholarship should and indeed can only progress by argument, and this implies also: trying to understand someone else's arguments. Those who are not willing or able to do this, would have done better to ignore the book,[5] rather than pronounce facile judgments about it.

The first edition of this book was published in 1986, by Franz Steiner Verlag Wiesbaden GmbH, Stuttgart. The preparation of this second edition has permitted me to correct a number of, usually minor, mistakes, and make other improvements. For ease of comparison, the page numbers of the first edition are indicated in the margin in the present edition. The help provided by Yves Ramseier in the preparation of this edition is here gratefully acknowledged.

5. This is done in some recent surveys of Buddhism, such as Harvey, 1990; and Klimkeit, 1990.

Addendum:

The numbers in the margins refer to the page numbering in the first edition of the book.

Acknowledgements to the first edition

This book was written with the financial assistance of the Netherlands Organisation for the Advancement of Pure Research (ZWO). This organisation also enabled me to visit India in order to work with various Jainas, laymen and monks. From among these I like to thank in particular Prof. N. Tatia and Muni Jambūvijayaji for their help. In Europe I received help and encouragement from many friends and colleagues. Here I can mention but a few: Professors L. Schmithausen and T. E. Vetter, and Dr. H. Tieken. I like to thank Prof. A. Wezler for his support and enthusiasm in getting this book published in Germany, when ZWO refused to finance its publication.

Introduction

[XI]

The main aim of the present study is to find out what early Buddhist meditation was by ascertaining what it was not. The results are therefore largely negative, but not any less interesting.

The fact is that everyone who wishes to form an opinion on early Buddhism has to choose from a bewildering mass of often contradictory statements in the Buddhist canon. This choice is in danger of being arbitrary, for little is known about the relative chronology of the different parts of the canon. There can be no doubt that the canon – including the older parts, the *Sūtra*- and *Vinaya-Piṭaka* – was composed over a long period of time. Only by assuming this can we make sense of its often glaring contradictions. But which parts are the oldest ?

In the following pages I shall try to answer this question in so far as it concerns Buddhist meditation by a method which, to my knowledge, has never yet been employed. At a number of places the Buddhist canon criticizes alternative practices which are claimed by others to lead to the highest good. These alternative practices can be identified in the early scriptures of Jainism and Hinduism. The idea behind this method is that those alternative practices, even when they are described and approved of in other parts of the Buddhist canon, cannot be considered to be authentic to Buddhism; they must be looked upon as later borrowings from outside. Traces of earliest Buddhism therefore must be sought among the practices which are opposed to those alternative ones.

Does this deny the possibility that early Buddhism shared certain features with the other religious movements that existed in India in its time ? Clearly not! We do not wish to exclude features from early Buddhism simply because they are present elsewhere. We wish to exclude such features only if other, contrasting or even contradictory, features exist in the early Buddhist scriptures which are explicitly preferred to the former ones in those scriptures.

Why should features which are peculiar to Buddhism have greater likelihood to belong to early Buddhism than features which also occur

elsewhere ? This is partly a matter of definition. By 'early Buddhism' we mean the beginning of the tradition peculiar to Buddhism. The question will remain whether all these peculiar features came more or less at the
[XII] same time and can therefore be ascribed to a single founder of this tradition, i.e., to the historical Buddha. All we can say is that the Buddhist tradition clearly points to such a person. Moreover, it is known that religious traditions tend to be conservative. They may inadvertently borrow elements from outside; they may also develop and undergo modifications. They will not as a rule introduce complete novelties. This privilege is reserved for the founder of such a tradition.

The execution of the above program will enable us to reach a better understanding of early Buddhist meditation. It also allows us to obtain more insight into the alternative, non-Buddhist, practices, especially of the early period. The circumstance that the two traditions intermingled at a rather early date had hidden from previous investigators the ideas underlying the non-Buddhist practices. It also obscured the influence which these ideas had on virtually all systems of Hindu philosophy.

A few words must be said about methodology. This book presents a *theory* about what early Buddhism – or rather, certain aspects of it – was and what it was not. That is to say, this book does not merely reproduce the texts on which it is based, and is not simply the result of 'just reading the texts' (if such a thing is at all possible; cf. Bronkhorst, 1986 : Introduction). In a way it contains *more* than what can be found in the texts. In return, it *explains* contradictions and other features of the texts which would otherwise remain obscure. There is no way to *prove* that the theory presented in this book is right. But this does not by itself detract from its value. A great deal, if not all, we know about the world is of such a theoretical nature.

Such a starting point has consequences for those who wish to disagree with my theory. It will not just be enough to say that it has not been proved. It may be more worthwhile to try and show that the theory does not fit certain facts. Criticism of this kind, though not without value, will at best bring us back to the situation where the contradictions in the Buddhist canon are, again, unexplained. Really constructive criticism of my theory will present *an even better theory*.

Part I: Two traditions of meditation. [1]

I. The ascetic practices of the Bodhisattva.

1.1. At three places[1] in the *Majjhima Nikāya* of the Pāli Buddhist canon an episode is found in which the Buddha describes how he, before his enlightenment, tried out two methods which he then discovered did not lead to the desired end. The two methods are 'meditation without breath' and 'reduced intake of food'. The episode reads[2] in the *Mahāsaccaka Sutta*:[3]

MN I.120-121 { (p. 242, l. 23:) Then, Aggivessana, I thought : 'Let me, closing my teeth, pressing my palate with my tongue, restrain my thought with my mind, let me coerce and torment it'. Then indeed, Aggivessana, closing my teeth and pressing my palate with my tongue, I restrained my thought with my mind, coerced and tormented it. } While I, Aggivessana, closing my teeth and pressing my palate with my tongue, restrained my thought with my mind, coerced and tormented it, sweat came from my armpits.

MN I.121 { Just as when, Aggivessana, a strong man, taking a weaker

---

1. Mahāsaccaka Sutta, MN I. 242-46, Nālandā ed. vol. I, p. 301-05; Bodhirājakumāra Sutta, MN II.93, Nālandā ed. vol. II, p. 326-31; Saṅgārava Sutta, MN II.212, Nālandā ed. vol. II, p. 490-94.
2. References to other parts of the Pāli canon where identical or closely similar passages occur are given to the left of the passages concerned.
3. (p. 242, l. 23:) *tassa mayhaṃ aggivessana etad ahosi: yan nūnāhaṃ dantehi dantam ādhāya jivhāya tāluṃ āhacca cetasā cittaṃ abhiniggaṇheyyaṃ abhinippīḷeyyaṃ abhisantāpeyyan ti / so kho ahaṃ aggivessana dantehi dantam ādhāya jivhāya tāluṃ āhacca cetasā cittaṃ abhiniggaṇhāmi abhinippīḷemi abhisantāpemi / tassa mayhaṃ aggivessana dantehi dantam ādhāya jivhāya tāluṃ āhacca cetasā cittaṃ abhiniggaṇhato abhinippīḷayato abhisantāpayato kacchehi sedā muccanti / seyyathā pi aggivessana balavā puriso dubbalataraṃ purisaṃ sīse vā gahetvā khandhe vā gahetvā abhiniggaṇheyya abhinipīḷeyya abhisantāpeyya,*

MN I. 121 man by his head or taking him by his shoulder, may
restrain, coerce and torment him, just so indeed,
Aggivessana, while I, closing my teeth and pressing my
palate with my tongue, restrained my thought with my
mind, coerced and tormented it, sweat come from my
armpits. But, Aggivessana, my energy was aroused, not
MN I. 21; 117; 186 shrinking, my mindfulness was alert, not distracted, but[4]
my body was impetuous, not calmed, while I was
harassed by that painful exertion. Even such a painful
experience, Aggivessana, when it happened to me, did not
completely take hold of my mind.

(p. 243, 1. 4:) Then, Aggivessana, I thought: 'Let me
perform meditation without breath'. Then indeed,
Aggivessana, I stopped breathing out and breathing in,
both through the mouth and through the nose. When,
Aggivessana, my breathing out and breathing in had been
stopped, both through the mouth and through the nose,
there came about the extremely strong noise of winds
[2] which went out through my ears. Just as when an
SN I. 106 extremely strong noise comes about when the bellows of
a smith are blown, just so indeed, Aggivessana, there

---

evam eva kho me aggivessana dantehi dantam ādhāya jivhāya tāluṃ āhacca cetasā cittaṃ abhiniggaṇhato abhinippīḷayato abhisantāpayato kacchehi sedā muccanti / āraddhaṃ kho pana me aggivessana viriyaṃ hoti asallīnaṃ, upaṭṭhitā sati asammuṭṭhā, sāraddho ca pana me kāyo hoti appaṭippasaddho ten'eva dukkhappadhānena padhānābhitunnassa sato / evarūpā pi kho me aggivessana uppannā dukkhā vedanā cittaṃ na pariyādāya tiṭṭhati /

(p. 243, l. 4:) *tassa mayhaṃ aggivessana etad ahosi: yan nūnāhaṃ appānakaṃ jhānaṃ jhāyeyyan ti / so kho ahaṃ aggivessana mukhato ca nāsato ca assāsapassāse uparundhiṃ / tassa mayhaṃ aggivessana mukhato ca nāsato ca assāsapassāsesu uparuddhesu kaṇṇasotehi vātānaṃ nikkhamantānaṃ adhimatto saddo hoti / seyyathā pi nāma kammāragaggariyā dhamamānāya adhimatto saddo hoti, evam eva kho me aggivessana mukhato ca nāsato ca assāsapassāsesu /*

---

4. MN I.21, 117, 186 have: "my energy was aroused, not shrinking, my mindfulness was alert, not distracted, my body was calmed, not impetuous, ...". This justifies the translation 'but' for *ca*.

came about the extremely strong noise of winds which
SN I. 106 went out through the ears, when my breathing out and
breathing in had been stopped both through the mouth and
through the nose. But, Aggivessana, my energy was
MN I. 21; 117; aroused, not shrinking, my mindfulness was alert, not
186 distracted, but my body was impetuous, not calmed, while
I was harassed by that painful exertion. Even such a
painful experience, Aggivessana, when it happened to me,
did not completely take hold of my thought.

(p. 243 l. 18): Then, Aggivessana, I thought: 'Let me perform meditation fully without breath'. Then indeed, Aggivessana, I stopped breathing out and breathing in through mouth, nose and ears. When, Aggivessana, my breathing out and breathing in had been stopped through mouth, nose and ears, extremely strong winds shook up
MN II.193 my head. Just as when, Aggivessana, a strong man may
SN IV.56 destroy a head with the sharp edge of a sword, just so
AN III.379 indeed, Aggivessana, extremely strong winds shook up
my head, when breathing out and breathing in had been stopped through mouth, nose and ears. But, Aggivessana, my energy ... did not completely take hold of my mind.

(p. 243, l. 32:) Then, Aggivessana, I thought: 'Let me perform meditation fully without breath'. Then indeed,

---

uparuddhesu kaṇṇasotehi vātānaṃ nikkhamantānaṃ adhimatto saddo hoti āraddhaṃ kho pana me aggivessana viriyaṃ hoti asallīnaṃ, upaṭṭhitā sati asammuṭṭhā, sāraddho ca pana me kāyo hoti appaṭippassaddho ten'eva dukkhappadhānena padhānābhitunnassa sato / evarūpā pi kho me aggivessana uppannā dukkhā vedanā cittaṃ na pariyādāya tiṭṭhati /

(p. 243, l. 18:) *tassa mayhaṃ aggivessana etad ahosi: yan nūnāhaṃ appānakaṃ yeva jhānaṃ jhāyeyyan ti / so kho ahaṃ aggivessana mukhato ca nāsato ca kaṇṇato ca assāsapassāse uparundhiṃ / tassa mayhaṃ aggivessana mukhato ca nāsato ca kaṇṇato ca assāsapassāsesu uparuddhesu adhimattā vātā muddhānaṃ ūhananti / seyyathā pi aggivessana balavā puriso tiṇhena sikharena muddhānaṃ abhimantheyya, evam eva kho me aggivessana mukhato ca nāsato ca kaṇṇato ca assāsapassāsesu uparuddhesu adhimattā vātā muddhānaṃ ūhananti / āraddhaṃ kho pana me aggivessana viriyaṃ ... na pariyādāya tiṭṭhati /*

(p. 243, l. 32:) *tassa mayhaṃ aggivessana etad ahosi: yan nūnāhaṃ appānakaṃ*

Aggivessana, I stopped breathing out and breathing in through mouth, nose and ears. When, Aggivessana, my breathing out and breathing in had been stopped through mouth, nose and ears, there came about extremely strong headaches in my head. Just as when, Aggivessana, a strong man may place a turban on a head with a strong strip of leather, just so indeed, Aggivessana, there came about extremely strong headaches in my head when breathing out and breathing in had been stopped through mouth, nose and ears. But, Aggivessana, my energy did not completely take hold of my mind.

MN II. 193; SN IV. 56; AN III. 380

[3] (p. 244, l. 9:) Then, Aggivessana, I thought: 'Let me perform meditation fully without breath'. Then indeed, Aggivessana, I stopped breathing out and breathing in through mouth, nose and ears. When, Aggivessana, my breathing out and breathing in had been stopped through mouth, nose and ears, extremely strong winds cut my belly all around. Just as when, Aggivessana, a skilled butcher or apprentice of a butcher may cut a belly all around with a sharp butcher's knife, just so indeed, Aggivessana, extremely strong winds cut my belly all around. But, Aggivessana, my energy ... did not completely take hold of my mind.

MN II. 193; SN IV. 56; AN III. 380

---

yeva jhānaṃ jhāyeyyan ti / so kho ahaṃ aggivessana mukhato ca nāsato ca kaṇṇato ca assāsapassāse uparundhiṃ / tassa mayhaṃ aggivessana mukhato ca nāsato ca kaṇṇato ca assāsapassāsesu uparuddhesu adhimattā sīse sīsavedanā honti / seyyathā pi aggivessana balavā puriso daḷhena varattakhaṇḍena sīse sīsaveṭhaṃ dadeyya, evam eva kho me aggivessana mukhato ca nāsato ca kaṇṇato ca assāsapassāsesu uparuddhesu adhimattā sīse sīsavedanā honti / āraddhaṃ kho pana me aggivessana viriyaṃ ... na pariyādāya tiṭṭhati /

(p. 244, l. 9:) *tassa mayhaṃ aggivessana etad ahosi: yan nūnāhaṃ appānakaṃ yeva jhānaṃ jhāyeyyan ti / so kho ahaṃ aggivessana mukhato ca nāsato ca kaṇṇato ca assāsapassāse uparundhiṃ / tassa mayhaṃ aggivessana mukhato ca nāsato ca kaṇṇato ca assāsapassāsesu uparuddhesu adhimattā vātā kucchiṃ parikantanti / seyyathā pi aggivessana dakkho goghātako vā goghātakantevāsī va tiṇhena govikantanena kucchiṃ parikanteyya, evam eva kho me aggivessana adhimattā vātā kucchiṃ parikantanti / āraddhaṃ kho pana me aggivessana viriyaṃ ... na pariyādāya tiṭṭhati /*

(p. 244, l. 23:) Then, Aggivessana, I thought: 'Let me perform meditation fully without breath'. Then indeed, Aggivessana, I stopped breathing out and breathing in through mouth, nose and ears. When, Aggivessana, my breathing out and breathing in had been stopped through mouth, nose and ears, there came about an extremely strong heat in my body. Just as when, Aggivessana, two strong men, taking a weaker man by both his arms, may burn and roast him on a pit of burning coal, just so indeed, Aggivessana, there came about an extremely strong heat in my body when my breathing out and breathing in had been stopped through mouth, nose and ears. But, Aggivessana, my energy ... did not completely take hold of my mind.

MN II. 193; SN IV. 56; AN III. 380

(p. 244, l. 37:) The gods moreover, Aggivessana, seeing me spoke thus: 'The recluse Gotama is dead'. Some gods spoke thus: 'the recluse Gotama is not dead, but he is dying'. Other gods spoke thus: 'The recluse Gotama is not dead, nor is he dying, the recluse Gotama is an *arahant*, that condition is exactly the one of an *arahant* '.

(p. 245, l. 6): Then, Aggivessana, I thought: 'Let me completely abstain from taking food'. Then indeed,

---

(p.244, l. 23) *tassa mayhaṃ aggivessana etad ahosi: yan nūnāhaṃ appānakaṃ yeva jhānaṃ jhāyeyyan ti / so kho ahaṃ aggivessana mukhato ca nāsato ca kaṇṇato ca assāsapassāse uparundhiṃ / tassa mayhaṃ aggivessana mukhato ca nāsato ca kaṇṇato ca assāsapassāsesu uparuddhesu adhimatto kāyasmiṃ ḍāho hoti / seyyathā pi aggivessana dve balavanto purisā dubbalataraṃ purisaṃ nānābāhāsu gahetvā aṅgārakāsuyā santāpeyyuṃ samparitāpeyyuṃ, evam eva kho me aggivessana mukhato ca nāsato ca kaṇṇato ca assāsapassāsesu uparuddhesu adhimatto kāyasmiṃ ḍāho hoti / āraddhaṃ kho pana me aggivessana viriyaṃ ... na pariyādāya tiṭṭhati /*

(p. 244, l. 37:) *api 'ssu maṃ aggivessana devatā disvā evam āhaṃsu: kālakato samaṇo gotamo ti / ekaccā devatā evam āhaṃsu: na kālakato samaṇo gotamo, api ca kālaṃ karotīti / ekaccā devatā evam āhaṃsu: na kālakato samaṇo gotamo na pi kālaṃ karoti, arahaṃ samaṇo gotamo, vihāro tv eva so arahato evarūpo hotīti /*

(p. 245, l. 6:) *tassa mayhaṃ aggivessana etad ahosi: yan nūnāhaṃ sabbaso*

Aggivessana, the gods, approaching me, said this: 'Don't you, Sir, completely abstain from taking food. If indeed,
[4] Sir, you will completely abstain from taking food, then we shall feed you divine nutritive essence through the pores of your skin, and thereby you will stay alive'. Then, Aggivessana, I thought: 'If I promised to completely abstain from taking food, these gods would feed me divine nutritive essence through the pores of my skin, and thereby I would stay alive; thus I would [speak] untruth'. Then indeed, Aggivessana, I rejected those gods, and said 'enough'.

(p. 245, l. 17:) Then, Aggivessana, I thought: 'Let me take food little by little, drop by drop, soup of kidney-beans, or soup of vetch, or soup of chick-peas, or soup of peas'. Then, Aggivessana, while I took food little by little, drop by drop, soup of kidney-beans, or soup of vetch, or soup of chick-peas, or soup of peas, my body became extremely thin. Just like the joints of the *āsītika* or the
MN I. 80 joints of the *kāla,* my limbs, great and small, became just so on account of taking so little food. Just like the foot of

---

āhārupacchedāya paṭipajjeyyan ti / atha kho maṃ aggivessana devatā upasaṅkamitvā etad avocuṃ: mā kho tvaṃ mārisa sabbaso āhārupacchedāya paṭipajji, sace kho tvaṃ mārisa sabbaso āhārupacchedāya paṭipajjissasi tassa te mayaṃ dibbaṃ ojaṃ lomakūpehi ajjhoharissāma, tāya tvaṃ yāpessasīti / tassa mayhaṃ aggivessana etad ahosi: ahañ c'eva kho pana sabbaso ajaddhukaṃ paṭijāneyyaṃ imā ca me devatā dibbaṃ ojaṃ lomakūpehi ajjhohareyyuṃ tāya cāhaṃ yāpeyyaṃ, taṃ mama assa musā ti / so kho ahaṃ aggivessana tā devatā paccācikkhāmi, halan ti vadāmi /

(p. 245, l. 17:) *tassa mayhaṃ aggivessana etad ahosi: yan nūnāhaṃ thokaṃ thokaṃ āhāraṃ āhāreyyaṃ pasataṃ pasataṃ, yadi vā muggayūsaṃ yadi vā kulatthayūsaṃ yadi vā kaḷāyayūsaṃ yadi vā hareṇukayūsan ti / so kho ahaṃ aggivessana thokaṃ thokaṃ āhāraṃ āhāresiṃ pasataṃ pasatam, yadi vā muggayūsaṃ yadi vā kulatthayūsaṃ yadi vā kaḷāyayūsaṃ yadi vā hareṇukayūsaṃ / tassa mayhaṃ aggivessana thokaṃ thokaṃ āhāraṃ āhārayato pasataṃ pasatam, yadi vā muggayūsaṃ yadi vā kulatthayūsaṃ yadi va kaḷāyayūsaṃ yadi vā hareṇukayūsaṃ, adhimattakasimānaṃ patto kāyo hoti / seyyathā pi nāma āsītikapabbāni vā kālāpabbāni vā evam eva 'ssu me aṅgapaccaṅgāni bhavanti tāy'ev'appāhāratāya, seyyathā pi nāma oṭṭhapadaṃ evam eva 'ssu me ānisadaṃ*

MN I. 80

a camel, my behind became just so on account of taking so little food. Just like a line of balls, my backbone became similarly bent up and bent down, on account of taking so little food. Just as the supporting beams in an old shed are breaking off and falling to pieces, just so my ribs were breaking off and falling to pieces on account of taking so little food. Just as in a deep well the glitter of water is seen, deep and low-lying, just so the glitter of my eyes was seen, deep and low-lying in the sockets, on account of taking so little food. Just as a bitter gourd, cut off while still unripe, becomes shrivelled and withered on account of wind and heat, just so the skin of my head became shrivelled and withered on account of taking so little food. Then indeed, Aggivessana, [thinking:] 'I shall touch the skin of my belly', I got hold of my backbone, [thinking:] 'I shall touch my backbone', I got hold of the skin of my belly, since, Aggivessana, the skin of my belly had become stuck to my backbone on account of taking so little food. Then indeed, Aggivessana, [thinking:] 'I shall defecate or urinate', I fell down, head forward, at that very place, on account of taking so little food. Then indeed, Aggivessana, soothing this my body I rubbed over my limbs with my hand. While I, Aggivessana, rubbed over

[5]

hoti tāy'ev'appāhāratāya, seyyathā pi nāma vaṭṭanāvaḷī evam eva 'ssu me piṭṭhikaṇṭako unnatāvanato hoti tāy'ev'appāhāratāya, seyyathā pi nāma jarasālāya gopānasiyo oluggaviluggā bhavanti evam eva 'ssu me phāsuḷiyo oluggaviluggā bhavanti tāy'ev'appāhāratāya, seyyathā pi nāma gambhīre udapāne udakatārakā gambhīragatā okkhāyikā dissanti evam eva 'ssu me akkhikūpesu akkhitārakā gambhīragatā okkhāyikā dissanti tāy'ev'appāhāratāya, seyyathā pi nāma tittakālābu āmakacchinno vātātapena sampuṭito hoti sammilāto evam eva 'ssu me sīsacchavi sampuṭitā hoti sammilātā tāy'ev'appāhāratāya / so kho ahaṃ aggivessana udaracchaviṃ parimasissāmī 'ti piṭṭhikaṇṭakaṃ yeva parigaṇhāmi, piṭṭhikaṇṭakaṃ parimasissāmī 'ti udaracchaviṃ yeva parigaṇhāmi / yāva 'ssu me aggivessana udaracchavi piṭṭhikaṇṭakaṃ allīnā hoti tāy'ev'appāhāratāya / so kho ahaṃ aggivessana vaccaṃ vā muttaṃ vā karissāmīti tattheva avakujjo papatāmi tāy'ev'appāhāratāya / so kho ahaṃ aggivessana imam eva kāyaṃ assāsento pāṇinā gattāni anomajjāmi / tassa mayhaṃ aggivessana pāṇinā gattāni anomajjato

MN I.80 my limbs with my hand, the hairs, having fetid roots, fell down from my body on account of taking so little food.

(p. 246, l. 12:) People moreover, Aggivessana, seeing me spoke thus: 'The recluse Gotama is black'. Some people spoke thus: 'The recluse Gotama is not black, the recluse Gotama is brown'. Other people spoke thus: 'The recluse Gotama is not black, nor is he brown, the recluse Gotama has a fair[5] skin (*manguracchavi*)'. So much, Aggivessana, the colour of my skin, [though] fully clean and fully pure, had become destroyed on account of taking so little food.

(p. 246, l. 20:) Then, Aggivessana, I thought: 'The recluses or Brahmins of the past who experienced painful, sharp, severe sensations [which were] due to [self-inflicted] torture,[6] [experienced] this much at the most, not more than this. Also the recluses or Brahmins of the future who will experience painful, sharp, severe sensations [which will be] due to [self-inflicted] torture, [will experience] this much at the most, not more than this. Also the recluses or Brahmins of the present who experience painful, sharp, severe sensations [which are]

---

pūtimūlāni lomāni kāyasmā papatanti tāy'ev'appāhāratāya /

(p. 246, l. 12:) *api 'ssu maṃ aggivessana manussā disvā evam āhaṃsu: kāḷo samaṇo gotamo ti* / *ekacce manussā evam āhaṃsu: na kāḷo samaṇo gotamo, sāmo samaṇo gotamo ti* / *ekacce manussā evam āhaṃsu: na kāḷo samaṇo gotamo na pi sāmo, manguracchavi samaṇo gotamo ti* / *yāva'ssu me aggivessana tāva parisuddho chavivaṇṇo pariyodāto upahato hoti tāy'ev'appāhāratāya* /

(p. 246, l. 20:) *tassa mayhaṃ aggivessana etad ahosi: ye kho keci atītaṃ addhānaṃ samaṇā vā brāhmaṇā vā opakkamikā dukkhā tippā kaṭukā vedanā vedayiṃsu, etāvaparamaṃ nayito bhiyyo; ye pi hi keci anāgatam addhānaṃ samaṇā vā brāhmaṇā vā opakkamikā dukkhā tippā kaṭukā vedanā vedayissanti,*

---

5. See below, point (iv).
6. *opakkamika*. The parallel passages in the *Mahāvastu* (II, p. 130) and *Lalitavistara* (p. 263) have *ātmopakramika*; see also *Mahāvastu* II, p. 121-23, *Lalitavistara* p. 246-48.

> due to [self-inflicted] torture, [experience] this much at the most, not more than this. But indeed I do not attain, through these severe and difficult practices, excellence in knowledge and insight which is truly noble and transcends the human condition. Could there be another road toward enlightenment ?'

This episode contains two features which suggest that non-Buddhist, most probably Jaina, practices are described :

(i) After the "meditation fully without breath", some gods think that Gotama is dead, others that he is dying, others again observe that "that condition is exactly the one of an *arahant*". Obviously Gotama's condition is not "exactly the one of an *arahant*" in the Buddhist sense of [6]
this word. Here the term *arahant is* reserved[7] for those who have followed to the end the road to salvation taught by the Buddha, as also for the Buddha himself after his enlightenment. The practices described in the present passage are without value for the attainment of (Buddhist) salvation, and to be discarded by Buddhist *arahants*. However, this same term (or its equivalent, in Sanskrit *arhant,* in Ardha-Māgadhī *araha, arihaṃta*) was also used by the Jainas, and perhaps the Ājīvikas (see Basham, 1951: 56, 140), to designate those who have reached the highest

---

etāvaparamaṃ nayito bhiyyo; ye pi hi keci etarahi samaṇā vā brāhmaṇā vā opakkamikā dukkhā tippā kaṭukā vedanā vediyanti, etāvaparamaṃ nayito bhiyyo / na kho panāhaṃ imāya kaṭukāya dukkarakārikāya adhigacchāmi uttariṃ manussadhammā alamariyañāṇadassanavisesaṃ, siyā nu kho añño maggo bodhāyāti /

7. A few possible exceptions occur in the *Pāṭika Sutta* (nr. 24) of the *Dīgha Nikāya* (III, 7, 10, 11), where the term is used - by Sunakkhadatta, who has left the Buddhist order - in connection with certain ascetics. It is hard to decide if the term is used here, for once, in its literal sense ('deserving, respectable'), or if it is used to indicate the foolishness of Sunakkhadatta, who indeed is repeatedly called *moghapurisa* 'foolish man' in that Sūtra. T.W. and C.A.F. Rhys Davids' (1921: 3-6) contention that in the *Pāṭika Sutta* as well as in our *Mahāsaccaka Sutta* the term is used in its supposedly pre-Buddhistic sense ("we may take it that ... the word ... had come to be popularly applied, not only to priests and kings, but also to ascetics") is unacceptable, the more so since this part of the *Mahāsaccaka Sutta* cannot be very early; see below, § 1.4. Some more places where *arahant* may be used in its literal sense have been noted by Franke (1913: 300-301). See further Horner, 1936: 77-95.

stage possible while still embodied as human beings.[8] Both the Jainas and the Ājīvikas are known for their inclination towards asceticism, so that we must conclude that the gods used the word *arahant* in the sense current among these religious wanderers.

(ii) The reduced intake of food is preceded by the intention to completely abstain from taking food. The reduced intake of food, with all its horrors, is therefore no more than a second choice. The story loses much of its force by the fact that the exalted initial intention comes to nothing. Why then was it added?[9] The question resolves itself once we assume that our episode is directed against the Jainas, among whom the most respected way of dying is by voluntary starvation.[10]

The following feature points in the same direction:

(iii) The phrase "painful, sharp, severe sensations [which are] due to [self-inflicted] torture" (*opakkamikā dukkhā tippā kaṭukā vedanā*) occurs, apart from this episode, in two and only two other contexts in the Pāli canon, both times in connection with Jainas (Nigaṇṭha; see below): in the *Devadaha Sutta* (nr. 101 of the *Majjhima Nikāya*, vol. II, p. 218-19) and in the *Cūḷadukkhakkhandha Sutta* (nr. 14 of the *Majjhima Nikāya*, vol. I, p. 92).

Perhaps we may add:

(iv) The reduced intake of food is said to evoke three kinds of reactions from onlookers. Some say that Gotama is black, others that he is brown, others again that he has a fair skin (*maṅguracchavi*). The exact

8. Also the Vrātyas used the term; see Weber, 1876: 85.
9. It is not present in the parallel passage in the *Mahāsīhanāda Sutta* of the *Majjhima Nikāya* (I.80).
10. Cf. Schubring, 1935: 182-83; Kamptz, 1929; and ch. III below. Perhaps we may look at the following as a confirmation that our episode is directed against the Jainas : the gods assure Gotama that they will keep him alive in a way which is familiar from the Jaina scriptures. They want to feed Gotama divine nutritive essence through the pores of his skin (*lomakūpesu*). Feeding of this kind (*lom' āhāra*) is known from the (late) *Paṇṇavaṇā Sutta* (ch. 28, § 1859-61). "Here we learn that infernal beings, celestial beings and one-sensed beings undertake feeding through skin (1859-60). The two-sensed up to the five-sensed human beings undertake the feeding through skin as well as mouth (1861)." (*Paṇṇavaṇā*, part 2, Intr. p. 396-97). Cf. *Sūtrakṛtaṅganiryukti* p. 228-29, gāthās 171f.

significance of *maṅguracchavi* is not known. It occurs always[11] (DN I. 193; 242; MN I. 429; II. 33; and here) in the company of *kāḷa*, "black", *sāma* "brown". The three terms seem intended to cover among them the whole range of colours a human being can have: in three of the five cases they enumerate the varieties of complexion that an unknown beautiful girl can have, so that "having a fair skin" seems to be a reasonable translation. In the circumstances, only the first two terms are appropriate. The third [7]
one may have been added[12] under the influence of and in order to ridicule the belief which survived among the Digambaras, that Mahāvīra shone like a crystal (Jaini, 1979:35; cf., e.g., Raviṣeṇa's *Padmapurāṇa* II.92 (vol. I, p. 18)). [This idea is not totally foreign to the ancient Buddhist scriptures. Sn 548 describes the Buddha as 'golden coloured' (*suvaṇṇa-vaṇṇa*), Sn 550 as 'shining like the sun' (*ādicco va virocasi*), Sn 551 as 'whose skin resembles gold' (*kañcanasannibhattaca*); see also Th 818f. See however ch. X below.]

However, it is not impossible that the disagreement among the onlookers does not concern the present colour of Gotama, but rather his original colour which had now become unrecognizable.[13]

1.2. The episode on meditation without breath and reduced intake of food occurs in the *Ekottara Āgama* preserved in Chinese, as well. It reads (T.125, p. 670c18-671b4):[14]

---

11. That is to say, in the Pāli canon. Prof. K.R. Norman informs me that *maṅguracchavi* occurs with *kāla* and *odāta* at Vism 184 and Sp 238, and observes that it "presumably represents a colour (half-way) between black and white", perhaps '(dark) brown'. Norman further suggests a connection with *maṅgula* / *maṅgulī*, which seems to be used only in a bad sense.
It seems however dubious to attach too much worth to the opinions of the commentators, who may often, like us, have tried to make sense of the material before them and may occasionally have failed to draw the correct conclusions. Moreover, *maṅgura* may be connected with *maṅkura*, which has been preserved by the Sanskrit lexicographers in the sense 'mirror'; this suggests 'shining' for *maṅgura*.
12. It is hard to believe that *maṅguracchavi* was added by the redactors of the Pāli canon in their efforts to unify the texts, since the *Mahāvastu* (II, p. 126-30) and the *Lalitavistara* (p. 255) use the corresponding term *madguracchavi* in the same context.
13. This was pointed out to me by Prof. Schmithausen in a written communication.
14. Prof. E. Zürcher was kind enough to lend assistance in reading this passage. The responsibility for the translation remains however mine.

(670c18:) Then I thought: 'Why should I still eat ? I can completely abstain from taking food'. Because this thought arose in me, the gods came to me and said: 'Do not now stop eating. If you'll stop eating, we'll prolong and preserve your life with the pure force of nectar'. Then again I thought: 'What reason is there now to stop eating, [since] it will instigate the gods to give me nectar. I would deceive [others and myself]'. At that time I thought: 'Now I can eat a residue of sesamum[15] and rice'. Then I ate per day one [seed of] sesamum and one [grain of] rice. My body became deteriorated and weak, and my bones were joined together. A sore grew on top of my head, so that the skin [of my head] fell down of its own, piece after piece, and my head resembled a broken bottle-gourd. [The sore] did not leave my head intact.[16] At that time I was like this : a sore grew on top of my head, so that the skin [of my head] fell down of its own, piece after piece, all because I did not eat. And just like stars which are seen [reflected] in deep water, so were my eyes at that time, all because I did not eat. My body resembled an old cart which breaks down. It was entirely destroyed and could not support and obey me. And my two buttocks were like the foot of a camel. When I put my hand on my belly, I got hold of the bones of my spine; and when I placed my hand on my spine, I got
[8] hold of the skin of my belly. My body was emaciated and weak, all because I did not eat. At that time, when I ate one [seed of] sesamum and one [grain of] rice and considered it my food, I did not in the end derive any benefit [from it]. And I did not attain to the most honourable dharma. When I wished to defecate or urinate, then I fell over on the earth and could not myself stand up and sit down.

(671a7:) Gods, seeing me, thought this, saying: 'This recluse (*śramaṇa*) Gautama, he has come to extinction'. But there were some gods who said: 'This recluse, his life has not yet ended, [but] today his life will certainly end'. Other gods again said: 'This recluse is not at the end of his life. This recluse is really an *arhat*.

15. 麻 'hemp' short for 芝麻 'sesamum'?
16. Unclear.

The dharma of a sage [called] *arhat* contains this painful practice'. At that time I still was conscious and knew the factors that came to me from outside.

(671a12:) Then again I thought: 'Now I can enter into meditation without breath'. I then entered into meditation without breath, and counted my exhalations and inhalations. Counting my exhalations and inhalations, I noticed that there was air coming out from my ears. The sound of [this] wind resembled the roll of thunder.

(671a15:) Then again I thought: 'Now I close my mouth and block my ears, [so that] my breath [can] not escape'. When my breath [could] not escape, the air inside came out from my hands and feet. Truly, I did not let my breath go out through my ears, nose and mouth. The inner sound [resulting from this] resembled the roar of thunder. Yet my consciousness revolved [through all this] along with my body.[17]

(671a19:) Then again I thought: 'I ought to enter into meditation without breath once more'. I then completely blocked all apertures [of my body]. Having blocked all exhalations and inhalations, I then suffered pain in my forehead. As if a man, taking hold [of me], pierced my head with a drill, so did I have extremely painful headaches. At that time, like before, I retained consciousness.

(671a23:) Then again I thought: 'Now again I can sit down and meditate [such that] my breath cannot go out or in'. Then I blocked my exhalations and inhalations. Thereupon all my breaths gathered together in my belly. The breaths which then whirled around had extremely few points of support.[17] Just as when a skilled butcher slaughters a cow with a knife, so did I suffer extremely severe pains. And as when two strong men together hold one weak man and toast him before a fire, [so that] he suffers extreme pains which he cannot bear, so did I [suffer such pains]. These severe pains [9]
cannot be wholly described. Yet I retained consciousness.

(671a29:) On that day, while I sat in meditation, my body did not have a human colour. At that occasion there were people who, seeing me, said: 'The colour of this recluse is extremely black'.

17. Unclear.

> There were other people who, seeing me, said: 'The colour of this recluse resembles green'.
> (671b3:) Monks (*bhikṣu*), you should know that in the six years that I did these painful practices I did not attain to the most honourable dharma.

The episode from the *Ekottara Āgama* and the one from the *Majjhima Nikāya* clearly come from a common source. It seems a priori likely that the former is a later version, for the *Ekottara Āgama* is said to have been profoundly influenced by Mahāyāna, and to contain an "abundance of composite Sūtras, artificially forged together by placing one after the other Sūtras or portions of Sūtras borrowed from other canonical texts" (cf. Lamotte,1967: 106; Bareau, 1963: 9). Some facts support this.

The episode in the *Ekottara Āgama* reverses meditation without breath and reduced intake of food. Reduced intake of food comes here first, and this has given rise to an absurdity. At the beginning of his reduced intake of food the future Buddha decides not to undertake a complete fast, because the gods would keep him alive, would not let him die. But at the end of the reduced intake of food the gods are made to think that Gautama has died, or is about to die, without their having done a thing to prevent this. This inconsistency is absent from the Pāli version where these thoughts on the part of the gods occur after Gautama's meditation without breath. We may assume that the story got muddled up in the course of the longer tradition which underlay the version in the *Ekottara Āgama*.

The statement at the end of the episode in the *Ekottara Āgama* that these painful practices were performed for six years is another indication that this is a later stage in the development of the story. The Pāli canon does not, to my knowledge, indicate anywhere how long the future Buddha tried alternative methods. In the later literature,[18] however, it is often said that it lasted six years.

The *Ekottara Āgama* version of our episode preserves, in spite of its

18. E.g., Aśvaghoṣa's *Buddhacarita* 12.95; *Lalitavistara* p. 250, 256, 257, 259, 260, 264, 265; *Mahāvastu* II, p. 241. It is also mentioned in the introduction to the Jātakas (Ja I.67), which is late. For a comparative study of all these and other versions of our story, see Dutoit, 1905.

lateness, the two main indications that it originally dealt with non-Buddhist, probably Jaina, practices:

(i) The gods call Gautama an *arhat* [10]

(ii) The future Buddha intends to fast to death but abandons this idea.

The third indication which we might expect, viz., something corresponding to *maṅguracchavi,* is not found in the *Ekottara Āgama.*

One thing is lacking in the *Ekottara Āgama*. The Pāli version introduces the description of meditation without breath with an account of the Bodhisattva's attempt to "restrain my thought with my mind, [to] coerce and torment it". This is the only part of the whole episode which can properly be called a description of meditation. It is absent from the Chinese version.

The explanation of this absence lies no doubt in the circumstance that the practice to "restrain one's thought with one's mind, to coerce and torment it" – here criticized – was taken over by the Buddhists themselves at an early date. This is most clearly shown by the fact that almost the same words which are used in the autobiographical account of the Buddha to ridicule this practice, are used elsewhere in the *Majjhima Nikāya* (I. 120-21; similarly MĀC p. 582c7-10) to recommend that same practice. Even the accompanying simile is there. This explains sufficiently the omission in the *Ekottara Āgama.*

1.3. The *Ekottara Āgama* gives no real context to the autobiographical account which contains our episode. Only an introduction accompanies it, which reads (p. 670c2-3): "Thus it has been heard. At one time the Buddha was in a grove outside the city of Vaiśālī. Then the world-honoured one spoke to the monks: 'Formerly, when I had not yet attained enlightenment,[19] ...'." Following this comes the autobiographical account which contains our episode and which reaches up to the end of this unit.

The *Majjhima Nikāya* gives the episode in three different contexts, one of which is of particular interest to us. The *Mahāsaccaka Sutta* may well contain the original context of the episode; at the very least it shows

19. Lit. 'the way of a Buddha'.

that early in the Buddhist tradition there was a clear awareness that our episode served the purpose of criticizing others, i.e., Jainas, for which a suitable context was created. The following points go to show this:

(i) The *Mahāsaccaka Sutta* mainly describes a conversation between the Buddha and Saccaka Nigaṇṭhaputta, alias Aggivessana. The Nigaṇṭhas of the Pāli canon are – as has been shown by Jacobi (1895: xivf.) – the Jainas. Saccaka is called 'Nigaṇṭhaputta', i.e., 'son of a Nigaṇṭha', which indicates that he was a Jaina.[20]

[11] (ii) Saccaka points out that there are two extremes into which certain recluses and Brahmins fall. Some are devoted to the cultivation of the body, at the expense of the cultivation of the mind. Others are devoted to the cultivation of the mind, at the expense of the cultivation of the body. Both suffer the horrible consequences of this omission because they fail respectively to cultivate the mind or the body. Saccaka specifies that the disciples of the Buddha are devoted to the cultivation of the mind, at the expense of the cultivation of the body. Those who are devoted to the cultivation of the body, at the expense of the cultivation of the mind, are, apparently, Nanda Vaccha, Kisa Saṅkicca, and Makkhali Gosāla. These three persons are mentioned at the beginning of a passage which gives an enumeration of ascetic practices. These practices fit very well with what we know about the Jainas (Jacobi, 1895: xxxi), yet neither Nigaṇṭha Nātaputta, i.e. Mahāvīra, nor his followers are here mentioned. The reason seems clear: Saccaka, himself a Jaina, cannot ascribe to the Jainas the extreme of only cultivating the body at the expense of cultivating the mind. The tenor of Saccaka's exposition indicates that others such as Nanda Vaccha, Kisa Saṅkicca, and Makkhali Gosāla – all of whom are normally associated with the Ājīvikas (Basham, 1951: 27–30) – are guilty of this extreme, while the Jainas give mind and body their proper share. It is certainly significant that this same enumeration of ascetic practices occurs often in the Pāli canon (see Franke, 1913: 135n.1), but never in connection with these three persons![21] Note that according to the composer of this

20. On the pleonastic use of *-putta / putra*, see Alsdorf, 1969: 18 (375) n. 9, and esp. Alsdorf, 1951: 357-60 (587-90).

21. Jacobi (1895: xxxi-xxxii), not taking into account the context, mistakenly thinks that this passage is "most easily ... accounted for by our assuming that the original

part of the *Mahāsaccaka Sutta* the episode of meditation without breath and reduced intake of food is not directed against the Ājīvikas. (MN I. 237-39, esp. p. 238, l. 12-28).

Perhaps the following point should be added:

(iii) Towards the end of the Sūtra (MN I. 249-50) Saccaka directs a final criticism at the Buddha. The Buddha, he points out, sleeps sometimes by day. This criticism makes sense against the background of the Jaina rule that monks should abstain from sleeping by day (Jaini, 1979: 251; cf. Āyār. 106 (1.3.1.1): *suttā amuṇī muṇiṇo sayā jāgaraṃti* "The unwise sleep, the sages always wake" (tr. Jacobi, 1884: 28); Sūy. 585 (1.14.6); Pūjyapāda's *Sarvārthasiddhi* 9.19; Hemacandra's *Yogaśāstra* with the own commentary (vol. II, p. 726); etc.).[22]

The other two Sūtras of the *Majjhima Nikāya* provide no context worth the name. The autobiographical account containing our episode is given in the *Bodhirājakumāra Sutta* in reply to the faulty observation that [12]
"happiness should not be reached through happiness, happiness should be reached through hardship" (see however note 5 to ch. II). Here the features which point to specific non-Buddhistic, probably Jaina, practices remain unexplained. In the *Saṅgārava Sutta* the autobiographical account follows the Buddha's statement that he has achieved perfection of wisdom in this world (*diṭṭhadhammābhiññāvosānapāramippatta*) by having recognized the *dhamma* himself (MN II.211). This is hardly a fitting context for our episode.

However, in all the three Sūtras our episode is part of the same autobiographical account, portions of which do not appear to make sense in the *Mahāsaccaka Sutta*. One of those portions seems to fit much better in the *Saṅgārava Sutta*. This is the story of the Bodhisattva's training under Āḷāra Kālāma and Uddaka the son of Rāma, which he then discarded as useless. This story has nothing to do with the point which the Buddha wants to make to Saccaka. It is, on the other hand, a suitable

---

Nigaṇṭhas ... were not the section of the church, which submitted to the more rigid rules of Mahāvīra, but those followers of Pārśva, who, without forming a hostile party, yet continued ... to retain within the united church some particular usages of the old one."

22. The idea is also found in Brahmanical sources, e.g. ĀpDhS 1.2.24.

introduction to the message which the Buddha wants to get across in the *Saṅgārava Sutta*, viz., that he reached his goal all alone.[23] One gets the impression that the long autobiographical account which is repeated in three contexts, contains some portions which at an earlier time occurred separately in those different contexts.

Be this as it may, the autobiographical account in the *Mahāsaccaka Sutta* contains some further portions which do not make sense in the conversations with Saccaka, and which may therefore be later additions. They are the following:

(i) Immediately after the account of the training under Āḷāra Kālāma and Uddaka the son of Rāma, the Buddha describes how three similes occurred to him which, briefly stated, showed him that no progress would be possible as long as desire for the objects of the senses were not abandoned (MN I. 240-42). This description serves no purpose in the reply to Saccaka.

(ii) At the end of the *Mahāsaccaka Sutta* (MN I. 250-51) Saccaka contrasts the composed behaviour of Gotama with the evasive reactions of the six heretics, which include, as ever, Nigaṇṭha Nātaputta. Since there is no mention in the text that Saccaka was converted to Buddhism, he was still a follower of Nigaṇṭha Nātaputta. This episode is therefore inexplicable in this context.

[13] If we remove the portions indicated above from the *Mahāsaccaka Sutta*, we are left with what may be called the 'Original Mahāsaccaka Sūtra'. It is very likely that it once had an existence of its own, while additions were made to it later. From the beginning this Original Mahāsaccaka Sūtra must have contained the episode on meditation without breath and reduced intake of food. This episode itself may or may not have existed before the composition of the Original Mahāsaccaka Sūtra.

1.4. Something can be said about the date of composition of the episode on meditation without breath and reduced intake of food. It must have been well before the final redaction of the Pāli canon, because, as we have seen, the Original Mahāsaccaka Sūtra suffered a number of additions. The Pāli

23. This story occurs again in the *Ariyapariyesana Sutta* (MN I. 163-67).

canon was written down in the first century B.C.[24] Our episode must be much earlier than this.

One feature of our episode allows us to tentatively push this date back considerably. The Bodhisattva, we know, abandoned his intention to fast to death. The author of the episode really did not have much choice here, for if he had let the Bodhisattva die as a result of these hardships, the latter could not have reached enlightenment in the same life. Embarrassment could however have been avoided by placing the episode in an earlier existence of the Bodhisattva. In that case the Bodhisattva could finish his fast to death completely. Why was this not done ?

Stories about previous existences of the Buddha are a late feature of the canonical literature. Very few of them occur in the collections of Sūtras (*Kūṭadanta Sutta*: DN I. 134-43, cf. DĀ^{C} p. 98b-100b; *Mahāsudassana Sutta*: DN II. 169-98, cf. DĀ^{C} p. 21b-24b, MĀ^{C} p. 515b-518b; *Mahāgovinda Sutta*: DN II. 220-51, cf. DĀ^{C} p. 30b-34a; *Makhādeva Sutta*: MN II. 74-82, cf. MĀ^{C} p. 511c-515a, EĀ^{C} p. 806c-810a; *Ghaṭīkāra Sutta*: MN II. 46-49, 54, cf. MĀ^{C} p. 499a-503a; see Winternitz, 1920: 91f.; Bareau, 1980: 5). A whole collection of such stories (the Jātakas) came to be accepted in the Pāli canon. We may assume that this happened before the time that these Jātakas (Lüders, 1941: 136f.; but cf. Lamotte, 1958: 444-45) were depicted at Buddhist monuments, especially in Bhārhut. These sculptures may be dated between 150 and 100 B.C. (Barua, 1934: 29-37; Rowland, 1967: 88). It seems that we must date our episode long before this time, i.e., in the third century B.C. at the latest (cf. Bareau, 1980: 5-6).[25]

This conclusion seems supported by the fact that many Jātakas contain verses in the new Āryā metre (Alsdorf, 1967: 23-51) and must therefore perhaps be dated before the supposed migration of Pāli to [14]
Ceylon, in the middle or second half of the third century B.C. (Alsdorf, 1965: 70; 1967: 5). This last consideration is however weakened by the possibility that the early Pāli works which originated after this date may

24. Dates vary from between 35 and 32 B.C. (Lamotte, 1958: 404-05) to about 89-77 B.C. (Bechert, 1974: 131).
25. A possible objection would be that the Bodhisattva is said to abandon a full fast *merely* to indicate that he would be kept alive by receiving divine food through his pores. This point of view does not however seem to do full justice to our episode.

also have been composed on the mainland, not in Ceylon; cf. Frauwallner, 1971: 105-06.[26]

With regard to the above conclusion some caution must be exercised. It is likely that some kind of tradition regarding the pre-enlightenment hardships of the Buddha existed prior to the composition of our episode (see below). This may have prevented the transposition of this episode to an earlier life of the Bodhisattva even at a time that stories about such earlier lives started playing a role.

The episode on meditation without breath and reduced intake of food does not belong to the earliest layer of Buddhist literature. There is reason to believe that its composer made use of already existing passages ('pericopes'), which may have been more or less freely floating.

The Pāli account of meditation fully without breath contains four comparisons:

(i) "Just as when a strong man may destroy a head with the sharp edge of a sword, just so indeed extremely strong winds shook up my head"

(ii) "Just as when a strong man may place a turban on a head with a strong strip of leather, just so indeed there came about extremely strong headaches in my head"[27]

(iii) "Just as when a skilled butcher or apprentice of a butcher may cut a belly all around with a sharp butcher's knife, just so indeed extremely strong winds cut my belly all around"

(iv) "Just as when two strong men, taking a weaker man by both his arms, may burn and roast him on a pit of burning coal, just so indeed there came about an extremely strong heat in my body."

These comparisons also occur in the *Ekottarāgama* version, even though there (i) and (ii) have been condensed into one:

---

26. It is not likely that our episode was part of the original Skandhaka which Frauwallner (1956b: 67) dates a century after the death of the Buddha. Mukherjee (1966: 130-32) argues convincingly that the original Skandhaka may not have contained any biographical material regarding the period preceding the enlightenment of the Buddha.
27. Jha (1979: 276) observes: "The traditional scholars from South India very often say: *kimarthaṃ śiroveṣṭana-prāṇāyāmaḥ* ?" What could be the connection ?

(i)-(ii) "As if a man, taking hold of me, pierced my head with a drill, so did I have extremely painful headaches"

(iii) "Just as when a skilled butcher slaughters a cow with a knife, so did I suffer extremely severe pains"

(iv) "And as when two strong men together hold one weak man and toast [15
him above a fire, so that he suffers extreme pains which he cannot bear, so did I suffer such pains."

These four[28] comparisons must have occurred in the original version of our episode.

But the same comparisons occur in the exact words elsewhere in the Pāli canon and always in connection with a sick person: MN II. 193; SN IV. 56; AN III. 379-80. There can be no doubt that the comparisons fit a sick person much better than one engaged in meditation fully without breath. The important role allotted to wind in Indian medical treatises is well-known.[29] Further, it is difficult to see why meditation without breath should bring about the extreme heat of the fourth comparison, which appears to describe fever, which is connected with bile (*pitta*) and not wind (see note 28). It is however clear how the four comparisons could come to be transferred from a sick person to one engaged in meditation fully without breath; the first and the third mention wind, and winds are not allowed to leave the body in this kind of meditation.

Another apparently borrowed part in the episode is the description of the horrible effects of the future Buddha's reduced intake of food, which occurs in both the Pāli and the Chinese versions. It occurs again in the *Mahāsīhanāda Sutta* of the *Majjhima Nikāya* (nr. 12, MN I.80) and, in a somewhat different form, in the *Shên mao hsi shu ching* (身毛喜豎經);

---

28. Four, not three. The Pāli version must be closer to the original because two of its comparisons make a mention of winds, which the whole passage really is about. The mention of winds cannot be an adjustment après coup, for the four comparisons were taken from another context. See below.

29. According to Agniveśa's *Caraka Saṃhitā*, Sūtrasthāna 20.11 (p. 113), headache (*śiroruc*) and belly-ache (*udarāveṣṭaḥ*; the commentator Cakrapāṇidatta explains: *udarasyāveṣṭanam ivodarāveṣṭaḥ*) are caused by wind (*vāta*). This corresponds to comparisons (i)-(iii). Heat (*dāha*), on the other hand, is caused by bile (*pitta*); see Sūtrasthāna 20.14 (p. 114).

originally *Romaharṣaṇīya Sūtra*, cf. Lévi, 1932: 158n5; T. 757, p. 598a 25f.).[30] In both these Sūtras it is part of an account of the extreme ascetic practices which the Bodhisattva tried out. These practices include much besides fasting, but no meditation with or without breath. Since it is hard to see in what other context this part could originally have existed, we may assume that some sort of tradition regarding the pre-enlightenment hardships of the Buddha existed prior to the composition of our episode.[31] The portion on meditation in our episode may not have been part of this tradition (it occurs nowhere except in our episode), and appears to have been composed for this episode.

1.5. The most interesting result of the above observations is that, probably in the third century B.C., a Buddhist gave a description of a non-Buddhist, probably Jaina, method of cultivating the mind, called 'meditation' (*jhāna* / *dhyāna*). Stripped from obvious exaggerations and
[16] repetitions it presents this picture : Among the non-Buddhists (Jainas), meditation was a forceful effort to restrain the mind and bring it to a standstill. Along with it, but perhaps only in a more advanced stage of meditation, breathing is stopped.

This form of non-Buddhist meditation is contrasted with Buddhist meditation in the *Mahāsaccaka Sutta*, and probably also in the Original Mahāsaccaka Sūtra which may have constituted the original context of our episode. The Bodhisattva is said to recall the First Dhyāna in a passage which appears to contain very old elements (Horsch, 1964; Bareau, 1963: 47-48, 52-53). It reads (MN I. 246-47; cf. T. 1428, p. 781a4-11):[32]

> Then, Aggivessana, I thought: 'I remember, indeed, that [once], during the work of my father the Sakka, while sitting in the cool

30. The *Romaharṣaṇīya Sūtra* in its Chinese version is clearly influenced by our episode. It includes the remarks by onlookers regarding Gautama's black or brown colour (p. 598b24) and is aware of the feeding of *ojas* through the pores (p. 599a24).

31. This tradition, too, may have been strongly influenced by Jaina and similar practices. See Bollée, 1971; Verclas, 1978: 156-60.

32. *tassa mayhaṃ aggivessana etad ahosi: abhijānāmi kho panāhaṃ pitu sakkassa kammante sītāya jambucchāyāya nisinno vivicc'eva kāmehi vivicca akusalehi*

> shade of the rose-apple tree, separated from desires, separated from bad things (*dhamma*), I reached the First Dhyāna, which is accompanied by thought and reflection, born from separation, consists of joy and bliss, and remained [there]. Could this perhaps be the road toward enlightenment ?' Then, Aggivessana, following this memory I had this knowledge: 'This is really the road toward enlightenment'. Then, Aggivessana, I thought: 'Indeed, I do not fear that bliss, a bliss which is apart from desires, apart from bad psychic states'.

One cannot fail to be struck by the relaxed and friendly atmosphere which emanates from this passage, and which contrasts with the violent spirit ascribed to Jaina meditation.

In the opinion of the author of the Original Mahāsaccaka Sūtra Buddhist meditation consists of the so-called Four Dhyānas. This is shown by the fact that the autobiographical account in the Mahāsaccaka Sutta concludes with a description of the final enlightenment of the Buddha which follows his ascent through the Four Dhyānas. They are described as follows (MN I. 247):[33]

> Then indeed, Aggivessana, having taken ample food, and having recovered strength, being separated from desires, separated from bad things, I reached the First Dhyāna, which is accompanied by thought and reflection, born from separation, and consists of joy and bliss, and resided [there]. Even such a blissful experience, Aggivessana, when it happened to me, did not completely take hold of my mind. As a result of appeasing thought and reflection I

---

dhammehi savitakkaṃ savicāraṃ vivekajaṃ pītisukhaṃ paṭhamaṃ jhānaṃ upasampajja viharitā, siyā nu kho eso maggo bodhāyā'ti / tassa mayhaṃ aggivessana satānusāri viññāṇaṃ ahosi: eso va maggo bodhāyā'ti / tassa mayhaṃ aggivessana etad ahosi: kin nu kho ahaṃ tassa sukhassa bhāyāmi yan taṃ sukhaṃ aññatr 'eva kāmehi aññatra akusalehi dhammehī 'ti / tassa mayhaṃ aggivessana etad ahosi: na kho ahaṃ tassa sukhassa bhāyāmi yan taṃ sukhaṃ aññatr 'eva kāmehi aññatra akusalehi dhammehī 'ti /

33. *so kho ahaṃ aggivessana oḻārikaṃ āhāraṃ āhāretvā balaṃ gahetvā vivicc'eva kāmehi vivicca akusalehi dhammehi savitakkaṃ savicāraṃ vivekajaṃ pītisukhaṃ paṭhamaṃ jhānaṃ upasampajja vihāsiṃ / evarūpā pi kho me aggivessana uppannā sukhā vedanā cittaṃ na pariyādāya tiṭṭhati / vitakkavicārānaṃ vūpasamā*

> reached the Second Dhyāna, which is an inner tranquillization, a
> [17] unification of the mind, free from thought and reflection, consisting of joy and bliss that is born from concentration (*samādhija*), and resided [there]. Even such a blissful experience, Aggivessana, when it happened to me, did not completely take hold of my mind.
> As a result of detachment from joy, I remained indifferent, attentive and mindful. I experienced with my body the bliss which the noble ones describe [in these terms]: 'indifferent, with attentiveness, residing in bliss'; thus I reached the Third Dhyāna and resided [there]. Even such a blissful experience, Aggivessana, when it happened to me did not completely take hold of my mind.
> As a result of abandoning bliss, and abandoning pain, as a result of the earlier disappearance of cheerfulness and dejection, I reached the Fourth Dhyāna, which is free from pain and bliss, the complete purity of equanimity and attentiveness, and resided [there]. Even[34] such a blissful experience, Aggivessana, when it happened to me, did not completely take hold of my mind.

When we compare what we learned about non-Buddhist meditation with this description of the Buddhist Four Dhyānas (which is standard, and recurs numerous times in the Buddhist canon; see Schmithausen, 1981: 203-04), we notice many differences. The one that is emphasized by the author of the Original Mahāsaccaka Sūtra is that Buddhist meditation[35] is a pleasant experience,[36] accompanied by joy (*pīti*) and bliss (*sukha*), or

---

ajjhattaṃ sampasādanaṃ cetaso ekodibhāvaṃ avitakkaṃ avicāraṃ samādhijaṃ pītisukhaṃ dutiyaṃ jhānaṃ upasampajja vihāsiṃ / evarūpā pi kho me aggivessana uppannā sukhā vedanā cittaṃ na pariyādāya tiṭṭhati / pītiyā ca virāgā upekhako ca vihāsiṃ sato ca sampajāno, sukhañ ca kāyena paṭisaṃvedesiṃ yan taṃ ariyā ācikkhanti : upekhako satimā sukhavihārīti tatiyaṃ jhānaṃ upasampajja vihāsiṃ / evarūpā pi kho me aggivessana uppannā sukhā vedanā cittaṃ na pariyādāya tiṭṭhati / sukhassa ca pahānā dukkhassa ca pahānā pubbeva somanassa-domanassānaṃ atthagamā adukkhaṃ asukhaṃ upekhāsatipārisuddhiṃ catutthaṃ jhānaṃ upasampajja vihāsiṃ / evarūpā pi kho me aggivessana uppannā sukhā vedanā cittaṃ na pariyādāya tiṭṭhati /

34. This sentence is here rather absurd, and shows the unifying, but non-understanding hand of a redactor.
35. By this I mean, of course, the Four Dhyānas.
36. Note that SN I.1 claims that Nirvāṇa is reached without effort; cf. Karunaratne, 1976.

bliss alone, in all but its highest stages, whereas non-Buddhist meditation is not described as pleasurable.

[24] II. Further Buddhist criticism of alternative practices.

2.1. More information about the Jainas that is of interest to us can be gathered from various places in the Buddhist canon. Of particular interest is MN I. 92-95 (cf. T. 55, p. 850c-851a; MĀ^{C} p. 587b13f.; EĀ^{C} p. 744a27f.) where the Buddha is in conversation with the Sakka named Mahānāma:[1]

> At one time, Mahānāma, I resided in Rājagaha on the mountain Gijjhakūṭa. At that time there were many Nigaṇṭhas on the black rock on the slope of [the mountain] Isigili, standing erect,[2] refusing to sit down, and they experienced painful, sharp, severe sensations [which were] due to [self-inflicted] torture.[3] Then, Mahānāma, having arisen in the evening from my retirement, I went to the black rock on the slope of [the mountain] Isigili where those Nigaṇṭhas were; having gone there I said to those Nigaṇṭhas: 'Why, dear Nigaṇṭhas, are you standing erect, refusing to sit down, and do you experience painful, sharp, severe sensations [which are] due to [self-inflicted] torture?' When this was said, Mahānāma, those Nigaṇṭhas said to me: 'Friend, Nigaṇṭha Nāthaputta, who knows all and sees all, claims complete knowledge and insight [saying:] "Always and continuously knowledge and insight are present to

1. *ekam idāhaṃ mahānāma samayaṃ rājagahe viharāmi gijjhakūṭe pabbate / tena kho pana samayena sambahulā nigaṇṭhā isigilipasse kāḷasilāyaṃ ubbhaṭṭhakā honti āsanapaṭikkhittā, opakkamikā dukkhā tippā kaṭukā vedanā vediyanti / atha kho 'haṃ mahānāma sāyanhasamayaṃ paṭisallāṇā vuṭṭhito yena isigilipassaṃ kāḷasilā yena te nigaṇṭhā ten 'upasaṅkamiṃ, upasaṅkamitvā te nigaṇṭhe etad avocaṃ : kin nu tumhe āvuso nigaṇṭhā ubbhaṭṭhakā āsanapaṭikkhittā opakkamikā dukkhā tippā kaṭukā vedanā vediyathā'ti ? evaṃ vutte mahānāma te nigaṇṭhā maṃ etad avocuṃ : nigaṇṭho āvuso nāthaputto sabbaññū sabbadassāvī aparisesaṃ ñāṇadassanaṃ paṭijānāti : carato ca me tiṭṭhato ca suttassa ca jāgarassa ca*

2. T. 55 (p. 850c4) has 'standing on their knees' (跪), EĀ^{C} (p. 744b1) 'squatting on the heels' (蹲)
3. See note 6 to ch. I, above.

me, whether I walk, stand still, sleep or be awake." He (i.e., Nigaṇṭha Nāthaputta) says: "Formerly, Nigaṇṭhas, you performed sinful activities; you must exhaust that [sinful activity] by means of this severe and difficult practice. Being here and now restrained in body, speech and mind, amounts to not performing sinful activity in the future. Thus, as a result of the annihilation of former actions by asceticism, and of the non-performing of new actions, there is no further effect in the future; as a result of no further effect in the future there is destruction of actions; as a result of the destruction of actions there is destruction of suffering; as a result of the destruction of suffering there is destruction of sensation; as a result of the destruction of sensation all suffering will be exhausted." And this [word of Nigaṇṭha Nāthaputta] pleases us and is approved of by us, and therefore we are delighted. ... Happiness, dear Gotama, should not be reached through happiness,[4] happiness should be reached through hardship.[5] If happiness should be reached through happiness, dear Gotama, king Seniya Bimbisāra of Magadha would reach happiness [hereafter, because] king Seniya Bimbisāra of Magadha lives in greater happiness than the venerable

satataṃ samitaṃ ñāṇadassanaṃ paccupaṭṭhitan ti / so evaṃ āha: atthi kho vo nigaṇṭhā pubbe pāpaṃ kammaṃ katam, taṃ imāya kaṭukāya dukkarakārikāya nijjaretha; yaṃ pan'ettha etarahi kāyena saṃvutā vācāya saṃvutā manasā saṃvutā taṃ āyatiṃ pāpassa kammassa akaraṇaṃ; iti purāṇānaṃ kammānaṃ tapasā byantibhāvā, navānaṃ kammānaṃ akaraṇā āyatiṃ anavassavo, āyatiṃ anavassavā kammakkhayo, kammakkhayā dukkhakkhayo, dukkhakkhayā vedanākkhayo, vedanākkhayā sabbaṃ dukkhaṃ nijjiṇṇaṃ bhavissatī'ti / tañ ca pan'amhākaṃ ruccati c'eva khamati ca, tena c'amhā attamanā'ti / ... na kho āvuso gotama sukhena sukhaṃ adhigantabbaṃ, dukkhena kho sukhaṃ adhigantabbaṃ / sukhena ca āvuso gotama sukhaṃ adhigantabbaṃ abhavissa, rājā māgadho seniyo bimbisāro sukhaṃ adhigaccheyya, rājā māgadho seniyo bimbisāro sukha-vihāritaro āyasmatā gotamenāti / ...

4. The Jaina text *Sūyagaḍa* 230 (I.3.4.6) criticizes some who say that happiness is reached through happiness (*iham ege u bhāsaṃti sātaṃ sāteṇa vijjatī*). Śīlāṅka (p. 64) identifies these as 'Buddhists etc.' (*śākyādayaḥ*).
5. The *Ekottara Āgama* completely reverses the situation and makes the Buddha say that happiness can only be reached through hardship, not through happiness ($E\bar{A}^C$ p. 744b9-10, 20-21). This must be due to outside influence; see § 1.2 above.

[25] Gotama.' [The Buddha replies:]
'With respect to this I should be asked: "Who of the [two] venerable ones lives in greater happiness, King Seniya Bimbisāra of Magadha or the venerable Gotama?" ... Therefore, dear Nigaṇṭhas, I shall ask you [a question] which you may answer as seems right to you. What do you think, dear Nigaṇṭhas, is king Seniya Bimbisāra of Magadha able to experience unalloyed happiness for seven (six ... five ... four ... three ... two ... one) nights and days [at a stretch] without moving his body and without saying a word?' 'No, friend.' 'But I, dear Nigaṇṭhas, am able to experience unalloyed happiness[6] for one (two ... three ... four ... five ... six ... seven) night and day [at a stretch] without moving my body and without saying a word. What do you think, dear Nigaṇṭhas, who lives in view of this in greater happiness, king Seniya Bimbisāra of Magadha or I ?' 'In view of this the venerable Gotama lives in greater happiness than king Seniya Bimbisāra of Magadha'.

We observe that here again the painful practices of the Jainas are contrasted with the happiness of the Buddhists. Unfortunately the contrast is not validly illustrated, because the Buddha himself – who has already reached the goal – is said to be happy, and those who have not yet reached

---

api ca aham eva tattha paṭipucchitabbo : ko nu kho āyasmantānaṃ sukhavihāritaro, rājā vā māgadho seniyo bimbisāro āyasmā vā gotamo ti / ... tena h'āvuso nigaṇṭhā tumhe va tattha paṭipucchissāmi, yathā vo k!ameyya tathā naṃ byākareyyātha / taṃ kiṃ maññath'āvuso nigaṇṭhā: pahoti rājā māgadho seniyo bimbisāro aniñjamāno kāyena abhāsamāno vācaṃ satta (cha ... pañca ... cattāri ... tīṇi ... dve ... ekaṃ) rattindivāni (rattindivaṃ) ekantasukhapaṭisaṃvedī viharitun ti / no h'idaṃ āvuso / ahaṃ kho āvuso nigaṇṭhā pahomi aniñjamāno kāyena abhāsamāno vācaṃ ekaṃ (dve ... tīṇi ... cattāri ... pañca ... cha ... satta) rattindivaṃ (rattindivāni) ekantasukhapaṭisaṃvedī viharituṃ / taṃ kiṃ maññath'āvuso nigaṇṭhā : evaṃ sante ko sukhavihāritaro, rājā vā māgadho seniyo bimbisāro ahaṃ vā'ti / evaṃ sante āyasmā va gotamo sukhavihāritaro raññā māgadhena seniyena bimbisārenā'ti /

---

6. EĀ[c] p. 744b14-15 seems to miss the point and makes the Buddha boast of being able "to sit cross-legged for seven days and nights without stirring the body", not mentioning happiness.

the goal but are practising in the right way are not mentioned.

Nevertheless, this passage contains one more piece of information about the Jainas as viewed by the Buddhists. The Jainas, we read, were "standing erect,[7] refusing to sit down". We may look upon this as an expression of their desire for 'non-performing of new actions' and 'annihilation of former actions by asceticism'.[8]

The emphasis on bodily practices among the Jainas is explicitly mentioned in the Upāli Sutta/Sūtra (MN no. 56, I.371f.; MĀC no. 133, p. 628a f.). The Nigaṇṭha Dīghatapassī tells the Buddha that of the three kinds of bad activities – of body, speech, and mind – bodily activities are the worst. The Buddha, on the other hand, is of the opinion that mental bad activities are the worst.

2. 2. The *Indriyabhāvanā Sutta* of the *Majjhima Nikāya* (III. 298f.; cf. SĀC p. 78a22f.) criticizes such 'cultivation of the senses' (*indriya-bhāvanā*) as leads to their non-functioning. Uttara explains, at the request of the Buddha, that his teacher Pārāsariya teaches such cultivation of the senses that "one sees no form with the eye, hears no sound with the ear"
(MN III.298: *...cakkhunā rūpaṃ na passati, sotena saddaṃ na suṇāti*). [26]
The Buddha responds that then the blind and deaf will have cultivated the

7. Or 'standing on their knees' and 'squatting on their heels' in the Chinese parallels.
8. These words are again ascribed to Nigaṇṭha Nāthaputta and his followers at AN I. 220-21; MN II.214; cf. SĀC p. 147c8f.; MĀC p. 442c2f.

It is noteworthy that almost the same words are placed in the mouth of the Buddha at AN I.221, II.197-98 (cf. MĀC p. 434b23; SĀC p.147c27): *so navañ ca kammaṃ na karoti, purāṇaṃ kammaṃ phussa phussa vyantikaroti*; the effects of activities are now said to wear out with death (AN II. 198-99; MĀC p. 434c5f.). At Ud 21, similarly, we are confronted with a monk "in a cross-legged position, with body erect, mindful and conscious, and bearing without a murmur, acute, piercing and terrible pains, the result of deeds done in the past" (*pallaṅkaṃ ābhujitvā ujuṃ kāyaṃ paṇidhāya purāṇakammavipākajaṃ dukkhaṃ tippaṃ kharaṃ kaṭukaṃ vedanaṃ adhivāsento sato sampajāno avihaññamāno*; tr. Strong, 1902: 27). At AN V.292, 294, 297, 298 (cf. MĀC p. 437b26f.) the Buddha is made to declare "that of intentional deeds done and accumulated there can be no wiping out without experiencing the result thereof, and that too whenever arising, either in this same visible state or in some other state hereafter" (*nāhaṃ bhikkhave sañcetanikānaṃ kammānaṃ katānaṃ upacitānaṃ appaṭisaṃviditvā vyantibhāvaṃ vadāmi, tañ ca kho diṭṭhe va dhamme upapajjaṃ vā apare vā pariyāye;* tr. Woodward, 1936: 189, 191). In all these cases we can be sure of outside influence on Buddhism. See ch. VII, below.

senses (*bhāvitindriya*), because they do not see with the eye, nor hear with the ear. The Buddha then explains to Ānanda that the best cultivation of the senses (*anuttarā indriyabhāvanā*) consists in equanimity (*upekkhā*) with respect to what is experienced through the senses.

2.3. The main conclusions to be drawn from the material presented in chapters I and II are as follows. Certain non-Buddhist ascetics, in particular the Jainas, performed practices which are described as 'non-performing of new actions' and 'annihilation of former actions by asceticism'. The 'non-performing of new actions' implied apparently such feats of motionlessness as standing erect without ever sitting or lying down. The accompanying feelings of displeasure are probably what is meant by 'annihilation of former actions by asceticism'.

These practices on the part of the Jainas and other non-Buddhist religious ascetics were, in the view of the Buddhists, accompanied by others, of equally negative intent. One of these is the abstention from all food, until its inevitable result, death. Another one is described as 'meditation without breath'. The meditation-part of this practice consisted in a complete restraint of all mental processes. Along with this went an attempt to stop breathing.

One more practice was described and assigned to non-Buddhists. Here the attempt is made to halt the functioning of the senses in such a way that "one sees no form with the eye, hears no sound with the ear".

The common denominator in all these practices is easily discerned. All of them aim at non-activity of a part, or of the whole, of the aspirant. Given the fact that many of the religious movements in the time of the Buddha and later strove to discard the evil consequences of activity (*karman*), this goal should not surprise us.

It is perhaps more surprising that the early Buddhists are against all these practices. In some cases they contrast the non-Buddhist practices aiming at non-activity with what are, in their opinion, the practices to be performed in their stead. Rather than fasting, restraining the mind and stopping the breath, one should perform the Four Dhyānas. And rather than aiming at the non-functioning of the senses, one should remain equanimous in the face of the experiences they offer.

Part II: The main stream. [29]

III. Early Jaina meditation.

3.1. Probably the earliest surviving detailed description of the road leading to liberation in the Jaina scriptures is *Āyāraṃga* (Āyār.) 1.8(7).7.2-8 / 228-53:[1]

> When[2] a monk thinks: 'I am indeed tired of carrying around this body in these circumstances', he should gradually reduce his food; having gradually reduced his food and diminished his passions, his body being prepared, standing like a plank, his body pacified, ... he should ask for grass; having asked for grass and received it, he should go away to a lonely place; having gone away to a lonely place ... he should spread the grass; and having spread the grass, at that occasion, he should reject body, activity, and movement ... (228).
>
> The[3] firm ones, having reached the [ways of] liberation, powerful and wise,[4] knowing all that is excellent, (229)

---

1. *jassa ṇaṃ bhikkhussa evaṃ bhavati 'se gilāmi ca khalu ahaṃ imammi samae imaṃ sarīragaṃ aṇupuvveṇaṃ parivahittae' se aṇupuvveṇaṃ āhāraṃ saṃvaṭṭejjā, aṇupuvveṇaṃ āhāraṃ saṃvaṭṭettā kasāe pataṇue kiccā samāhiyacce phalagāvayaṭṭhī uṭṭhāya bhikkhū abhiṇivvuḍacce ... taṇāiṃ jāejjā, taṇāiṃ jāettā se ttam āyāe egaṃtam avakkamejjā, egaṃtam avakkamettā ... taṇāiṃ saṃtharejjā, [taṇāiṃ saṃtharettā] ettha vi samae kāyaṃ ca jogaṃ ca iriyaṃ ca paccakkhāejjā / ... //228//*
   aṇupuvveṇa vimohāiṃ jāiṃ dhīrā samāsajja /
   vasumaṃto matimaṃto savvaṃ ṇaccā aṇelisam //229//
2. The meaning of the passage is not always clear. The translation often follows Schubring, 1926 : 111-15, and also owes much to the advice of Dr. H. Tieken. The suggestions of N. Balbir (*Bulletin d'études indiennes* 4, 1986, p.23*) have been gratefully incorporated.
3. The remainder of this passage consists of verses which have been added to explain "body, activity and movement". See Schubring, 1926: 113 n.3.
4. Schubring takes *vasumanto maimanto* to be nom. sing., but there is nothing against it being nom. plural (Pischel, 1900: § 396, pp. 324-25). On *vasuma(t)* < Skt. **vaśamat*, see Norman, 1976:49.

Having conquered the twofold (birth and death?), the awakened ones have gone to the other shore of the doctrine. And one rids oneself of activity when he has thought [about this] in due order. (230)

(1) Having diminished his passions he bears with little food. In case the monk gets ill in the presence of food, (231)
He should not long for life, nor strive after death; he should not be attached to either, life or death. (232)
Impartial, intent on the destruction of activity (*ṇijjarā*) he should preserve his concentration. Renouncing internally as well as externally he strives after a pure heart. (233)
Whatever means he may know to secure his life [for another while, let the wise one quickly avail of that for an intervening period.[5] (234)
Having looked for a place in a village or in the wilderness,[6] and knowing it to be with little life, the monk should spread out the grass. (235)
He should lie without food; when affected [by discomfort] in that [position] he should bear it. He should not go beyond the boundary

---

duvihaṃ pi viittā (so Schubring; Jambuvijaya reads *viditttā*) *ṇaṃ buddhā dhammassa pāragā* /
aṇupuvvīe saṃkhāe āraṃbhā ya tiuṭṭati //230//
kasāe payaṇue kiccā appāhāro titikkhae /
aha bhikkhū gilāejjā āhārasseva aṃtiyaṃ //231//
jīviyaṃ ṇābhikaṃkhejjā maraṇaṃ ṇo vi patthae /
duhato vi ṇa sajjejjā jīvite maraṇe tahā //232//
majjhattho ṇijjarāpehī samāhim aṇupālae /
aṃto bahiṃ viyosajja ajjhatthaṃ suddham esae //233//
jaṃ kiṃcuvakkamaṃ jāṇe āukhemassa appaṇo /
tasseva aṃtaraddhāe khippaṃ sikkhejja paṃḍite //234//
gāme aduvā raṇṇe thaṃḍilaṃ paḍilehiyā /
appapāṇaṃ tu viṇṇāya taṇāiṃ saṃthare muṇī //235//
aṇāhāro tuvaṭṭejjā puṭṭho tattha hiyāsae /

---

5. Śīlāṅka (p. 194) and Schubring (1926: 114 n. 1) point out that this extension of life is meant to make the monk ready for the death he has chosen.
6. On the opposition between 'village' (*grāma*) and 'wilderness' (*araṇya*) in Vedic literature, see Sprockhoff, 1981: 32-43.

[which he has set himself], even when he has been affected[7] by things human. (236)
He should not hurt nor rub away living creatures which creep on the ground, or fly high or low, and eat his flesh and blood. (237)
Creatures injure his body, yet he should not walk from his place. Being pained by all kinds of outside influences, he should bear [it all], (238)
going to the other shore of his span of life, [free] from all kinds of knots. This is well-accepted by the self-controlled and understanding person. (239)

(2) The following is another practice taught by the son of Ṇāya (= Mahāvīra). One should abandon movement in the threefold three ways, except for [keeping] himself [alive]. (240)
He should not sit down on green plants, but lie on the bare ground after inspecting it; renouncing, taking no food, he should bear [discomfort] when affected [by it] in that [position]. (241)
While feeling aversion to his senses, the monk may take [as much food] as is appropriate.[8]
Nevertheless, he is blameless who is motionless and concentrated. (242)
He may step forward and backward, contract and stretch [his

ṇātivelaṃ uvacare māṇussehiṃ vi puṭṭhavaṃ //236//
saṃsappagā ya je pāṇā je ya uḍḍha-m-ahecarā /
bhuṃjaṃte maṃsasoṇiyaṃ ṇa chaṇe ṇa pamajjae //237//
pāṇā dehaṃ vihiṃsaṃti thāṇāto ṇa vi ubbhame /
āsavehiṃ vivittehiṃ tippamāṇo 'dhiyāsae //238//
gaṃthehiṃ vivittehiṃ āyukālassa pārae /
paggahitataragaṃ cetaṃ daviyassa viyāṇato //239//
ayaṃ se avare dhamme ṇāyaputteṇa sāhite /
āyavajjaṃ paḍiyāraṃ vijahejjā tidhā tidhā //240//
hariesu ṇa ṇivajjejjā thaṃḍilaṃ muṇiā sae /
viyosajja aṇāhāro puṭṭho tattha 'dhiyāsae //241//
iṃdiehiṃ gilāyaṃto samiyaṃ sāhare muṇī /
tahāvi se agarahe acale je samāhie //242//

7. *puṭṭhavaṃ*; cf. Pischel, 1900: § 396.
8. *samiyaṃ* = *samyak*. See Schubring, 1910 : 105.

limbs], in order to keep body [and soul] together; or, alternatively, he [may become] unconscious in that same position. (243)
He may walk around when tired, or [remain] standing as before. When tired of standing he may finally sit down. (244)
While sitting he directs his senses to the excellent death [which he is going to die]. In case he stumbles upon a termite hill [for support], he should search for something different. (245)
He does not lean on something from which something avoidable could originate. He should pull himself up from there and bear all that affects him. (246)

(3) This one is [even] more intent (*āyatatare*) [on reaching the goal] who keeps to the following. While controlling all his limbs, let him not move away from his place. (247)
This is the best practice, better than the preceding. Having cleansed [the place] for a short time, the Brahmin should remain there standing. (248)
Having reached a place free from living beings, he should place himself there. He should renounce his body; thinking 'there are no afflictions in my body, afflictions and troubles [last] as long as life', he should bear them, being restrained, realizing that they lead to the destruction of the body. (249-50)

---

abhikkame paḍikkame saṃkucae pasārae /
kāyasāhāraṇaṭṭhāe etthaṃ vā vi acetaṇe //243//
parikkame parikilaṃte aduvā ciṭṭhe ahāyate /
ṭhāṇeṇa parikilaṃte ṇisīejja ya aṃtaso //244//
āsīṇe 'ṇelisaṃ maraṇaṃ iṃdiyāṇi samīrate /
kolāvāsaṃ samāsajja vitahaṃ pādur esae //245//
jato vajjaṃ samuppajje ṇa tattha avalaṃbae /
tato ukkase appāṇaṃ savve phāse 'dhiyāsae //246//
ayaṃ cātatare (v.l. *cāyatatare*) *siyā je evaṃ aṇupālae* /
savvagāyaṇirodhe vi ṭhāṇāto ṇa vi ubbhame //247//
ayaṃ se uttame dhamme puvvaṭṭhānassa paggahe /
aciraṃ paḍilehittā vihare ciṭṭhaṁ (so Schubring; Jambuvijaya reads *ciṭṭha*) *māhaṇe* //248//
acittaṃ tu samāsajja ṭhāvae tattha appagaṃ /
vosire savvaso kāyaṃ ṇa me dehe parīsahā //249//
jāvajjīvaṃ parīsahā uvasaggā ya iti saṃkhāya /

He should not be attached to desires for transitory things, even when [they become] more numerous. He should not nourish wishes and greed, since he is looking for the unchanging character. (251)

[A god] may offer him eternal things,[9] [but] he should not trust this divine trick. Brahmin, recognize this, shaking off all that is inferior. (252)

Not stupefied by all things he reaches the other shore of his span of life. Knowing that endurance is highest, each of the [three ways] of liberation is good. (253).

Here we find a description of a voluntary starvation to death, accompanied by an as complete as possible restraint with regard to all activity and movement. It is the culmination of a life of training and preparation.[10]

The emphasis on restraint of activity and movement should not surprise us. We read repeatedly in the Āyār. that suffering is the result of activity (*āraṃbha, kamma*): "knowing that all this suffering is born from activity" (1.3.1.3 / 108 and 1.4.3.1/140; *āraṃbhajaṃ dukkham iṇaṃ ti ṇaccā);* "no action is found in him who has abandoned activity, the condition [for rebirth] originates on account of activity, (1.3.1.4 / 110; *akammassa vavahāro ṇa vijjati, kammuṇā uvādhi jāyati*).

The most obvious remedy against such a situation is to abstain from

---

saṃvuḍe dehabhedāe iti paṇṇe 'dhiyāsae //250//
bhiduresu ṇa rajjejjā kāmesu bahutaresu vi /
icchālobhaṃ ṇa sevejjā dhuvavaṇṇaṃ sapehiyā //251//
sāsaehiṃ ṇimaṃtejjā divvamāyaṃ ṇa saddahe /
taṃ paḍibujjha māhaṇe savvaṃ nūmaṃ vihūṇiyā (so Schubring, Jambuvijaya reads *vidhūṇitā*) *//252//*
savvaṭṭhehiṃ amucchie āyukālassa pārae /
titikkhaṃ paramaṃ ṇaccā vimohaṇṇataraṃ hitam //253//

9. Prof. Tatia draws my attention to *Yogasūtra* 3.51 and the Bhāṣya thereon, where the gods are made to say to the yogin, among other things: "Have entrance to this high-place which is unfading and ageless and deathless and dear to the gods." (*pratipadyatām idam akṣayam ajaram amarasthānaṃ devānāṃ priyam;* tr. Woods, 1914: 286.)

10. In these respects the above description contrasts with the later canonical descriptions of voluntary death contained in the *Paiṇṇayas*. This has been pointed out by Caillat (1977).

activity: "therefore he who does not act has ceased [from activity]; he who has ceased from that is called 'homeless'" (1.1.5.1/40; *taṃ je ṇo karae esovarate, etthovarae esa aṇagāre tti pavuccati*); "free from activity he knows and sees, he does not long for [anything] because of his insight; he is called 'homeless'" (1.2.2.1 / 71; *esa akamme jāṇati pāsati, paḍilehāe ṇāvakaṃkhati, esa aṇagāre tti pavuccati*); "But he is wise and awakened [who] has ceased from activity. ... Looking at those among the mortals in this world who are free from activity, having seen the result connected with activity, he who really knows turns away from that [activity]" (1.4. 4. 3 / 145; *se hu pannāṇamaṃte buddhe āraṃbhovarae ... ṇikkammadaṃsī iha macciehiṃ kammuṇā saphalaṃ daṭṭhūṇa*[11] *tato ṇijjāti vedavī*); etc.

[32] All this gives us a clear and intelligible picture of the way to liberation in early Jainism. Activity being the source of all unhappiness,[12] the attempt is made to put a stop to activity.[13] This is done in a most radical way. The monk abstains from food and prepares for death in a position which is as motionless as possible.

The passage translated above does not say a word about meditation (*jhāṇa* / Skt. *dhyāna*). This does not mean that nothing is said about the mental attitude of the monk. The monk is supposed to have diminished his passions, he should not long for life or death, must preserve his concentration and strive after a pure heart, etc. It is easy to guess that in the mental realm as in the bodily, cessation of activity is sought, but no detailed information is given in the *Āyāraṃga*.

3.2. For such information we turn to a slightly younger text, the *Uttarajjhayaṇa*, chapter 29. This chapter deals with the effects of a number of practices. Some of these are comparable with what we learned in the preceding section, others throw additional light on it.

---

11. This v.l. *daṭṭhūṇa* seems to make more sense than *daṭṭhuṃ*, which Schubring (1926: 89 n. 4) takes as "grammatisch ungenau fur pāsai od. dergl."
12. Injury to living beings seems to be the intermediate link between activity and the resulting unhappiness. This explains the always repeated emphasis in the Jaina scriptures on abstention from injury.
13. This is perhaps most concisely expressed at Sūy. 1.15.7 / 613: "For him who does not act there is no new *karman*" (*akuvvato ṇavaṃ natthi kammaṃ*). Old *karman*, be it noted, is cut off by asceticism (Uttar. 29.27 / 1129) as well as by non-activity (Uttar. 29.37 / 1129; see below).

Comparable with our earlier findings are the following statements: "What does the soul produce by renouncing activity? By renouncing activity it produces a state without activity. By being without activity the soul does not bind new *karman* and destroys the *karman* that was bound before". (29.37 / 1139; *jogapaccakkhāṇeṇaṃ ... jīve kaṃ jaṇayaï? jogapaccakkhāṇeṇaṃ ajogattaṃ jaṇayaï / ajogī ṇaṃ jīve navaṃ kammaṃ na baṃdhaï, puvvabaddhaṃ nijjarei*) "By renouncing food it stops the many hundreds of existences (which it would otherwise be doomed to live)" (29.40 / 1142; *bhattapaccakkhāṇeṇaṃ aṇegāiṃ bhavasayāiṃ niruṃbhaï*). "By the possession of right conduct [the soul] produces the state [of motionlessness] of the king of mountains. Having reached the state [of motionlessness] of the king of mountains, the homeless [monk] destroys the four parts of *karman* which [even] a *kevalin* possesses. After that [the soul] becomes perfected, awakened, freed, completely emancipated, and puts an end to all suffering" (29.61/1163; *caritta-saṃpannayāe ṇaṃ selesībhāvaṃ jaṇayaï / selesiṃ paḍivanne aṇagāre cattāri kevalikammaṃse khavei / tao pacchā sijjhaï bujjhaï muccaï parinivvāi savvadukkhāṇam aṃtaṃ karei /.*) These passages confirm our idea that liberation is effected by bringing all activity to a standstill.

The culmination of this process is described in Uttar. 29.72 / 1174:[14]

> Then having preserved his life [long enough], the remainder of life being less than the time of a *muhūrta*, he stops [all] activities and enters pure meditation (*sukkajjhāṇa*) in which only subtle activity remains and from which one does not fall back; he first stops the [33]
> activity of his mind, then of his speech and body, then he puts a stop to breathing out and breathing in. During the time needed to pronounce hardly five short syllables the homeless [monk], being in pure meditation in which [all] activity has been cut off and from which there is no return, simultaneously destroys the four parts of

14. *ahāuyaṃ pālaïttā aṃtomuhuttaddhāvasesāue joganirohaṃ karemāṇe suhumakiriyaṃ appaḍivāi sukkajjhāṇaṃ jhāyamāṇe tappaḍhamayāe maṇajogaṃ niruṃbhaï, vaïjogaṃ niruṃbhaï, kāyajogaṃ niruṃbhaï, āṇāpāṇunirohaṃ karei, īsipaṃcahrassakkharuccāraṇaddhāe ya ṇaṃ aṇagāre samucchinnakiriyaṃ aṇiyaṭṭiṃ sukkajjhāṇaṃ jhiyāyamāṇe veyaṇijjaṃ āuyaṃ nāmaṃ goyaṃ ca ee cattāri kammaṃse jugavaṃ khavei.*

karman [which remain]: pertaining to experience, span of life, name and lineage.

Here we meet with the term 'pure meditation' (*sukkajjhāṇa* / Skt. *śukladhyāna*). It is clear from the text that in this stage of pure meditation little or no activity remains. Initially only subtle activity remains, later all activity is cut off. The text adds, almost superfluously, that the monk stops the activities of his mind, speech and body, and even stops breathing. All this is exactly what we had expected on the basis of the supposition that early Jainism strives to obtain complete inactivity. This inactivity includes, we now know for certain, cessation of the mental processes. Let us however note that meditation, i.e. the attempt to stop the mental processes, constitutes here no more than one relatively minor aspect of the road to liberation.

3.3. A more detailed description of 'pure meditation' is found in the no doubt later *Ṭhāṇaṃga Sutta* (Ṭhāṇ.) which, like the *Aṅguttara Nikāya* of the Pāli canon, classifies and orders subject matters on the basis of the number of their subdivisions. At Ṭhāṇ. 4.1.69-72 / 247 we read:[15]

> Pure meditation is of four kinds and has four manifestations: 1. in which there is consideration of multiplicity and changes of object; 2. in which there is consideration of oneness and no change of object; 3. in which activity has become subtle and from which there is no return; 4. in which [all] activity has been cut off and from which one does not fall back. These are the four characteristics of pure meditation: absence of agitation, absence of delusion, discriminating insight, renunciation. These are the four supports of pure meditation: forbearance, freedom, softness, straightness. These are the four reflections of pure meditation: reflection on

15. *sukke jhāṇe caüvvihe caüppaoāre pannatte, taṃjahā – puhattavitakke saviyārī* (1), *egattavitakke aviyārī* (2), *suhumakirie aṇiyaṭṭī* (3), *samucchinnakirie appaḍivātī* (4) / *sukkassa ṇaṃ jhāṇassa cattāri lakkhaṇā pannattā, taṃjahā – avvahe asammohe vivege viussagge / sukkassa ṇaṃ jhāṇassa cattāri ālaṃbaṇā pannattā, taṃjahā – khaṃtī muttī maddave ajjave / sukkassa ṇaṃ jhāṇassa cattāri aṇuppehāo pannattāo, taṃjahā – aṇaṃtavattiyāṇuppehā vippariṇāmāṇuppehā asubhāṇuppehā avāyāṇuppehā /*

infinity, reflection on change, reflection on what is inauspicious, reflection on sin.

The third and fourth kind of pure meditation are here described as in the passage from the *Uttarajjhayaṇa* (29.72 / 1174) studied above. The only difference is that the words "from which one does not fall back" (*appaḍivātī*/*-vāi*) and "from which there is no return" (*aṇiyattī*) have changed place. There is therefore no reason to doubt that the *Ṭhāṇaṃga* [34]
Sutta follows in this point an older tradition.

In order to find out whether the other kinds of pure meditation also existed in early Jainism, we shall compare the above description with some passages from Āyār. I, certainly one of the oldest texts of the Jaina canon. The few occurrences of 'meditation' (*jhāṇa*), 'meditate' (*jhāti*) etc. in Āyār. I are all of them found in the ninth (in some editions eighth) chapter which describes the vicissitudes of Mahāvīra and may be a later addition. Of this Great Hero it is said that "he meditates with care and concentration, exerting himself day and night" (1.9.2.4 / 280; *rāiṃdivaṃ pi jayamāṇe appamatte samāhite jhātī*). Meditation is here said to be possible for long stretches of time, not, e.g., merely for a *muhūrta* as maintained by the later tradition.

Āyār. 1.9.4.14 / 320 reads: "Further, the Great Hero meditates on what is above, below, beside, while remaining in his position, motionless, observing his concentration, without desires."[16] This indicates that meditation can have an object in the outside world. This fits the second kind of pure meditation described in the *Uttarajjhayaṇa*. In this form of meditation there is "consideration of oneness and no change of object". A single object, we may assume, is made the focus of attention and this causes the mind to come to a standstill. The first kind of pure meditation must then be an introductory stage to the second kind.

We see that the four kinds of pure meditation can be looked upon as stages on the road to complete motionlessness and physical death. At the first stage the mind still moves from one object to another. At the second stage it stops doing so and comes to a standstill. At the third and fourth

16. *avi jhāti se mahāvīre āsaṇatthe akukkue jhāṇaṃ / uḍḍhaṃ adhe ya tiriyaṃ ca pehamāṇe samāhim apaḍiṇṇe /*

stages motionlessness of the body comes about in addition to motionlessness of the mind. When complete motionlessness of body and mind has been reached, physical death takes place.

It is characteristic for the emphasis on the body in early Jainism that even in the above description of pure meditation two of the four kinds of pure meditation are described in physical rather than mental terms. The third and fourth kind of pure meditation are characterized by little or no activity of the body, in addition to that of the mind. Only this interpretation, so it seems, makes satisfactory sense, and agrees with the earlier passages which we discussed.

[35] 3.4. The description of pure meditation in the *Ṭhāṇaṃga Sutta* does not stand alone. Pure meditation is presented as one (the last) of four types of *dhyāna*, viz. *ārta* (AMg. *aṭṭa;* afflicted), *raudra* (*rodda;* wrathful), *dharmya* (*dhamma;* pious), and *śukla* (*sukka;* pure). The first three are described as follows (Ṭhāṇ. 4.1.61-68 / 247):[17]

> Afflicted *dhyāna* is of four kinds: 1. [one] is joined with what is not liked and also accompanied by the thought of separation therefrom; 2. [one] is joined with what is liked and also accompanied by the thought of non-separation therefrom; 3. [one] is joined with disease and also accompanied by the thought of separation therefrom; 4. [one] is joined with the experience of agreeable pleasures and also accompanied by the thought of non-separation therefrom. These are the four characteristics of afflicted *dhyāna:* crying, grief, weeping, lamentation.
>
> Wrathful *dhyāna* is of four kinds: connected with injury, connected

17. *aṭṭe jhāṇe caüvvihe pannatte, taṃjahā amaṇunnasaṃpaogasaṃpaütte tassa vippaogasatisamaṇṇāgate yāvi bhavati* (1), *maṇunnasaṃpaogasaṃpaütte tassa avippaogasatisamaṇṇāgate yāvi bhavati* (2), *ātaṃkasaṃpaogasaṃpaütte tassa vippaogasatisamaṇṇāgate yāvi bhavati* (3), *parijusitakāmabhogasaṃpaoga-saṃpaütte tassa avippaogasatisamaṇṇāgate yāvi bhavati* (4) / *aṭṭassa ṇaṃ jhāṇassa cattāri lakkhaṇā pannattā, taṃjahā kaṃdaṇatā sotaṇatā tippaṇatā paridevaṇatā* /

rodde jhāṇe caüvvihe pannatte, taṃjahā hiṃsāṇubaṃdhi mosāṇubaṃdhi

with robbery, connected with theft, connected with the protection [of worldly goods]. These are the four characteristics of wrathful *dhyāna:* [one] has abundant hatred, much hatred, hatred due to ignorance, hatred until the end which is death.

Pious *dhyāna* is of four kinds and has four manifestations: examination of the commandments [of the Jinas], examination of sins, examination of the results [of actions], examination of the forms [of the constituents of the world]. These are the four characteristics of pious *dhyāna:* liking for the commandments [of the Jinas],[18] liking for the natural state, liking for the scriptures, liking for pervasive study [of the scriptures]. These are the four supports of pious *dhyāna:* recitation, questioning, repetition, reflection. These are the four reflections of pious *dhyāna:* reflection on being alone, reflection on transitoriness, reflection on there being no refuge, reflection on birth and rebirth of living beings.

It is clear that in this passage *dhyāna* refers to a pondering over, a thinking about certain things, and not to the process of stopping the mind which we have designated 'meditation'. Yet the term *dhyāna* covers both 'pondering' and 'meditation'. This is the reason that a classificatory text like the *Ṭhāṇaṃga* can distinguish four types of *dhyāna:* afflicted, wrathful, pious, and pure.[19] Only the last type – *śukla dhyāna* – is of interest for our study of early Jaina meditation.

---

teṇāṇubaṃdhi sārakkhaṇāṇubaṃdhi / roddassa ṇaṃ jhāṇassa cattāri lakkhaṇā pannattā, taṃjahā – osaṇṇadose bahudose annāṇadose āmaraṇaṃtadose /

dhamme jhāṇe caüvvihe caüppaḍoyāre pannatte, taṃjahā āṇāvijate avāyavijate vivāgavijate saṃṭhāṇavijate / dhammassa ṇaṃ jhāṇassa cattāri lakkhaṇā pannattā, taṃjahā – āṇāruī ṇisaggaruī suttaruī ogāḍharuī / dhammassa ṇaṃ jhāṇassa cattāri ālaṃbaṇā pannattā, taṃjahā – vāyaṇā paḍipucchaṇā pariyaṭṭaṇā aṇuppehā / dhammassa ṇaṃ jhāṇassa cattāri aṇuppehāo pannattāo, taṃjahā – egāṇuppehā aṇiccāṇuppehā asaraṇāṇuppehā saṃsārāṇuppehā /

18. Or: "liking for knowledge" (Alsdorf, 1966: 203-04 ((51)-(52))).

19. The idea of four types of *dhyāna* may have been derived from a verse in the *Uttarajjhayaṇa* (30.35/1211): *aṭṭaroddāṇi vajjettā jhāejjā susamāhie / dhamma-sukkāiṃ jhāṇāiṃ jhāṇaṃ taṃ tu buhā vae //* It is not clear from this śloka whether there is a distinction between *dhamma jhāṇa* and *sukka jhāṇa*. Perhaps pure meditation (*sukka jhāṇa*) is 'in accordance with the doctrine' (*dhamma*). It is certainly clear that afflicted and wrathful *dhyāna* are to be avoided.

[36] However, these four types of *dhyāna* came to be looked upon as four types of meditation, and this led to peculiar results. The *Viyāhapaṇṇatti Sutta* (25.7.217 / 580) and the *Uvavāiya Sutta* (§ 30) distinguish six kinds of inner asceticism. The fifth is meditation (*dhyāna*). What is this meditation? That is explained at Viy. 25.7.237-49 / 600-12 and Uvav. § 30 V′, both of which are virtually identical with Ṭhāṇ. 4.1.61-72 / 247 studied above; both therefore describe all four types of *dhyāna*. This is a plain absurdity. Afflicted and wrathful *dhyāna* at any rate cannot possibly be considered forms of asceticism.

Interestingly, the confusion about *dhyāna* also found expression in an altogether different manner. The *Āvassaya Sutta* contains a sūtra (4.23.4) where the confessing monk is made to repent for "the four *dhyānas:* afflicted *dhyāna,* wrathful *dhyāna,* pious *dhyāna,* pure *dhyāna*" (*paḍikkamāmi caühiṃ jhāṇehiṃ – aṭṭeṇaṃ jhāṇeṇaṃ, ruddeṇaṃ jhāṇeṇaṃ, dhammeṇaṃ jhāṇeṇaṃ, sukkeṇaṃ jhāṇeṇaṃ*).[20]

All this makes sufficiently clear that the four types of *dhyāna* distinguished in the later texts of the Jaina canon are of no value for the study of meditation in early Jainism.

3.5. Some more information about early Jaina meditation is gained from *Uttarajjhayaṇa* 29:

"By making the mind onepointed [the soul] brings about the destruction of thought" (29.25 / 1127; *egaggamaṇasannivesaṇayāe ṇaṃ cittaniroham karei*). "By renouncing existence [the soul] brings about [the state] from which there is no return. And the homeless [monk] who has reached [the state] from which there is no return destroys the four parts of *karman* which [even] a *kevalin* possesses, viz. pertaining to experience, span of life, name, and lineage. After that [the soul] becomes perfected, awakened, freed, completely emancipated, and puts an end to all suffering." (29.41 / 1143; *sabbhāvapaccakkhāṇeṇaṃ aniyaṭṭiṃ jaṇayaï / aniyaṭṭipaḍivanne ya aṇagāre cattāri kevalikammaṃse khavei, taṃ jahā – veyaṇijjaṃ āuyaṃ nāmaṃ goyaṃ / tao pacchā sijjhaï bujjhaï muccaï parinivvāi savvadukkhāṇaṃ aṃtaṃ karei /*.)

20. The *ekottarikā*-pattern of Āv. 4 (Bruhn, 1981:23) excludes the possibility that this sūtra originally enumerated fewer (or more) than four *dhyānas*.

"By watchfulness of the mind the soul brings about onepointed [thought]. When thought is onepointed and the mind is watched the soul becomes devoted to control." (29.53 / 1155; *maṇaguttayāe ṇaṃ jīve egaggaṃ jaṇayaï / egaggacitte ṇaṃ jīve maṇagutte saṃjamārāhae bhavaï /.*)

"By holding the mind together[21] [the soul] brings about onepointed- [37]
ness. Having brought about onepointedness it brings about modifications of knowledge. Having brought about modifications of knowledge it purifies right belief and destroys wrong belief. ... By holding speech together [the soul] purifies the modifications of belief which are mixed with speech. Having purified the modifications of belief which are mixed with speech [the soul] easily reaches enlightenment, and is no longer such that it reaches enlightenment with difficulty. ... By holding the body together [the soul] purifies the modifications of conduct. Having purified the modifications of conduct it purifies the conduct which is in accord with the word [of the *tīrthaṅkaras*]. Having purified the conduct which is in accord with the word [of the *tīrthaṅkaras*, the soul] destroys the four parts of *karman* which [even] a *kevalin* possesses. After that [the soul] becomes perfected, awakened, freed, completely emancipated, and puts an end to all suffering." (29.56-58 / 1158-60; *maṇasamāhāraṇayāe ṇaṃ egaggaṃ jaṇayaï / egaggaṃ jaṇaïttā nāṇapajjave jaṇayaï / nāṇapajjave jaṇaïttā sammattaṃ visohei, micchattaṃ ca nijjarei / ... vaïsamāhāraṇayāe ṇaṃ vaïsāhāraṇadaṃsaṇapajjave visohei / vaïsāhāraṇadaṃsaṇapajjave visohittā sulabhabohiyattaṃ nivvattei, dullabhabohiyattaṃ nijjarei / ... kāyasamāhāraṇayāe ṇaṃ carittapajjave visohei / carittapajjave visohittā ahakkhāyacarittaṃ visohei / ahakkhāyacarittaṃ visohettā cattāri kevalikammaṃse khavei / tao pacchā sijjhaï bujjhaï muccaï parinivvāi savvadukkhāṇam aṃtaṃ karei /.)* "By subjugating the organ of hearing [the soul] brings about the subjugation of its likes and dislikes for pleasant and unpleasant sounds, it does not bind the *karman* which results therefrom, and destroys [the *karman*] which has been bound before. ... By subjugating the organ of sight [the soul] brings about the subjugation of its likes and dislikes for pleasant and unpleasant colours, it does not bind the *karman* which results therefrom, and destroys [the *karman*] which has

21. *samāhāraṇayā* = Skt. *samādhāraṇatā* ?

been bound before. With regard to the organ of smelling it is the same, as also with the organ of taste, and the organ of touch." (29.62-66 / 1164-68; *soiṃdiyaniggaheṇaṃ maṇunnāmaṇunnesu saddesu rāgadosaniggahaṃ jaṇayaï, tappaccaïyaṃ kammaṃ na baṃdhaï, puvvabaddhaṃ ca nijjarei / ... cakkhiṃdiyaniggaheṇaṃ maṇunnāmaṇunnesu rūvesu rāgadosa-niggahaṃ jaṇayaï, tappaccaïyaṃ kammaṃ na baṃdhaï, puvvabaddhaṃ ca nijjarei / ghāṇiṃdie evaṃ ceva / jibbhiṃdie vi / phāsiṃdie vi /.*)

3.6. We can summarize the results of the above as follows. Early Jaina meditation was only one aspect of a more general attempt to stop all activities of body and mind, including even breathing. In order to bring
[38] about this mental state a number of means were employed. Reflections on infinity, on change, on what is inauspicious, and on sin were probably preparatory. More immediate precursors of meditation proper, we may assume, were certain mental states, viz. forbearance, freedom, softness, and straightness. Other supportive practices were onepointedness of the mind, watchfulness of the mind, holding the mind together, and subjugation of the sense-organs. Meditation itself was characterized by absence of agitation, absence of delusion, discriminating insight, and renunciation.

Meditation was said to have four kinds of manifestations, which must be understood to be four steps on the ladder to perfection. They are described thus: 1. in which there is consideration of multiplicity and change of object; 2. in which there is consideration of oneness and no change of object; 3. in which activity has become subtle and from which there is no return; 4. in which [all] activity has been cut off and from which one does not fall back.

The fourfold division of meditation into afflicted, wrathful, pious and pure, is not reliable. Undoubtedly this division was made by early systematisers and must initially have been meant to be a division of *dhyāna,* which word means both 'thought' and 'meditation'. Later theoreticians mistakenly took it to be a division of meditation only, and this did not fail to influence the later history of Jaina meditation.

IV. Meditation as part of asceticism in early Hindu scriptures. [42]

4.1. The main idea of the road to liberation in early Jainism is also expressed in *Bhagavad Gītā* (BhG) 18.3 :[1] "Some wise men say that [all] activity is to be abandoned as evil."

More details are given at *Mahābhārata* (MBh) 1.86.14-16 :[2]

> But the *muni* who behaves like a *muni* by abandoning desires, renouncing activity, and conquering his senses, he reaches perfection in the world (14). Who should not honour him who has clean teeth, whose nails are cut, who is always bathed and adorned, is not bound and performs [only] pure actions ?[3] (15) Emaciated by austerities, patient, his flesh, bones and blood wasted away, when the *muni* becomes free from the pairs (of opposites, such as heat and cold), then he really behaves like a *muni*. Then, having conquered this world, he gains the other world (16).

Briefly stated: "Such a *muni* reaches perfection which is the most important [thing there is], by living in the forest, his food and movements being restrained."[4]

---

1. *tvājyaṃ doṣavad ity eke karma prāhur manīṣiṇaḥ.*
2. *yas tu kāmān parityajya tyaktakarmā jitendriyaḥ /*
ātiṣṭheta munir maunaṃ sa loke siddhim āpnuyāt //14//
dhautadantaṃ kṛttanakhaṃ sadā snātam alaṃkṛtam /
asitaṃ sitakarmasthaṃ kas taṃ nārcitum arhati //15//
tapasā karśitaḥ kṣāmaḥ kṣīṇamāṃsāsthiśoṇitaḥ /
yadā bhavati nirdvandvo munir maunam samāsthitaḥ /
atha lokam imaṃ jitvā lokaṃ vijayate param //16//
3. *sitakarmastham.* This expression is not fully clear. Nīlakaṇṭha's explanation (his text reads *sitakarmāṇam*) does not help much: *sitakarmāṇaṃ hiṃsāyuktaṃ dharmam api tyajantam* (p. 170, on 1.91.15).
4. MBh 1.86.4: *tādṛn muniḥ siddhim upaiti mukhyāṃ vasann araṇye niyatāhāra-ceṣṭaḥ //*

Motionlessness of body and mind is emphasized at MBh 12.294. 13-18:[5]

> Freed from all attachments, taking little food, having conquered the senses , he should fix his mind on his self in the first and last part of the night (13). Having made his senses firm with his mind, oh lord of Mithilā, and having made his mind (*manas*) firm with his intellect (*buddhi*), he is motionless like a stone (14). He should be without trembling like a pillar, and motionless like a mountain; the wise who know to follow the precepts then call him 'one engaged in Yoga' (*yukta*) (15). He neither hears nor smells nor tastes nor sees; he notices no touch, nor does [his] mind form conceptions (16). Like a piece of wood, he does not desire anything, nor does he notice [anything]. When he has reached the Original Nature (*prakṛti*), then sages call him 'engaged in Yoga' (*yukta*) (17). And he looks like a lamp shining in a place without wind; not flickering and motionless it will not move upward or sideward (18).

The *Kaṭha Upaniṣad* (KU) is probably the earliest Upaniṣad which gives some detailed information about meditation. The concluding verse
[43] (6.18) declares that 'the whole method of Yoga' (*yogavidhiṃ kṛtsnam*) has been presented. The most informative verses are KU 6.10-11:[6]

> When the five organs of knowledge stand still together with the mind (*manas*), and the intellect (*buddhi*) does not stir, that they call

---

5. *vimuktaḥ sarvasaṅgebhyo laghvāhāro jitendriyaḥ /*
pūrvarātre pare caiva dhārayeta mano ''tmani //13//
sthirīkṛtyendriyagrāmaṃ manasā mithileśvara /
mano buddhyā sthiraṃ kṛtvā pāṣāṇa iva niścalaḥ //14//
sthāṇuvac cāpy akampaḥ syād girivac cāpi niścalaḥ /
budhā vidhividhānajñās tadā yuktaṃ pracakṣate //15//
na śṛṇoti na cāghrāti na rasyati na paśyati /
na ca sparśaṃ vijānāti na saṃkalpayate manaḥ //16//
na cābhimanyate kiṃcin na ca budhyati kāṣṭhavat /
tadā prakṛtim āpannaṃ yuktam āhur manīṣinaḥ //17//
nivāte ca yathā dīpyan dīpas tadvat sa dṛśyate /
niriṅgaś cācalaś cordhvaṃ na tiryag gatim āpnuyāt //18//

6. *yadā pañcāvatiṣṭhante jñānāni manasā saha /*
buddhiś ca na viceṣṭati tām āhuḥ paramāṃ gatim //10//
tāṃ yogam iti manyante sthirām indriyadhāraṇām /
apramattas tadā bhavati yogo hi prabhavāpyayau //11//

> the highest course (10). This they consider as Yoga, a firm fixing of the senses. Then one becomes careful, for Yoga is the origin and the end (11).

KU 3.6 has the same tenor:[7]

> But he who has discernment, with an ever controlled (*yukta*) mind (*manas*), his senses are subdued, like the good horses of a charioteer.

The following description in the *Śvetāśvatara Upaniṣad* (2.8-9) gives also the bodily practices their due:[8]

> Holding the body straight, three parts of it stretched up, causing the senses to enter into the heart by means of the mind, the wise one should cross over all the frightening streams with the help of the raft which is Brahman (8). Having here suppressed his breaths and having brought his movements under control (*yuktaceṣṭa*), when his breath has been diminished, he should take breath through his nose. Being careful, the wise one should restrain (*dhārayeta*) his mind like that chariot yoked with vicious horses (9).

The *Maitrāyaṇīya Upaniṣad* (MU 6.18)[9] speaks of a six-membered Yoga, consisting of restraint of the breath, withdrawal of the senses, meditation, fixing the mind, insight (*tarka*),[10] concentration. All these terms, with the single exception of *tarka*, are known from the other early

---

7. *yas tu vijñānavān bhavati yuktena manasā sadā /*
tasyendriyāṇi vaśyāni sadaśvā iva sāratheḥ //
8. *trir unnataṃ sthāpya samaṃ śarīraṃ hṛdīndriyāṇi manasā saṃniveśya /*
brahmoḍupena pratareta vidvān srotāṃsi sarvāṇi bhayāvahāni //8//
prāṇān prapīḍyeha sa yuktaceṣṭaḥ kṣīṇe prāṇe nāsikayocchvasīta /
duṣṭāśvayuktam iva vāham enaṃ vidvān mano dhārayetāpramattaḥ //9//
9. *prāṇāyāmaḥ pratyāhāro dhyānaṃ dhāraṇā tarkaḥ samādhiḥ ṣaḍaṅga ity ucyate yogaḥ.*
10. The use of *tarka* here is surprising. The only meaning which seems to fit both here and at MU 6.20 (see below) is 'insight'. A similar meaning is assigned to this term in Abhinavagupta's Tantrāloka (III.13-15, 34, 40); see Pandey, 1963: 535; Pensa, 1973: 11-13.

passages on meditation which we have studied. The explanation of 'fixing the mind' (*dhāraṇā*) is interesting (MU 6.20):[11]

> And elsewhere also it has been said: After this, the fixing of it (i.e., of the mind). As a result of pressing the tip of the tongue against the palate and suppressing speech, mind and breath, one sees Brahman through insight (?; *tarka*)[12].

The tip of the tongue is here said to be pressed against the palate. The same is said at *Viṣṇusmṛti* 97.1 and *Triśikhibrāhmaṇa Upaniṣad* 93 and 146. But this is exactly what the early Buddhist critic ridiculed the Jainas for in the Original Mahāsaccaka Sūtra (above, § 1.1). A point of difference is that the *Viṣṇusmṛti* (97.1) and the *Triśikhibrāhmaṇa Upaniṣad* (92 and
[44] 146) add that the teeth do not touch each other, whereas the Original Mahāsaccaka Sūtra said they do. Here, however, the *Mahā Upaniṣad* (5.75) and the *Muktikā Upaniṣad* (2.42) agree with the account in the Original Mahāsaccaka Sūtra, by talking about 'grinding the teeth' (*dantair dantān vicūrṇya*). We see that the description of meditation in the Original Mahāsaccaka Sūtra corresponds with these texts in this respect.

Details of meditation are found in a few verses given at MU 6. 34 (Van Buitenen, 1962: 105):[13]

> When [someone], having made his mind (*manas*) completely motionless, without dissolution or distraction, goes to a state without mind, that is the highest place (7). The mind has to remain suppressed until it is destroyed in the heart. This is knowledge, this is liberation; the rest, on the other hand, is bookish proliferation[14] (8). The bliss, purified by concentration, which arises when the

---

11. *athānyatrāpy uktam – ataḥ parāsya dhāraṇā / tālurasanāgranipīḍanād vāṅmanaḥ-prāṇanirodhanād brahma tarkeṇa paśyati /*. The readings *ataḥ* and *tālurasanāgra-nipīḍanād* (so Limaye-Vadekar, 1958: 343) seem to make more sense than *atha* and *tālurasanāgre nipīḍanād* (so Van Buitenen, 1962: 112).
12. See note 10 above.
13. *layavikṣeparahitaṃ manaḥ kṛtvā suniścalam /*
yadā yāty amanobhāvaṃ tadā tat paramaṃ padam //7//
tāvan mano niroddhavyaṃ hṛdi yāvat kṣayaṃ gatam /
etaj jñānaṃ ca mokṣaś ca śeṣas tu granthavistarāḥ //8//
samādhinirdhautam amalasya cetaso, niveśitasyātmani yat sukhaṃ bhavet /
na śakyate varṇayituṃ girā tadā, svayaṃ tad antaḥkaraṇena gṛhyate //9//
14. So Van Buitenen, 1962: 133.

> spotless mind (*cetas*) has been made to enter into the self, cannot be described with words. It is in that state (*tadā*) itself experienced by the inner organ (9).

It is remarkable that here bliss is said to accompany meditation which is clearly of the type also met with in early Jainism. The author of the Original Mahāsaccaka Sūtra had denied experiences of bliss to Jaina meditation and reserved them for Buddhist meditation. Is the mention of bliss here due to influence from Buddhist meditation? It is possible, for influence from Buddhism in the *Maitrāyaṇīya Upaniṣad* seems likely (Horsch, 1966: 197-203; Pande, 1974: 575-76). It is however strange that not more features of Buddhist meditation are found in this Upaniṣad.

4.2. Restraint of breath has been referred to a few times in the passages discussed in § 3.1. It recurs more emphatically in certain others. BhG 4. 29 speaks of those "who having stopped the movements of breathing in (*prāṇa*) and breathing out (*apāna*) are devoted to *prāṇāyāma*" (*prāṇāpānagatī ruddhvā prāṇāyāmaparāyaṇāḥ*). This suggests that the term *prāṇāyāma* can refer to a complete cessation of breathing. This agrees with the definition of *prāṇāyāma* in *Yoga Sūtra* (YS) 2.49 as "cutting off the movement of breathing out and breathing in" (*śvāsapraśvāsayor gativicchedaḥ*).

The following passage brings restraint of breath in connection with fixing the mind (MBh 12.304.8-10):[15]

> But they say in accordance with the teaching of the sacred books that the highest Yoga-activity among [the different forms of] Yoga is of two kinds: with properties (*saguṇa*) and without properties [45]
> (*nirguṇa*) (8). [These two are] fixing the mind and restraint of breath (*prāṇāyāma*), oh king; restraint of breath is with properties,

15. *dviguṇaṃ yogakṛtyaṃ tu yogānāṃ prāhur uttamam /*
saguṇaṃ nirguṇaṃ caiva yathāśāstranidarśanam //8//
dhāraṇā caiva manasaḥ prāṇāyāmaś ca pārthiva /
prāṇāyāmo hi saguṇo nirguṇaṃ dhāraṇaṃ (v.l. *dhārayen*) *manaḥ //9//*
yatra dṛśyeta muñcan vai prāṇān maithilasattama /
vātādhikyaṃ bhavaty eva tasmād dhi na samācaret //10//

> fixing the mind[16] is without properties (9). Where [a Yogin] would be seen leaving his breaths free, oh best among the people of Mithilā, there is certainly an excess of air (*vāta*); therefore one should not act [in such a manner] (10).

The passage is obscure, but seems to consider *prāṇāyāma* less than and probably preparatory to fixing the mind. Verse 10 seems to indicate the need for *prāṇāyāma;* otherwise there would be an excess of air. This indicates that apparently *prāṇāyāma* remains a necessity also in the state 'without properties', i.e., fixing the mind. It certainly shows that here too *prāṇāyāma* concerns the breath, not, or not only, the senses.[17]

The following passage comes closer to the idea that saints stop their breathing moments before death (MBh 12.207.25):[18]

> Having reached equilibrium of the *guṇas*, performing [only] such actions as concern sustaining the body, and pushing at the time of death the breaths into the artery of the heart (*manovahā*) with merely the mind, one is liberated.

The same may be intended at MBh 13.154.2, where in describing the death of Bhīṣma it is said:[19]

> The breaths of that great soul, forced together, went up.

4.3. Fasting to death was practised by Yayāti (MBh 1.81.10-16):[20]

> King Yayāti the son of Nahuṣa anointed his younger son Pūru king and then gladly departed for the forest (10). Having sent his sons Yadu etc. to the borders [of the kingdom], the king lived for a long

---

16. The reading *dhāraṇaṃ manaḥ* is hard to construe grammatically; the v.l. *dhārayen manaḥ* is better, but not completely satisfactory. Perhaps however we may accept a construction action noun + accusative as permissible for epic Sanskrit, as it is for Pāli (Hinüber, 1968: 54-55).
17. This is maintained by Edgerton (1924: 41 n. 46).
18. *guṇānāṃ sāmyam āgamya manasaiva manovaham* (v.l. *manovahām*) / *dehakarma* (v.l. *dehakarmā*) *nudan prāṇān antakāle vimucyate* //
19. *tasyordhvam agaman prāṇāḥ saṃniruddhā mahātmanaḥ.*
20. *yayātir nāhuṣo rājā pūruṃ putraṃ kanīyasam /*
rājye 'bhiṣicya muditaḥ pravavrāja vanaṃ tadā //10//
anteṣu sa vinikṣipya putrān yadupurogamān /
phalamūlāśano rājā vane saṃnyavasac ciram //11//

> time in the forest, eating [only] fruits and roots (11). Firmly resolved, having conquered anger, satisfying manes and gods, and duly pouring oblations into the fires, [all] in accordance with the rules of forest-dwellers (12), the mighty one honoured guests with oblations obtained from the forest. Adopting the mode of life by way of gleaning, eating remains of food (13),[21] the king accepted this mode of life for a full thousand years. Eating [only] water for thirty autumns, he kept his speech and mind under restraint (14). Then he ate [only] wind for a year, free from lassitude. And the king performed asceticism in the midst of five fires for a year (15). And he stood on one foot for six months, eating [only] air. Then, [46]
> having a reputation of virtue, he went to heaven, ...

Fasting to death is prescribed, after a preparatory course of asceticism, at *Yājñavalkyasmṛti* II.3.50-55 :[22]

> He should spend the time with fasts regulated by the moon, or he should continually be engaged in painful exercises. Or, alternatively, he should eat when a fortnight has passed, or when a month, or a day, has passed (50). Being pure he should sleep on the earth at night, the day he should spend [standing] on the tip of his toes, or standing, sitting, or walking about, or again by practising Yoga

---

saṃśitātmā jitakrodhas tarpayan pitṛdevatāḥ /
agnīṃś ca vidhivaj juhvan vānaprasthavidhānataḥ //12//
atithīn pūjayām āsa vanyena haviṣā vibhuḥ /
śiloñchavṛttim āsthāya śeṣānnakṛtabhojanaḥ //13//
pūrṇaṃ varṣasahasraṃ sa evaṃvṛttir abhūn nṛpaḥ /
abbhakṣaḥ śaradas triṃśad āsīn niyatavāṅmanāḥ //14//
tataś ca vāyubhakṣo 'bhūt saṃvatsaram atandritaḥ /
pañcāgnimadhye ca tapas tepe saṃvatsaraṃ nṛpaḥ //15//
ekapādasthitaś cāsīt ṣaṇmāsān anilāśanaḥ /
puṇyakīrtis tataḥ svargam jagām[a] ...

21. On the meaning and implication of this term (*śeṣānnakṛtabhojana*) see Wezler, 1978, esp. p. 87-88.

22. *cāndrāyaṇair nayet kālaṃ kṛcchrair vā vartayet sadā /*
pakṣe gate vāpy aśnīyāt māse vāhani vā gate //50//
śucir bhūmau svaped rātrau divasaṃ prapadair nayet /
sthānāsanavihārair vā yogābhyāsena vā punaḥ //51//

> (51). He should perform asceticism in the midst of five fires in summer, lying on the bare ground during the rains, and wearing wet clothes in winter, or he should perform asceticism according to his power (52). If someone pricks him with thorns, or anoints him with sandal, he is neither angry nor satisfied with all and with that man (53). Or having placed the fires upon himself, living under a tree, taking limited food, he should go for alms in order to prolong his life,[23] only in the houses of forest-dwellers (54). Or, taking eight mouthfuls from a village, he should eat it, his speech remaining restrained. Or, eating [only] wind he should go to the north-east, until the destruction of his body (55).

It deserves notice that the final fast is here not accompanied by motionlessness.[24]

Death through fasting and restraint of breath is described at *Āpastambīya Dharma Sūtra* 2.9.23.1-2:[25]

> Or, if he desires [to perform] more restraint, he should collect things (i.e., food) every day, morning and evening, in a vessel (1). After that he should wander, surviving on roots, fruits, leaves, or grass; in the end he should live on what happens [to come to him], then on water, [then] air, [then] ether. Each next undertaking brings greater reward (2).

---

grīṣme pañcāgnimadhyastho varṣāsu sthaṇḍil eśayaḥ /
ārdravāsāś ca hemante śaktyā vāpi tapaś caret //52//
yaḥ kaṇṭakair vitudati candanair yaś ca limpati /
akruddho 'parituṣṭaś ca samastasya ca tasya ca //53//
agnīn vāpy ātmasāt kṛtvā vṛkṣāvāsī mitāśanaḥ /
vānaprasthagṛheṣv eva yatrārtham bhaikṣam ācaret //54//
grāmād āhṛtya vā grāsān aṣṭau bhuñjīta vāgyataḥ /
vāyvaśanaḥ prāgudīcīṃ gacched vā varṣmasaṃkṣayāt //55//

23. I understand, following Wezler in a private communication, *yātrā* ° as ellipsis for *dehayātrā* °.

24. This and the preceding case have affiliations with 'Vedic asceticism'; see my *The Two Sources of Indian Asceticism*, forthcoming.

25. *bhūyāṃsaṃ vā niyamam icchann anvaham eva pātreṇa sāyaṃ prātar artham āharet //1// tato mūlaiḥ phalaiḥ parṇais tṛṇair iti vartayaṃś cared antataḥ pravṛttāni tato 'po vāyum ākāśam ity abhiniśrayet teṣām uttara uttaraḥ saṃyogaḥ phalato viśiṣṭaḥ //2//.*

4.4. It is clear that all the important features of early Jaina meditation are found in the early Hindu scriptures. Here too meditation is only one aspect of a more general process in which all bodily and mental activities are stopped. Fasting to death and stopping the breath, both of which we had come to know as characteristic accompaniments of early Jaina meditation, are also present in the Hindu scriptures. The same is true of bodily [47] motionlessness, which is compared with the state of a stone, of a pillar, of a mountain.

As in early Jainism, meditation itself aims at the motionlessness of the mind. Here as well the sense organs are conquered. As a result the adept is said not to hear, smell, etc.

There can be no doubt that the early Jaina and Hindu scriptures describe forms of meditation which belong to the same tradition. Therefore we shall speak of main stream meditation. It cannot be denied that this kind of meditation, and more in particular its accompaniments, have been described remarkably well, although not fully, by the author of the Original Mahāsaccaka Sūtra and elsewhere in the Buddhist canon.

[51] **V. Theory and practice in the main stream.**

5.1. The idea that liberation from the effects of activity is obtained by abstaining from activity may have been criticized from the earliest period. We find it in the *Bhagavad Gītā* 3.4-6:[1]

> A man does not reach the state free from activity by not performing actions; and he does not attain perfection by merely abandoning [activity] (4). For no one ever remains without activity even for a moment, because everyone, being powerless, is made to perform activity by the *guṇas* which are born from Original Nature (*prakṛti*) (5). He who sits, restraining his organs of action [but] thinking with his mind of the objects of the senses, he is said to be deluded and of improper demeanour (6). But he, Arjuna, who performs discipline of action (*karmayoga*) with his organs of action, restraining his senses with his mind, unattached, he excels (7).

The same criticism is expressed in BhG 18.11: "For it is not possible for an embodied being to abandon completely all actions" (*na hi dehabhṛtā śakyaṃ tyaktuṃ karmāṇy aśeṣataḥ*).

Criticism of this kind has to answer the question whether liberation can be attained in another way, and if yes, which way. The answer which is given is surprisingly simple. Liberation from the results of one's actions is possible because in reality no actions are ever performed. They are not performed because man's inner self, his soul, is completely different from

---

1. *na karmaṇām anārambhān naiṣkarmyaṃ puruṣo 'śnute /*
na ca saṃnyāsanād eva siddhiṃ samadhigacchati //4//
na hi kaś cit kṣaṇam api jātu tiṣṭhaty akarmakṛt /
kāryate hy avaśaḥ karma sarvaḥ prakṛtijair guṇaiḥ //5//
karmendriyāṇi saṃyamya ya āste manasā smaran /
indriyārthān vimūḍhātmā mithyācāraḥ sa ucyate //6//
yas tv indriyāṇi manasā niyamyārabhate 'rjuna /
karmendriyaiḥ karmayogam asaktaḥ sa viśiṣyate //7//

his body and never acts.[2] The *Bhagavad Gītā* (3.27) puts it like this:[3]

> Actions are, all of them, undertaken by the *guṇas* of Original Nature (*prakṛti*). He who is deluded by egoism thinks 'I am the doer'.

It is sufficient to know that in reality one never performs any actions:[4]

> But he, oh long-armed one, who knows the truth about the category *guṇa* and the category action, knowing that the *guṇas* move about among the *guṇas*, he does not get attached (28). Those who are confused by the *guṇas* of Original Nature (*prakṛti*) get attached to the *guṇas* and their actions. He who knows all should not disturb those dull [people] who do not know all.

It is clear that in this way an altogether different road to liberation is introduced. The *Bhagavad Gītā* (3.3) calls it *jñānayoga* 'discipline of knowledge' and mentions it together with the 'discipline of action' [52
(*karmayoga*) which enjoins disinterested activity:[5]

> In this world a two-fold foundation (of religious salvation) has been expounded by Me of old : by the discipline of knowledge of the followers of Sāṅkhya, and by the discipline of action of the followers of Yoga. (tr. Edgerton, 1924: 1).

This 'discipline of knowledge' is, of course, the *sāṃkhya*[6] which is so often referred to in the *Mahābhārata*, as has been shown by Edgerton

---

2. This idea is already known to *Sūyagaḍaṃga* 13-14 (1.1.1.13-14); see Bollée, 1977: 15 and 66f. In Buddhist literature the idea is primarily connected with Pūraṇa Kassapa (Basham, 1951: 13), but sometime with others, such as Saṃjayin Vairāṭīputra (Vogel, 1970: 25f.). The idea is perhaps also present in MN III.19 and SN III.103, where the question is asked (and rejected) what self is affected by actions which have not been performed by a self, since the five skandhas are not the self; see however Schmithausen, 1986: 228-29 n. 122.
3. *prakṛteḥ kriyamāṇāni guṇaiḥ karmāṇi sarvaśaḥ /*
ahaṃkāravimūḍhātmā kartāham iti manyate //
4. BhG 3. 28-29: *tattvavit tu mahābāho guṇakarmavibhāgayoḥ /*
guṇā guṇeṣu vartanta iti matvā na sajjate //28//
prakṛter guṇasaṃmūḍhāḥ sajjante guṇakarmasu /
tān akṛtsnavido mandān kṛtsnavin na vicālayet //29//
5. *loke 'smin dvividhā niṣṭhā purā proktā mayānagha /*
jñānayogena sāṃkhyānāṃ karmayogena yogināṃ //
6. Different from the Sāṃkhya system of philosophy.

in an important article (1924). But there are also passages in the Upaniṣads which show that the knowledge that the soul is unchangeable and unaffected by actions was thought to bring about liberation. The soul is described at *Bṛhadāraṇyaka Upaniṣad* (BAU) 4.4.22:[7]

> That Soul (*ātman*) is not this, it is not that (*neti, neti*). It is unseizable, for it cannot be seized. It is indestructible, for it cannot be destroyed. It is unattached, for it does not attach itself. It is unbound. It does not tremble. It is not injured. Him (i.e., that Soul) these two do not overcome – neither the thought 'hence I did wrong', nor the thought 'hence I did right'. Verily, he overcomes them both. What has been done and what has not been done do not affect him. (cf. Hume, 1931: 143)

The result of knowing the soul is presented in BAU 3.8.10-11:[8]

> 10. Verily, O Gārgī, if one performs sacrifices and worship and undergoes austerity in this world for many thousands of years, but without knowing that Imperishable, limited indeed is that [work] of his. Verily, O Gārgī, he who departs from this world without knowing that Imperishable is pitiable. But, O Gārgī, he who departs from this world knowing that Imperishable is a Brahmin.
> 11. Verily, O Gārgī, that Imperishable is the unseen Seer, the unheard Hearer, the unthought Thinker, the ununderstood Understander. Other than It there is naught that sees. Other than It there is naught that hears. Other than It there is naught that thinks. Other than It there is naught that understands. ... (tr. Hume, 1931: 119)

---

7. *sa eṣa neti nety ātmā / agṛhyo na hi gṛhyate / aśīryo na hi śīryate / asaṅgo na hi sajyate / asito na vyathate / na riṣyati / etam u haivaite na tarata iti / ataḥ pāpam akaravam iti / ataḥ kalyāṇaṃ akaravam iti / ubhe u haivaiṣa ete tarati / nainaṃ kṛtākṛte tapataḥ //*
8. *yo vā etad akṣaraṃ gārgy aviditvā 'smiṃl loke juhoti yajate tapas tapyate bahūni varṣasahasrāṇy antavad evāsya tad bhavati / yo vā etad akṣaraṃ gārgy aviditvā 'smāl lokāt praiti, sa kṛpaṇaḥ / atha ya etad akṣaraṃ gārgi viditvā 'smāl lokāt praiti, sa brāhmaṇaḥ //10//*
tad vā etad akṣaraṃ gārgy adṛṣṭaṃ draṣṭr aśrutaṃ śrotr amataṃ mantr avijñātaṃ vijñātṛ / nānyad ato 'sti draṣṭṛ / nānyad ato 'sti śrotṛ / nānyad ato 'sti mantṛ / nānyad ato'sti vijñātṛ / ... //11//

Since knowledge of the soul is something which is attained while being alive, the idea of liberation in this life could arise. It is described in BĀU 4.4.6:[9]

> He who is without desire, who is freed from desire, whose desire [53]
> is satisfied, whose desire is the Soul – his breaths do not depart. Being very Brahma, he goes to Brahma. (tr. Hume, 1931: 141)

We may observe that this trend of thought exerted a lasting influence on later philosophical systems, most notably on the Sāṃkhya and Vedānta systems. In both these systems the soul is conceived as motionless and no party to the activity of body and mind.[10]

5.2. If the knowledge that one's real self is by its very nature free from activity is sufficient for being freed from the results of actions, one would think that no place is left for austerities and meditation. There can be no doubt that indeed knowledge fully replaced these alternative methods in the opinion of some. But others preferred a combination of knowledge and ascetic and meditative practices. Reasons for doing so are given at *Āpastambīya Dharma Sūtra* 2.9.21.13-16:[11]

> 13. Abandoning truth and falsehood, pleasure and pain, the Vedas, this world and the next, he shall seek the soul.
> 14. (Some say that) in a enlightened one there is obtainment of peace.
> 15. (But) that (opinion) is opposed to the Śāstras.
> 16. (For) if there were obtainment of peace in an enlightened one, then he ought not to feel pain even in this (world). (cf. Bühler, 1879: 153)

---

9. *yo 'kāmo niṣkāma āptakāma ātmakāmo na tasya prāṇā utkrāmanti / brahmaiva san brahmāpyeti /.* Sprockhoff (1962) sees in passages like this 'vage Ansätze' to the concept of *jīvanmukti*.

10. The soul is in these systems as a rule considered to be omnipresent. The exception is Rāmānuja, whose soul has the size of an atom; see Hohenberger, 1960: 67-68.

11. *satyānṛte sukhaduḥkhe vedān imaṃ lokam amuṃ ca parityajyātmānaṃ anvicchet //13// buddhe kṣemaprāpaṇam //14// tac chāstrair vipratiṣiddham //15// buddhe cet kṣemaprāpaṇam ihaiva na duḥkham upalebheta //16//*

That is to say, in addition to knowledge of the soul something more is required. This something is here[12] the ascetic mode of life described in the following Sūtras (2.9.21.18 - 23.2).

A different justification for combining the way of knowledge and the practice of bodily and mental restraint is given in the *Kaṭha Up.* (2.24):[13]

> Not one who does not abstain from bad acts, nor one who has not come to peace, nor one who is not concentrated, nor one whose mind has not come to peace, shall reach this [Self] by means of knowledge.

In this passage ascetic practices are a precondition for the acquisition of knowledge. Similarly, BAU 4.4.22 first gives a description of the soul and then states that austerities are performed in order to gain knowledge of it:[14]

[54]

> Verily, he is the great, unborn soul, who is this [person] consisting of knowledge among the senses. He lies in the space within the heart, the ruler of all, the lord of all, the king of all. He does not become greater by good actions nor inferior by bad actions. He is the lord of all, the overlord of beings, the protector of beings. He is the separating dam for keeping these worlds apart.
>
> Such a one the Brahmins desire to know by repetition of the Vedas, by sacrifices, by offerings, *by austerities, by fasting*. On knowing him, in truth, one becomes an ascetic (*muni*). (cf. Hume, 1931: 143)

---

12. We shall leave out of consideration other ways, such as *karmayoga* in the *Bhagavad Gītā*; they are not directly relevant to the present discussion. See also note 16 below.

13. *nāvirato duścaritān nāśānto nāsamāhitaḥ /*
nāśāntamānaso vā 'pi prajñānenainam āpnuyāt //

14. *sa vā eṣa mahān aja ātmā yo 'yaṃ vijñānamayaḥ prāṇeṣu / ya eṣo 'ntarhṛdaya ākāśas tasmiñ chete / sarvasya vaśī / sarvasyeśānaḥ / sarvasyādhipatiḥ / sa na sādhunā karmaṇā bhūyān / no evāsādhunā kanīyān / eṣa sarveśvaraḥ / eṣa bhūtādhipatiḥ / eṣa bhūtapālaḥ / eṣa setur vidharaṇa eṣāṃ lokānām asaṃbhedāya / tam etaṃ vedānuvacanena brāhmaṇā vividiṣanti yajñena dānena tapasā 'nāśakena / etam eva viditvā munir bhavati /*

The two ways are also combined, e.g. in MBh 12.212.14-19:[15]

> He who looks upon this collection of *guṇa*s as being the soul, due to wrong points of view, his suffering is infinite [and] does not cease (14). But when [suffering] for you (*te*) [= by you] is seen as not the soul, not as I, nor as mine, on what basis does [then] the stream of suffering continue ? (15) Hear in this connection the supreme teaching of renunciation called 'Right Mind', which when declared shall result in liberation for you (16). For mere renunciation (without knowledge of the soul) of all actions, also of the ones prescribed [by the Veda], is considered as an affliction of the wrongly educated which always brings suffering (17). When objects are renounced (*dravyatyāge*), however, [sacrificial] activities [are involved]; when property is renounced, also vows [are involved]; when happiness is renounced, this is the exertion of asceticism; when all is renounced, this is perfection (18). This one and only way of renunciation of all (viz. the one called 'Right Mind') is taught as leading to freedom from suffering; any other way leads to misery (19).

5.3. A consequence of the fact that practice leads to liberation only in combination with the knowledge of the immovable nature of the soul, is that practice does no longer have to be predominantly bodily.[16] Where practice is expected to bring about this knowledge, the mental part is bound to gain prominence. This means that now meditation can become

---

15. *imaṃ guṇasamāhāram ātmabhāvena paśyataḥ /*
asamyagdarśanair duḥkham anantaṃ nopaśāmyati //14//
anātmeti ca yad dṛṣṭam tenāhaṃ na mamety api /
vartate kimadhiṣṭhānā prasaktā duḥkhasaṃtatiḥ //15//
tatra saṃyaṅmano nāma tyāgaśāstram anuttamam /
śṛṇu yat tava mokṣāya bhāṣyamāṇaṃ bhaviṣyati //16//
tyāga eva hi sarveṣām uktānām (v. l. *yuktānām*) *api karmaṇām //*
nityaṃ mithyāvinītānāṃ kleśo duḥkhāvaho mataḥ //17//
dravyatyāge tu karmāṇi bhogatyāge vratāny api /
sukhatyāge tapoyogaḥ sarvatyāge samāpanā //18//
tasya mārgo 'yam advaidhaḥ sarvatyāgasya darśitaḥ /
viprahāṇāya duḥkhasya durgatir hy anyathā bhavet //19//
16. This opens the way for practices like the *karmayoga* of the *Bhagavad Gītā*, devotion to God, etc.

the main means of liberation, at the expense of physical austerities. It can virtually by itself lead to knowledge of the true nature of the self. The following passage, which describes Yoga-activity (*yogakṛtya*) according to verse 2, illustrates this (MBh 12.232.10-18):[17]

[55] Meditation, study, liberality, truth, modesty, sincerity, forbearance, purification, purity of food, and restraining the senses (10); by these [means] the fire increases and removes sin. To him [who practises these means] all things are obtained and knowledge comes about (11). Acting the same way toward all beings, with [things] obtained or not obtained, having shaken off sin, full of fire, taking little food, having conquered the senses, having brought desire and anger under control, he should wish to bring [himself] to the place of Brahman (12). Having brought about one-pointedness of his mind and senses, concentrated, he should fix his mind with his self in the first and last parts of the night (13). If one sense leaks of this man possessed of five senses, then his insight flows away, like water from the bottom of a bag (14). But he should first take hold of his mind, just as a killer of fish [first takes hold of] small fish; then the knower of Yoga [should take hold of] his ear, then his eye, tongue and nose (15). Then, holding these together, the ascetic should place them in his mind; removing in the same way his

17. *dhyānam adhyayanaṃ dānaṃ satyaṃ hrīr ārjavaṃ kṣamā /*
śaucam āhārasaṃśuddhir indriyāṇāṃ ca nigrahaḥ //10//
etair vivardhate tejaḥ pāpmānaṃ cāpakarṣati /
sidhyanti cāsya sarvārthā vijñānaṃ ca pravartate //11//
samaḥ sarveṣu bhūteṣu labdhālabdhena vartayan /
dhutapāpmā tu tejasvī laghvāhāro jitendriyaḥ /
kāmakrodhau vaśe kṛtvā ninīṣed brahmaṇaḥ padam //12//
manasaś cendriyāṇāṃ ca kṛtvaikāgryaṃ samāhitaḥ /
prāgrātrāpararātreṣu dhārayen mana ātmanā //13//
jantoḥ pañcendriyasyāsya yad ekaṃ chidram indriyam /
tato 'sya sravati prajñā dṛteḥ pādād ivodakam //14//
manas tu pūrvam ādadyāt kumīnān iva matsyahā /
tataḥ śrotraṃ tataś cakṣur jihvāṃ ghrāṇaṃ ca yogavit //15//
tata etāni saṃyamya manasi sthāpayed yatiḥ /
tathaivāpohya saṃkalpān mano hy ātmani dhārayet //16//

volitions, he should fix his mind in his self (16). Bringing the five [senses] together with his knowledge, the ascetic should place them in his mind; and when these [five senses] with the mind as sixth stay in the self, and come to rest staying together, then Brahman shines forth (17). Like a shining flame without smoke, like the bright sun, like the fire of lightning in the sky, he sees the self with the self.

5.4. A further theoretical adjustment to the situation where both knowledge and practice are required in order to find liberation, may be witnessed in the Nyāya-Vaiśeṣika system of philosophy. Here, to be sure, the soul is conceived as acting and undergoing the fruits of its actions. But a closer inspection brings to light that this should not be accepted at its face value, but in a technical sense which modifies the situation considerably.[18]

The soul, in Vaiśeṣika ontology, is an omnipresent and eternal substance *(dravya);* this implies that the soul is motionless. It is conceived as acting because it can have effort (*prayatna*) as a quality (*guṇa*); this quality is required in order to bring about activity of the body. Effort itself is the result of two other qualities of the soul, desire (*icchā*) and repulsion (*dveṣa*). The activity of the body gives rise to yet two more qualities of the
soul, virtue (*dharma*) and sin (*adharma*). Virtue and sin are responsible [56]
for rebirth and *saṃsāra.*

All these qualities inhere in the soul and cannot exist without it. The soul, on the other hand, can very well exist without them. Indeed, liberation is conceived of as freedom from the special qualities that inhere

---

pañca jñānena saṃdhāya manasi sthāpayed yatiḥ /
yadaitāny avatiṣṭhante manaḥṣaṣṭhāni cātmani /
prasīdanti ca saṃsthāya tadā brahma prakāśate //17//
vidhūma iva dīptārcir āditya iva dīptimān /
vaidyuto 'gnir ivākāśe paśyaty ātmānaṃ ātmanā /

18. Since the ontology of Nyāya-Vaiśeṣika derives from Vaiśeṣika, we shall confine ourselves to Vaiśeṣika texts, primarily Kaṇāda's *Vaiśeṣika Sūtra* and Praśastapāda's *Padārthadharmasaṅgraha.*

An analysis of the road to liberation in Pakṣilasvāmin's *Nyāya Bhāṣya* is given by Oberhammer (1984: 1-65), who however seems to misunderstand the nature of liberation adhered to by Pakṣilasvāmin.

in it. The complete list of these qualities is as follows: knowledge (*buddhi*), happiness (*sukha*), pain (*duḥkha*), desire (*icchā*), repulsion (*dveṣa*), effort (*pratyatna*), virtue (*dharma*), sin (*adharma*), subliminal impression (*saṃskāra*).[19] None of these survive in the liberated state. We see that the theoretical constructs of the Vaiśeṣikas, and following them the Naiyāyikas, force them to look at the liberated state as one without knowledge and happiness; a fact for which they have been often ridiculed.[20]

The order in the list of special qualities of the soul is not arbitrary. Knowledge of an object precedes the experience of happiness or pain connected with it; this in its turn gives rise to desire and repulsion respectively; then follows effort in order to obtain or avoid that object; as a result virtue and sin come into being, as well as subliminal impressions. The sequence also shows how liberation can be obtained. Right knowledge of the categories of reality, including the soul, prevents desire and repulsion from coming about. As a result no new virtue and sin arise. Life goes on until the old virtue and sin have produced experiences and consequently disappeared. Liberation is reached at the moment of death. Praśastapāda's *Padārthadharmasaṅgraha* (p.261-62) describes this process as follows:[21]

> When someone – as a consequence of knowledge and of the activity resulting therefrom, viz., [activity] without intended fruit –

---

19. *Dharma, adharma* and *saṃskāra* are not enumerated among the qualities in Kaṇāda's *Vaiśeṣika Sūtra* (VS 1.1.5) and were not yet considered such in the Vaiśeṣika known to the Jaina author Jinabhadra (c. 6th century; see Halbfass, 1980: 285n.55).

20. Already Pakṣilasvāmin (Vātsyāyana) notes as one example of wrong ideas in his *Nyāya Bhāṣya* on sūtra 1.1.2 (p. 11-12): "Emancipation (i.e., liberation) is dreadful. It consists, as a matter of fact, in the cessation of all effects. Since emancipation is separation from everything, much that is good is lost in it. How could therefore a wise man find pleasure in this state of emancipation, in which all happiness has been cut off and which is without consciousness?" (*apavargo bhīṣmaḥ / sa khalv ayaṃ sarvakāryoparamaḥ sarvaviprayoge 'pavarge bahu ca bhadrakaṃ lupyata iti kathaṃ buddhimān sarvasukhocchedam acaitanyam amum apavargaṃ rocayed iti /*) Some later Naiyāyikas preferred to look upon liberation as blissful (Mishra, 1936: 384-87).

21. *jñānapūrvakāt tu kṛtād asaṅkalpitaphalād viśuddhe kule jātasya duḥkha*

> is born in a virtuous family and desires to know means to get rid of suffering, goes to a teacher and acquires true knowledge about the six categories [of Vaiśeṣika], then he becomes free from passion because his wrong knowledge ceases. Because there is then no passion nor repulsion, virtue and sin which are born from those do not come into existence; and [the virtue and sin] which have been accumulated before disappear after producing experiences. When he has thus brought about contentment and happiness, as well as separation from the body, and passion etc. have ceased, only virtue characterized by inactivity remains. [This too,] after producing the happiness born from insight in the highest truth, ceases. Then the body etc. disappear of [this] soul which is free from seeds [for rebirth]. The tranquillity [which arises] since no body etc. come [57
> again into existence, and which resembles a fire whose fuel has been burnt, is liberation.

We see that the soul of the Vaiśeṣikas has something in common with the soul of the Sāṃkhyas. Both are in their deepest essence unconnected with what goes on in the world. But unlike the Sāṃkhyas, the Vaiśeṣikas admit that the soul can get into connection with the world, and into a close connection at that; the soul is connected with its qualities by the relation of inherence (*samavāya*), which is the closest relation that exists in this system of philosophy.

Yet, in its deepest essence the soul remains free from activity and its fruits. This is underlined by the circumstance that the soul is conceived as omnipresent. The soul, even though actor, remains in this way free from action. This is, as far as I can see, the only reasonable explanation of the otherwise rather queer attribute of omnipresence of the soul. This explanation gains in strength if it is true that the oldest Vaiśesika considered the soul as having the size of the body, as Frauwallner (1956a:

---

vigamopāyajijñāsor ācāryam upasaṅgamyotpannaṣaṭpadārthatattvajñāna-syājñānanivṛttau viraktasya rāgadveṣābhāvāt tajjayor dharmādharmayor anutpattau pūrvasañcitayoś copabhogān nirodhe santoṣasukhaṃ śarīraparicchedaṃ cotpādya rāgādinivṛttau nivṛttilakṣaṇaḥ kevalo dharmaḥ paramārthadarśanajaṃ sukhaṃ kṛtvā nivartate / tadā nirbījasyātmanaḥ śarīrādinivṛttiḥ / punaḥ śarīrādy-anutpattau dagdhendhanānalavad upaśamo mokṣa iti //

62) surmises.[22]

It is clear from the above passage from the *Padārthadharma-saṅgraha* that knowledge is but the beginning of the process leading to liberation. It is succeeded by some kind of practice of the type with which we are now familiar. This is confirmed by the *Vaiśeṣika Sūtra*,[23] which describes Yoga as a state where the mind (*manas*) resides only in the soul and therefore not in the senses, resulting in the absence of happiness and pain (5.2.17); liberation is attained when this contact of mind and soul is also no longer there (5.2.20). We recognize what is elsewhere called *pratyāhāra* 'withdrawal of the senses'. Again, liberation is the absence of contact of the soul with virtue and sin (6.2.19); the means thereto are, among other things, fasting, chastity, dwelling in a forest (6.2.2).

---

22. Frauwallner's (1956a: 95-97) attempt to explain the omnipresence of the soul on the basis of *adṛṣṭa*, a quality of the soul which is supposed to exert its influence almost everywhere, does not convince. The Vaiśeṣika Sūtra speaks already of the omnipresence of the soul (VS 7.1.29), but contains no indication that *adṛṣṭa* (mentioned in sūtras 5.1.15; 2.2; 4; 8; 14; 19; 6.2.2.; 15; in all but two cases in the compound *adṛṣṭakārita*) was considered a quality of the soul (cf. Halbfass, 1980: 285f.). Indeed, *adṛṣṭa* is not enumerated among the qualities (cf. note 19 above). Moreover, Nyāya Sūtra 3.2.69 uses the word *adṛṣṭa* – in the compound *adṛṣṭakārita*, so common in the *Vaiśeṣika Sūtra* – in a sense which contrasts with *karman* (67); here it is no quality of the soul, nor even the same as *dharma* and *adharma* .

Frauwallner's reason for believing that early Vaiśeṣika considered the soul as having the size of the body is that this idea was present and survived among the Jainas. The early connection between the two systems seems supported by the Jaina tradition that the *Vaiśeṣika Sūtra* was composed by a Jaina schismatic from the Ulūka lineage (Leumann, 1885a: 121; Mehta and Chandra, 1970-72: 646 (s.v. Rohagutta), 664 (s.v. Vaisesiya)). *Vaiśeṣika Sūtra* 5.2.18 has been presented as evidence that the soul of early Vaiśeṣika was deemed to have limited size. See Wezler, 1982: 653-55. A closer study of this sūtra, to be published in the Proceedings of the Bhartṛhari Conference held in Pune 1992 (*Asiatische Studien / Études Asiatiques* 1993), has convinced me that it constitutes no such evidence.

The omnipresence of the soul is explained by Vyomaśiva by arguing "that only on such a hypothesis can we explain the yogi's ability to inhabit many bodies simultaneously" (Potter, 1977: 98).

Other reasons why Brahmanical philosophies – unlike Jainism – introduced the idea of an omnipresent soul are given by Jaini (1980: 220).

23. Wezler (1982) argues that the sūtras on Yoga and liberation were later added, perhaps after Praśastapāda (p. 665). This does not however affect my argument.

5.5. The 'pure' forms of asceticism lived on, as in Haṭha Yoga,[24] beside the currents which emphasized meditation and knowledge of the soul. Where they had to confront these other currents, terms pertaining to meditation often were reinterpreted in such a manner that they came to refer to bodily practices. Elsewhere the mental practices were postponed until after the mastery of the – by now numerous and complex – bodily practices, i.e., postponed to a stage which few people would reach.

Reinterpretation of terms pertaining to meditation is witnessed in [58]
Śivānanda Sarasvatī's *Yogacintāmaṇi*. There we read that "restraint of breath itself, in accordance with the degree of practice, is called by the names *pratyāhāra, dhāraṇā, dhyāna* and *samādhi*" (p. 28: *prāṇāyāma evābhyāsakrameṇa pratyāhāradhāraṇādhyānasamādhiśabdenocyate*). Of the same tenor, but more specific, is *Skanda Purāṇa* 4.41.94-95:[25]

> By twelve restraints of breath (*prāṇāyāma*) *pratyāhāra* is named. By twelve *pratyāhāras dhāraṇā* is known (94). *Dhyāna* consists of twelve *dhāraṇās* and may lead to union with God. By twelve *dhyānas samādhi* is mentioned (95).

We recognize in the terms *pratyāhāra* ('withdrawal of the senses'), *dhāraṇā* ('fixing the mind'), *dhyāna* ('meditation'), and *samādhi* ('concentration') the last four limbs of the eightfold Yoga described in YS 2.29 (cf. also MU 6.18 discussed above, §4.1). We see that mental states are reinterpreted to be, or to be the result of, physical restrictions.

Postponement of meditation is seen in, e.g., Svātmārāma's *Haṭha Yoga Pradīpikā* (HYPr). We are told in verse 1.2 that Haṭha Yoga, which emphasizes bodily practices,[26] is only taught by way of preparation for Rāja Yoga:[27] "Bowing to the respected teacher and patron, Yogin Svātmārāma teaches the knowledge of Haṭha [Yoga] merely for the sake

---

24. On the ancient roots of Haṭha Yoga, see Nowotny, 1976: 5-10.
25. *prāṇāyāmadviṣaṭkena pratyāhāra udāhṛtaḥ /*
pratyāhārair dvādaśabhir dhāraṇā parikīrtitā //94//
bhaved īśvarasaṃgatyai dhyānaṃ dvādaśadhāraṇam /
dhyānadvādaśakenaiva samādhir abhidhīyate //95//
These verses occur in slightly different form in Gorakṣa's *Gorakṣaśataka* (114-15).
26. The *Gheraṇḍa Saṃhitā* (1.2) calls it *ghaṭasthayoga* 'bodily Yoga'.
27. *praṇamya śrīguruṃ nāthaṃ svātmārāmeṇa yoginā /*
kevalaṃ rājayogāya haṭhavidyopadiśyate //

of Rāja Yoga." And again (HYPr 4.103):[28] "All the means of Haṭha [Yoga] and Laya [Yoga] are for the attainment of Rāja Yoga." Rāja Yoga is the name of the unified mind (4.77);[29] it is the state without mind, *samādhi* (4.3-4). But a precondition for Rāja Yoga is mastery over Kevala-kumbhaka (2.74-75):[30] "Who is powerful through Kevala-kumbha[ka] because he [can] hold his breath as long as he likes, he obtains even the state of Rāja Yoga, there is no doubt about it." Holding one's breath as long as one likes is obviously beyond the reach of most (cf. Bernard, 1950: 57-58).

Haṭha Yoga belongs to the tradition of asceticism which we are investigating. The following verses (HYPr 4.106-09, 112) show this beyond doubt:[31]

> By virtue of the state without mind (*unmanī avasthā*)[32] the body becomes certainly like a piece of wood; it does not at any time hear the sounds of a conch-shell and of a large drum (106). Being free from all states and devoid of all thought, the Yogin is like a dead person; he is liberated, there is no doubt about it (107). The Yogin engaged in *samādhi* is not devoured by death and is not harassed
> [59] by *karman*, nor is he subdued by anyone (108). The Yogin engaged in *samādhi* is not aware of smell, taste, form, touch, and sound, nor of himself or another (109). ... He is certainly liberated who is healthy, as if sleeping while awake, and without breathing out and breathing in (112).

---

28. *sarve haṭhalayopāyā rājayogasya siddhaye /*
29. *ekībhūtaṃ tadā cittaṃ rājayogābhidhānakam /*
30. *śaktaḥ kevalakumbhena yatheṣṭaṃ vāyudhāraṇāt //*
rājayogapadaṃ cāpi labhate nātra saṃśayaḥ /
31. *śaṅkhadundubhinādaṃ ca na śṛṇoti kadācana /*
kāṣṭhavaj jāyate deha unmanyāvasthayā dhruvam //106//
sarvāvasthāvinirmuktaḥ sarvacintāvivarjitaḥ /
mṛtavat tiṣṭhate yogī sa mukto nātra saṃśayaḥ //107//
khādyate na ca kālena bādhyate na ca karmaṇā /
sādhyate na sa kenāpi yogī yuktaḥ samādhinā //108//
na gandhaṃ na rasaṃ rūpaṃ na ca sparśaṃ na niḥsvanam /
nātmānaṃ na paraṃ vetti yogī yuktaḥ samādhinā //109//...
svastho jāgradavasthāyāṃ suptavad yo 'vatiṣṭhate /
niḥśvāsocchvāsahīnaś ca niścitaṃ mukta eva saḥ //112//
32. This is the same as Rāja Yoga according to verses 4.3-4 (p. 125).

HYPr 4.31-32 amount to much the same:[33]

> Absorption (*laya*), in which breathing out and breathing in are destroyed and the grasping of objects has disappeared, in which there is no movement [of the body] nor modification [of the mind], is victorious in the Yogins (31). Some [state of] absorption comes about in which all conceptions are cut off and there are no movements whatever; it can only be experienced by oneself and is beyond words (32).

We find here most of the features which have characterized main stream meditation from early times: motionlessness of body and mind, cessation of breathing, non-functioning of the sense-organs.

It is interesting to quote in conclusion the final verse[34] of Svātmārāma's *Haṭha Yoga Pradīpikā* (4.114), because it evinces a sceptical attitude toward the claim that knowledge alone may lead to the goal:[35]

> As long as the breath, moving about, does not enter into the middle road; as long as the semen does not become steady as a result of binding the vital air; as long as in meditation reality does not become like the natural state;[36] so long the knowledge that [some] talk of is deceitful and false chattering.

---

33. *pranaṣṭaśvāsaniśvāsaḥ pradhvastaviṣayagrahaḥ /*
niśceṣṭo nirvikāraś ca layo jayati yogināṃ //31//
ucchinnasarvasaṃkalpo niḥśeṣāśeṣaceṣṭitaḥ /
svāvagamyo layaḥ ko 'pi jāyate vāgagocaraḥ //32//

34. In the Lonavla edition this is not the final verse. A whole (fifth) chapter follows which is found in some Mss., as explained on pp. (5) - (7) of the Introduction.

35. *yāvan naiva praviśati caran māruto madhyamārge*
yāvad bindur na bhavati dṛḍhaḥ prāṇavātaprabandhāt /
yāvad dhyāne sahajasadṛśaṃ jāyate naiva tattvaṃ
tāvaj jñānaṃ vadati tad idaṃ dambhamithyāpralāpaḥ //

36. This line is not very clear. The English translation in the Adyar Library edition, by Srinivasa Iyangar and revised by Radha Burnier and A. A. Ramanathan, reads (p. 83-84): "as long as the mind does not, in meditation, reflect the natural state [of the object contemplated upon, i.e. Brahman]". This translation depends on Brahmānanda's commentary *Jyotsnā* (p. 182): *yāvat tattvaṃ cittaṃ dhyāne dhyeyacintane sahajasadṛśaṃ svābhāvikadhyeyākāravṛttipravāhavan naiva jāyate naiva bhavati*. The Lonavla edition contains the translation (p. 176): "So long as ... the Supreme Reality does not appear as if it were its (the mind's) Sahaja (native) state."

[65] VI. The influence from Buddhist meditation.

6.1. It seems that main stream meditation remained unaffected by Buddhist meditation for a long time. Only in the case of the *Maitrāyaṇīya Upaniṣad* did we have to consider the possibility that there was some influence from the side of Buddhist meditation (above, § 4.1). And even in this case it concerned a rather minor point, not one pertaining to the actual technique of meditation, nor to its immediate aim. We may assume that main stream meditation owed its strong position primarily to two factors. The first one is that, apparently, it had far wider currency than Buddhist meditation. This is indicated by its presence in both Jaina and Hindu scriptures. The second factor explains to some extent the first one. The idea that the misery resulting from activity must be combated by inactivity is so clear and simple that its immediate appeal must have been greater than that of the rather abstruse methods propagated in Buddhist meditation.

Yet some influence from the side of Buddhist meditation is discernible. It is first noticeable in a passage of the *Mahābhārata*, but here the influence remains confined to terminology. Strong influence can be shown in the *Yoga Sūtra*. The important position acquired by this text explains that the Buddhist element in Hindu meditation came to stay.

We turn to the texts.

6.2. MBh 12.188.1-2, 5-10, 12-13, 15, 20-22 reads:[1]

> See, oh king, I tell you the fourfold Yoga of meditation, knowing which the supreme seers reach eternal perfection (1). Yogins, great seers satiated with knowledge whose minds are set on *nirvāṇa*, perform meditation that is well-practised (2). ... A sage, sitting like

---

1. *hanta vakṣyāmi te pārtha dhyānayogaṃ caturvidham /*
yaṃ jñātvā śāśvatīṃ siddhiṃ gacchanti paramarṣayaḥ //1//
yathā svanuṣṭhitaṃ dhyānaṃ tathā kurvanti yoginaḥ /
maharṣayo jñānatṛptā nirvāṇagatamanasaḥ //2//
...

a piece of wood, bundling his senses together, should fix his mind [so that it becomes] one-pointed and held together as a result of recitation, on that [own nature (?)] (5). He should not notice sound with his ear, nor should he feel touch with his skin; he should not perceive colour with his eye, nor tastes with his tongue (6). And the knower of Yoga should also abandon, by means of meditation, all odours; being energetic, he should not desire these things which trouble the five senses (7). Then, being wise and joining together his five senses in his mind, he should concentrate his wandering [66] mind together with the five senses (8). Being resolute, he should concentrate his interior mind, which is moving here and there, having no point of support, with five gates, unsteady, in the first course of meditation (9). When he bundles together his senses and his mind, this is the first course of meditation described by me (10). ... Like a drop of water on a leaf, moving here and there, going in all directions, just so is that mind of his on the road of meditation (12); being brought together (*samāhita*) for some moment on the road of meditation, it stands still, but again the mind roams about on the path of the wind, like the wind (13). ... When the sage concentrates on the first meditation from the beginning,

tatra svādhyāyasaṃśliṣṭam ekāgraṃ dhārayen manaḥ /
piṇḍīkṛtyendriyagrāmam āsīnaḥ kāṣṭhavan muniḥ //5//
śabdaṃ na vindec chrotreṇa sparśaṃ tvacā na vedayet /
rūpaṃ na cakṣuṣā vidyāj jihvayā na rasāṃs tathā //6//
ghreyāṇy api ca sarvāṇi jahyād dhyānena yogavit /
pañcavargapramāthīni necchec caitāni vīryavān //7//
tato manasi saṃsajya pañcavargaṃ vicakṣaṇaḥ /
samādadhyān mano bhrāntam indriyaiḥ saha pañcabhiḥ //8//
visaṃcāri nirālambaṃ pañcadvāraṃ calācalam /
pūrve dhyānapathe dhīraḥ samādadhyān mano 'ntaram //9//
indriyāṇi manaś caiva yadā piṇḍīkaroty ayam /
eṣa dhyānapathaḥ pūrvo mayā samanuvarṇitaḥ //10//
...
jalabindur yathā lolaḥ parṇasthaḥ sarvataś calaḥ /
evam evāsya tac cittaṃ bhavati dhyānavartmani //12//
samāhitaṃ kṣanaṃ kiṃcid dhyānavartmani tiṣṭhati /
punar vāyupathaṃ bhrāntam mano bhavati vāyuvat //13//
...
vicāraś ca vitarkaś ca vivekaś copajāyate /

> *vicāra, vitarka* and *viveka* come to him (15). ... He himself, oh descendant of Bharata, as well as his mind and five senses, comes to rest when he has reached the first course of meditation by the incessant practice of Yoga (20). That bliss of him whose self is thus controlled, will not be attained by means of any kind of human effort or fate (21). Endowed with that bliss he will delight in the activity of meditation. In this way Yogins attain to that *nirvāṇa* which is free from disease (22).

This passage speaks of a 'fourfold *dhyānayoga*' (v.1), and of a 'first Dhyāna' (*pūrva dhyānapatha,* vv. 9, 10, 20; *prathama dhyāna,* v. 15) in which *vicāra, vitarka* and *viveka* are present, as well as bliss (v. 21-22). Yogins performing this kind of meditation reach *nirvāṇa* (vv. 2, 22.) All this sounds like pure Buddhism (cf. § 1,5 above) and cannot be due to coincidence.[2]

But there are differences as well. It appears that the Four Dhyānas are really a foreign element in the Yoga of the Epic, which could only be made to fit clumsily. Note that only the First Dhyāna of the 'fourfold *dhyānayoga*' is mentioned – repeatedly – in the text, never the remaining three. The reason may well be that these later Dhyānas, especially the Third and Fourth, were an embarrassment for the author of this section because they go beyond his aim in discarding such desirable (see v. 21-22) states as joy (*prīti*) and bliss (*sukha*). The immediate aim in this section of

---

muneḥ samādadhānasya prathamaṃ dhyānam āditaḥ //15//
...
svayam eva manaś caiva pañcavargaś ca bhārata /
pūrvaṃ dhyānapathaṃ prāpya nityayogena śāmyati //20//
na tat puruṣakāreṇa na ca daivena kenacit /
sukham eṣyati tat tasya yad evaṃ saṃyatātmanaḥ //21//
sukhena tena saṃyukto raṃsyate dhyānakarmaṇi /
gacchanti yogino hy evaṃ nirvāṇaṃ tan nirāmayam //22//

This passage occurs with few changes in the *Bṛhan-Nāradīya Purāṇa* 44. 83-105. The differences are described on p. 2119 of the Poona ed. of MBh 12.

2. So Bedekar, 1963a; Pande, 1974: 534; Heiler, 1922: 46-47; Keith, 1923: 144; Oldenberg, 1915: 324; Barnes, 1976: 189 f. Nothing supports the contention that here the four stages of meditation are intended which figure in MBh 12.46.2-4, as maintained in the Critical Notes to the Poona ed. (p. 2161). In those stages no mention is made of *vicāra, viveka* and *nirvāṇa*.

the *Mahābhārata* – as elsewhere in the Epic – is control of the mind and the senses. This resembles the Second Dhyāna, where *vitarka* and *vicāra* come to rest. Our section of the Epic appears to be content with even less. The First Dhyāna is sufficient for its purposes because *vitarka* and *vicāra* [67]
are apparently looked upon as special faculties on the First Dhyāna, not as mere thought remaining from ordinary consciousness.[3]

Our passage contains clear indications that it belongs to the main, i.e., non-Buddhistic, tradition of meditation. The meditator sits 'like a piece of wood' (v. 5), tries to put his sense organs out of use (v. 6-7), wants to stop his mind (v. 20). The terminology of Buddhist meditation has been used, but its influence stopped at that.

6.3. Influence from Buddhist meditation, i.e., from the form Buddhist meditation acquired under the influence of main stream meditation (see ch. VII below), is noticeable in the first chapter of the *Yoga Sūtra* (YS).[4] This will be shown by bringing to light a contradiction between the sūtras.

Sūtra 1.2 defines: *yogaś cittavṛttinirodhaḥ* "Yoga is the suppression of the activities of the mind". This agrees with all we have come to know about main stream meditation in Jaina and Hindu scriptures. Sūtra 1.3 explains that then the self abides in its own form. This too tallies with main stream meditation and the accompanying speculations about the nature of the soul (above, chapter V). Subsequent sūtras (1.5-11) specify what are the activities of the mind. YS 1.12 indicates that the desired suppression comes about as a result of practice (*abhyāsa*) and passionlessness (*vairāgya*). These two terms are explained in sūtras 1.13-16. There can be no doubt that sūtras 1.2-16 belong together and give a short description of main stream meditation.

Sūtras 1.17-20 then continue:

YS 1.17: *vitarkavicārānandāsmitārūpānugamāt saṃprajñātaḥ* : "Because it is accompanied by the form of deliberation, reflexion, happiness and the

---

3. Note that also the *Yoga Sūtra* (1.44) appears to give *vicāra* a special sense, viz. of having subtle things as objects. Something similar is said in Vasubandhu's *Abhidharmakośa* and *Abhidharmakośabhāṣya* (II. 33) and in earlier Abhidharma works.
4. Cf. already Senart, 1900, and esp. La Vallée Poussin, 1937a.

feeling 'I am' [there is concentration (*samādhi*) which is] *saṃprajñāta*."

YS 1.18: *virāmapratyayābhyāsapūrvaḥ saṃskāraśeṣo 'nyaḥ* :"The other [*asaṃprajñāta* form of concentration (*samādhi*)] is preceded by practice on the notion of cessation, [and is such that only] subliminal impressions (*saṃskāra*) remain in it."

YS 1.19: *bhavapratyayo videhaprakṛtilayānām*: "In the case of the bodiless and the *prakṛtilayas*, it depends on their state."

YS 1.20: *śraddhāvīryasmṛtisamādhiprajñāpūrvaka itareṣām*: "It is preceded by trust, energy, mindfulness (*smṛti*), concentration (*samādhi*) and insight (*prajñā*) in the case of others."

We note, to begin with, that sūtra 1.17 is not complete. The author of the *Yoga Bhāṣya* supplies *samādhi*, a word which has not been used in the
[68] preceding sixteen sūtras. The incompleteness of sūtra 1.17 suggests that this sūtra together with the ones following it was taken from a different context. It is known that the Yoga sūtras were collected together, most probably by the author of the *Yoga Bhāṣya* (Bronkhorst, 1985a: § 1). The author of the *Yoga Bhāṣya* gives evidence at a few places that he knew the original meaning and context of the sūtras, and this allows us to accept tentatively his proposal to supply *samādhiḥ* in sūtra 1.17. It is true that sūtra 1.20 now comes to convey the peculiar sense that *asaṃprajñāta samādhi is* preceded by *samādhi*, but this may be due to the technical meaning assigned to *asaṃprajñāta samādhi*.

When we compare these four sūtras with the definition of Yoga given in sūtra 1.2, it becomes clear that *saṃprajñāta samādhi* cannot be considered the highest form of Yoga. Certainly deliberation (*vitarka*) and reflexion (*vicāra*), and perhaps also happiness (*ānanda*) and the feeling 'I am' (*asmitā*), must be looked upon as activities of the mind, even if it may be difficult to say how these must be brought in agreement with the five kinds of activity enumerated in sūtra 1.6. The case is different with *asaṃprajñāta samādhi*. Here only subliminal impressions (*saṃskāra*) remain, which cannot be looked upon as activities of the mind. Therefore *asaṃprajñāta samādhi* must be considered the completion of Yoga, the total suppression of all activity of the mind.

However, such an interpretation gives rise to difficulties. For it would mean that the bodiless – i.e., gods according to the *Yoga Bhāṣya* – and those called *prakṛtilaya* – those whose minds have been temporarily dissolved into primary matter – have reached the highest aim of Yoga, which seems an unlikely supposition. What is worse, sūtra 1.18 emphatically asserts that in *asaṃprajñāta samādhi* subliminal impressions (*saṃskāra*) remain, strongly suggesting that another state exists in which even these subliminal impressions are no longer present.

It is confirmed by the last sūtra of the first chapter, which I shall give in its immediate context, that such a further state exists. Sūtra 1.46 speaks about a concentration with seed (*sabījaḥ samādhiḥ*) and sūtra 1.47 about an inner tranquillity (*adhyātmaprasāda*). Sūtras 1.48-51 then continue:

YS 1.48: *ṛtaṃbharā tatra prajñā* : "There there is truthbearing insight."

YS 1.49: *śrutānumānaprajñābhyām anyaviṣayā viśeṣārthatvāt* : "It has [69] other objects than the insight from the scriptures and the insight from inference, because it concerns particulars."

YS 1.50: *tajjaḥ saṃskāro 'nyasaṃskārapratibandhī* : "From that [insight] arises a subliminal impression which obstructs the other subliminal impressions."

YS 1.51: *tasyāpi nirodhe sarvanirodhān nirbījaḥ samādhiḥ* : "When that [subliminal impression] too is destroyed,[5] because all [subliminal impressions] have been destroyed, there is concentration without seed."

It seems clear that the definition of Yoga given in the first chapter of the *Yoga Sūtra* does not fit the descriptions contained in that same chapter. The definition speaks merely of the suppression of mental activity, whereas the descriptions go far beyond this: they speak about a state also beyond happiness and the feeling 'I am', where even the subliminal impressions are destroyed.

The author of the *Yoga Bhāṣya* does not do much to solve the disagreement. On sūtra 1.18 he simply identifies *asaṃprajñāta samādhi*

5. *nirodha* carries both the meanings 'suppression' and 'destruction'. My choice of translation here and in YS 1.2 embodies a certain amount of interpretation.

with *nirbīja samādhi* ('concentration without seed'). And on sūtra 1.46 he justifies the expression *sabīja samādhi* 'concentration with seed' by stating that "outer objects are the seed". It is clear that in this way *nirbīja samādhi* 'concentration without seeds/outer objects' acquires a sense close to *asaṃprajñāta samādhi* . But the *Yoga Bhaṣya* does not explain how *asaṃprajñāta samādhi* can retain the subliminal impressions where *nirbīja samādhi* does not.

The *Yoga Bhāṣya* gets into more trouble while explaining sūtra 1.19. Obviously it does not want to grant the highest Yogic state – which it calls *kaivalya* 'isolation' – to the gods and the *prakṛtilayas,* free of charge, so to say. It 'solves' the problem by adding *iva* 'as if' in the explanation: it is *as if* the gods and *prakṛtilayas* experience isolation.

The clumsy procedure of the *Yoga Bhāṣya* further convinces us that two kinds of Yoga are being referred to in the first chapter of the *Yoga Sūtra*.[6]

The other kind of Yoga described in the first chapter of the *Yoga Sūtra* shows far-reaching agreement with Buddhist meditation. YS 1.17 says that deliberation (*vitarka*), reflection (*vicāra*), happiness (*ānanda*) and the feeling 'I am' (*asmitā*) are present in *saṃprajñāta* (*samādhi*).

[70] Deliberation (*vitarka*) and reflection (*vicāra*) are also present in the First Dhyāna of the Buddhists (above, § 1.5). Joy (*prīti*) is present in the First and Second Dhyāna, bliss (*sukha*) in the First, Second and Third; this corresponds to happiness (*ānanda*). Only the feeling 'I am' has nothing corresponding to it in the early Buddhist texts.[7]

Asaṃprajñāta samādhi (?) may be compared with the five states which came to be added after the Four Dhyānas in the Buddhist scriptures, and which are characterized by a weakening and ultimately disappearance of *samjñā* 'ideation'. The dependence on Buddhist ideas is confirmed by the fact that in YS 1.20 *asaṃprajñāta samādhi* (if it is that) is said to be

6. Frauwallner (1953: 437f.), too, distinguishes two kinds of Yoga in the *Yoga Sūtra*, but considers the first chapter as describing but one of them.

7. Unless we consider it equivalent to mindfulness *(smṛti)* and circumspection *(saṃprajanya)*, as Heiler, 1922: 46 does. Note that the Buddhist texts speak occasionally of liberation as a result of, among other things, the destruction of all dispositions to egoism, selfishness and pride *(sabbaahaṅkāramamaṅkāramānānusayānaṃ khayā)*; see MN I.486.

preceded by trust (*śraddhā*), energy (*vīrya*), mindfulness (*smṛti*), concentration (*samādhi*), and insight (*prajñā*). The last two of this list, *samādhi* and *prajñā*, are also the last two of the Buddhist triad *śīla, samādhi, prajñā*, which is often presented in the canon as the teaching of the Buddha in a nutshell (Eimer, 1976: 34f.; § 8.4.3, below). It is even more noticeable that all these five terms – *śraddhā, vīrya, smṛti, samādhi, prajñā*, or rather their Pāli equivalents – occur in the Pāli version of the account of the Bodhisattva's training under Āḷāra Kālāma and Uddaka the son of Rāma. Gotama proclaims to be the equal of his teachers in these five respects. (MN I.164-66; repeated I.240, II.212. Note that the Chinese parallels merely mention *śraddhā, vīrya* and *prajñā;* MĀ^{C} *p.* 776b14-17, c13-15; T 1428 p. 780b11-13, c4-5; cf. Bareau, 1963: 13-26). The terms occur also elsewhere in the canon (e.g. MN I.479), and frequently in the Abhidharma works.

YS 1.18 and 1.48-51 (when combined) tell us that *asaṃprajñāta samādhi* is not the final end. The subliminal impressions (*saṃskāra*) which remain are to be destroyed with the help of insight (*prajñā*). If we read *āsrava* for *saṃskāra*, this is pure Buddhism.[8] In addition to this, it can hardly be coincidence that the 'truthbearing insight' is said to follow an inner tranquillity (*adhyātmaprasāda*); the Buddhist texts speak about an inner tranquillization (*adhyātmasamprasādana*).

6.4. Traces of the influence from Buddhist meditation are visible in other works. *Yogakuṇḍalī Upaniṣad* 1-2 reads:[9]

> There are two causes for [the activity of] the mind: subconscious impression (*vāsanā*) and air. Of these two when one is destroyed, both get destroyed (1). Of these two, a man should always conquer

---

8. The Buddhist texts also speak about the destruction of *saṃskāras*, e .g. in Sn 731; cf. DN II.36, MN I.167, SN I.136, Vin I.5. See also the argument concerning the mental nature of *saṃkhāra* in Franke, 1913: 307-18; and Schneider, 1980: 100-01. Cf. Schumann, 1957; Johansson, 1979: 41-56.
9. *hetudvayaṃ hi cittasya vāsanā ca samīraṇaḥ* /
tayor vinaṣṭa ekasmiṃs tad dvāv api vinaśyataḥ //1//
tayor ādau samīrasya jayaṃ kuryān naraḥ sadā /

[71] air first. [The means thereto are:] moderate eating, [practising] postures, and setting the Śakti in motion as the third (2).

The words *vāsanā* ('subconscious impression') and *saṃskāra* ('subliminal impression') are virtual synonyms, in the *Yoga Bhāṣya* (Koelman, 1970: 154) and elsewhere.[10] Therefore the above verses refer to the destruction of subliminal impressions, like certain sūtras of the *Yoga Sūtra* (above, § 5.3). Similarly, the verses must be considered to have undergone influence from Buddhist meditation.

Note however, that the element 'destruction of subconscious impressions' is grafted upon techniques which clearly belong to main stream meditation. The destruction of subconscious impressions is said to result from the destruction of breath, one of the most characteristic accompaniments of main stream meditation. The Upaniṣad nowhere returns to the question of the destruction of the subconscious impressions, whereas much room is dedicated to breath control. We must conclude that in the *Yogakuṇḍalī Upaniṣad* the influence from Buddhist meditation is slight, and may even be merely terminological.

Buddhist meditation is more strongly represented in the *Muktikā Upaniṣad* (MuktU).[11] Verse 2.27 contains a statement very similar to the one above:[12]

> The tree which is the mind has two seeds: the movement of breath and subconscious impression. When one of these two is destroyed, both are quickly destroyed.

The remainder of this Upaniṣad talks much about the destruction of the subconscious impressions, more than about the control of breath. Destruction of the subconscious impressions is said to be equal to

---

mitāhāraś cāsanaṃ ca śakticālas tṛtīyakaḥ //2//

The first of these two verses occurs almost identically (*tu* for *hi*) in Svātmārāma's *Haṭhayogapradīpikā* (4.22).

10. E.g. in Vidyāraṇya's *Jīvanmuktiviveka*; see Sprockhoff, 1964: 226-27.

11. The *Muktikā Upaniṣad* is late and may date from the 15th century A.D. (Sprockhoff, 1976: 260-64, 286).

12. *dve bīje cittavṛkṣasya prāṇaspandanavāsane /*
ekasmiṃś ca tayoḥ kṣīṇe kṣipraṃ dve api naśyataḥ //
This verse occurs almost identically in the *Yogavāsiṣṭha* according to the commentary Jyotsnā on HYPr 4.22, p. 143.

liberation (MuktU 2.68). The subconscious impressions are of two kinds: pure and impure (MuktU 2.61); all are abandoned in the end (MuktU 2.68-71); etc. Yet abandonment of the *vāsanās* is said to be the same as suppression of the movement of breath (MuktU 2.45: *vāsanāsaṃparityāgaḥ prāṇaspandanirodhanam*). Moreover, the aim is to free the soul from attributes which do not really belong to it, such as 'being the actor': "Properties of the mind, such as being the actor, being the enjoyer, bliss and suffering, are fetters of the soul (*puruṣa*) because they are afflictions (*kleśa*) by nature; their destruction is liberation while being alive (*jīvanmukti*)" (MuktU 2 .1: *puruṣasya kartṛtvabhoktṛtvasukhaduḥkhādilakṣaṇaś cittadharmaḥ kleśarūpatvād bandho bhavati / tannirodhanaṃ*
jīvanmuktiḥ /). This shows that this Upaniṣad belongs to the main tradition [72]
of meditation, in spite of the influence from Buddhist meditation.

The notion of *vāsanā* and its destruction appears here and there in other late Upaniṣads as well, but not usually in the predominant position it has in the *Muktikā Upaniṣad*. Examples are: *Nādabindu Up.* 49c-d = *Yogaśikhā Up.* 6.71a-b; *Annapūrṇa Up.* 4.79; *Mahā Up.* 2.45; 5.78; etc.[13] Nothing like the Four Dhyānas of the Buddhists recurs in any of these Upaniṣads, as far as I know.

---

13. Cf. Sprockhoff, 1963: 200-201.

[75]

Part III: Buddhist meditation.

VII. Influence on Buddhist meditation (I).

7.1. We have seen that the main stream of ancient Indian meditation largely lived a life of its own, showing developments both theoretical and practical which could be explained without reference to Buddhism. Buddhist influence came late and remained marginal. The question is whether Buddhist meditation also remained unaffected by main stream meditation.

A priori this seems unlikely. Buddhist meditation had to live in surroundings where apparently the other form of meditation held undisputed sway. Moreover, the other form of meditation was so simple and perspicacious in its aim that Buddhist meditation could not compete with it in appeal.

There is another fact which supports this a priori supposition. The Buddhist scriptures, as we have seen, show that much attention was paid to other modes of meditation, or rather asceticism. We studied the most important passages in chapter I, above.[1] The Jaina canon, on the other hand, says very little about Buddhism, and nothing whatever about Buddhist meditation (Bollée, 1974: 27-28; cf. Jacobi, 1880: 161). Therefore Buddhism is more likely to have adopted parts of the meditation current among the Jainas and elsewhere than vice versa. The fact that Buddhism appears to have been 'a comparatively minor factor in the religious life of India before Asoka' lends further support to this supposition; see Basham, 1982: 139-41 .

A concrete instance of influence from mainstream asceticism on Buddhism is provided by the five demands of Devadatta to the Buddha (Mukherjee, 1966: 75-81). Three of them occur in a stereotyped description of heretics in the Buddhist canon. This has been discussed by Bollée (1971, esp. pp. 71, 76, 81, 83) and will not be repeated here. This

1. See further Bollée, 1971; Bhaskar, 1972; Jacobi, 1895: xv-xx; Tatia, date unknown.

case is particularly interesting because the five demands are in Buddhism not accepted as compulsory, but as optional. Four of them recur in the list of thirteen *dhutaṅgas* enumerated in the canon (Vin V. 131, 193) and in the post-canonical *Milindapañha* (ch. 6) and *Visuddhimagga* (ch. 2).[2]

Another instance occurs in the *Mahāparinirvāṇa Sūtra*, in the discussion with Putkasa / Pukkusa, the different versions of which have been compared by Bareau (1970: 282-95). Putkasa tells that Ārāḍa Kālāma at one occasion did not hear the sound of five hundred – in one version fifty – carts passing by, even though awake and conscious.[3] This ability, [76
we know, is ascribed to practitioners of main stream meditation, along with the ability not to see, smell, taste and feel. The Buddhist texts ridicule it, as we have seen (§ 2.2, above). Here however the Buddha is said to surpass Ārāḍa Kālāma in this respect. He tells Putkasa that once, in a violent thunderstorm when lightning killed two farmers and four oxen near him, he did not notice a thing. We see that a story of probably non-Buddhist origin (so Bareau) was accepted by the Buddhists. This could not fail to influence the way Buddhist meditation came to be looked upon subsequently.

One more instance of borrowing from main stream meditation was pointed out in § 1.2, above. We saw that at one place in the *Majjhima Nikāya* (*Vitakkasanthāna Sutta,* nr 20; MN I.120-21) monks are advised to do what is shown to be incorrect elsewhere (MN I.242; and therefore in the Original Mahāsaccaka Sūtra). It refers to the kind of meditation which consists of "closing the teeth, pressing his palate with the tongue, restraining thought with the mind, coercing and tormenting it", in short, main stream meditation.

Further cases were pointed out in notes 5 and 8 to ch. II. 'Non-performing of new actions' and 'annihilation of former actions' – two characteristics of Jaina meditation criticized at some places – were found to

---

2. On the *dhutaṅgas,* see Bapat, 1937; 1964: Introduction; and Dantinne 1991: esp. p. 25f. The tendency to accept painful practices is also apparent in the *Ekottara Āgama* where it makes the Buddha say that happiness can only be reached through hardship; elsewhere this point of view is ascribed to the Jainas; see note 5 to chapter II above.
3. Something closely similar is told about the grammarian Śākaṭāyana in Patañjali's *Vyākaraṇa-Mahābhāṣya* on P. 3.2.115, vol. II, p. 120, 1. 20-23.

be accepted at other places of the Buddhist canon.[4]

7.2. The above cases could relatively easily be shown to be due to outside influence. Each of them rests on at least two canonical passages which flatly contradict each other, while one agrees closely with what we know about main stream meditation and its accompaniments. We shall now turn to a few cases which are less immediately obvious. The idea remains the same: we shall propose outside influence where by this means contradictions in the Buddhist canon can be explained and where at the same time the origin of this influence can be indicated.

7.2.1. A number of meditational states are mentioned in the Buddhist canon. These, as a rule, occur in lists. We first look at the eight Liberations (*vimokṣa* / *vimokkha*).[5] They are the following:[6]

1) Having visible shape, one sees visible shapes
2) Having no ideation of visible shape in oneself, one sees visible shapes outside [oneself]
[77] 3) One becomes intent on what is beautiful
4) By completely going beyond ideations of visible shape and the coming to an end of ideations of aversion, by not fixing one's mind on different[7] ideations, [thinking] 'space is infinite', he reaches the Stage of Infinity of Space (*ākāśānantyāyatana* / *ākāsānañcāyatana*) and remains there
5) Having completely gone beyond the Stage of Infinity of Space, [thinking] 'knowledge is infinite', one reaches the Stage of

---

4. It is possible that the (first) stanza uttered by Anuruddha after the death of the Buddha (Bareau, 1971: 163-64), which stresses the latter's cessation of breathing, likewise betrays influence from main stream meditation.
5. See e.g. Saṅg VIII.9; Daśo VIII.7; DN II.70-71, 111-12; DĀ[C] p. 62b19-25; MN II.12-13; AN IV.306, 349; Lamotte, 1970: 1281-83. MN III.222 calls them *aṭṭhā disā* 'the eight directions'; cf . MĀ[C] p . 694a2-b9. According to *Mahāvibhāṣā* 77 (T. 1545, p. 399b20 f.; tr. La Vallée Poussin, 1937c: 12) heterodox teachers teach four liberations, viz. the four stages *ākāśānantyāyatana* until *naivasaṃjñānāsaṃjñāyatana*.
6. I translate the Pāli version. Small variations occur in the other versions which are of no relevance for the present study.
7. See note 14 below.

Infinity of Perception (*vijñānānantyāyatana* / *viññāṇañcāyatana*) and remains there

6) Having completely gone beyond the Stage of Infinity of Perception [thinking] 'there is nothing' one reaches the Stage of Nothingness (*ākiñcanyāyatana* / *ākiñcaññāyatana*) and remains there
7) Having completely gone beyond the Stage of Nothingness, one reaches the Stage of Neither Ideation nor Non-Ideation (*naivasaṃjñānāsaṃjñāyatana* / *nevasaññānāsaññāyatana*) and remains there
8) Having completely gone beyond the Stage of Neither Ideation nor Non-Ideation, one reaches the Cessation of Ideations and Feelings (*saṃjñāvedayitanirodha* / *saññāvedayitanirodha*) and remains there.

Even though it is difficult to understand fully what exactly is meant by this passage, one can easily see that it is a list of graded exercises by which the practitioner gradually puts an end to all ideations. In the Stage of Nothingness the most ethereal of ideations alone remain, described as "there is nothing". In the following two states even this ideation disappears.

It is not clear why two states follow the Stage of Nothingness. One might think that ideations are not yet completely absent in the Stage of Neither Ideation nor Non-Ideation, however unlikely that may be.[8] But even on this assumption the presence of feeling (*vedayita*) in the final Cessation of Ideations and Feelings must give rise to suspicion, since the

---

8. If we understand the term *naivasaṃjñānāsaṃjñāyatana* literally, there are no ideations in this 'Stage of Neither Ideations nor Non-Ideations'. This interpretation is supported by DN II.69, according to which beings without ideations occupy that stage (see note 15 below). DN I.184, moreover, speaks of the ideation accompanying the Stage of Nothingness as 'the topmost of ideations' (*saññagga*), after which follows the cessation of all ideations. See further Franke, 1917: 70. Note that the later dogmatists had different opinions on this issue, the Theravādins holding that there are ideations in the Stage of Neither Ideations nor Non-Ideations, their opponents that there are none (*Kathāvatthu* III.12). These opponents are identified as Andhakas in the *Kathāvatthuppakaraṇa-Aṭṭhakathā* (p. 72). See also Vasubandhu's *Abhidharmakośabhāṣya* 8.4 (La Vallée Poussin, 1923-31: ch. viii, p. 143-44).

whole list seems aimed at the dissolution of ideations and leaves no place for feelings. This suggests that the state of Cessation of Ideations and Feelings is an addition to the list. Other passages from the Buddhist canon confirm this.

The *Cūḷasuññata Sutta* of the *Majjhima Nikāya* (nr. 121; III. 104-09) gives a list of states in which more and more is experienced as empty (*suñña*). The list can be briefly given as follows:

[78] 1) He fixes his mind on the exclusive[9] ideation of forest (*araññasaññaṃ paṭicca manasikaroti ekattaṃ*)[10]
2) He fixes his mind on the exclusive ideation of earth (*paṭhavīsaññā*)
3) He fixes his mind on the exclusive ideation of the Stage of Infinity of Space (*ākāsānañcāyatanasaññā*)
4) He fixes his mind on the exclusive ideation of the Stage of Infinity of Perception (*viññāṇañcāyatanasaññā*)
5) He fixes his mind on the exclusive ideation of the Stage of Nothingness (*ākiñcaññāyatanasaññā*
6) He fixes his mind on the exclusive ideation of the Stage of Neither Ideation nor Non-Ideation (*nevasaññānāsaññāyatanasaññā*)
7) He fixes his mind on the exclusive mental concentration beyond [any ideation of] characteristics (or mental images)[11] (*animitta cetosamādhi*).

The numbers 3)-6) of this list correspond to the numbers 4)-7) of the list of the eight Liberations. What precedes and follows differ.

It is again possible to distinguish a list of graded exercises in which consciousness, by a process of ever increasing abstractions, is deprived of all content. The two introductory states fit well with this. But the last state,

---

9. See note 14 below.
10. The Pāli text adds *tassa araññasaññāya cittaṃ pakkhandati pasīdati santiṭṭhati / adhimuccati*, and the same appropriately adjusted to each of the following sentences. But the Chinese (MĀ^{C} p. 736c f.) and Tibetan (not accessible to me) parallels omit this (Schmithausen, 1981: 234 n. 124).
11. So Schmithausen, 1981: 235.

the *animitta cetosamādhi,* appears superfluous. Rather, in this list an unconvincing trick has been used which is apparently intended to provide a place for this *animitta cetosamādhi*. In all but the last states the mind is fixed on the exclusive ideation of something. In the final state the mind is fixed on the *animitta cetosamādhi* and now apparently goes beyond all forms of ideation. In the preceding state the mind is said to be fixed on "the exclusive ideation of the Stage of Neither Ideation nor Non-Ideation". This is absurd. Ideation is ascribed to a state which has no ideation. Perhaps we witness here an attempt to justify the final state, *animitta cetosamādhi*.

It seems dubious that *animitta cetosamādhi* is identical with *saṃjñā-vedayitanirodha* ('Cessation of ideations and Feelings').[12] Schmithausen (1981: 236 n. 133) gives one reference (SN 40.1-9) where the two terms seem to have been interchanged, as well as a few references (DN II. 100, AN 6.60 (III.397)) where the two denote different things. We note that, at any rate, the terms are different.

The two lists discussed thus far share in common a unit of four [79]
meditational states, which may be looked upon as their 'hard core': 1. the Stage of Infinity of Space (*ākāśānantyāyatana*); 2. the Stage of Infinity of Perception (*vijñānānantyāyatana*); 3. the Stage of Nothingness (*ākiñcanyāyatana*); 4. the Stage of Neither Ideation nor Non-Ideation (*naivasaṃjñānāsaṃjñāyatana*). This 'hard core' occurs by itself in the Buddhist canon under the name 'the four *arūpas* / *ārūpyas*' (DN III.224; Saṅg IV.8; DĀC p. 50c25f.).

One might expect that this list of four meditational states has to be reduced still further to account for the seven Places of Perception (*vijñānasthiti* / *viññāṇaṭṭhiti*):[13]

1) There are beings with different[14] bodies and different ideations, such as men, some gods and some inhabitants of hell

---

12. For a different opinion, see Vetter, 1988:67 n.8.

13. See e.g. DN III.253; DĀC p. 52a23 - 29; AN IV.39; Daśo VII.7. I translate the Pāli version, ignoring the small deviations which occur in other versions.

14. I translate *nānatta* (Skt . *nānātman*) and *ekatta* (Skt . *ekātman*) as proposed by Schmithausen (1981: 233-34, n. 122), even though the Sanskrit version has *nānātva* and *ekatva*.

2) There are beings with different bodies and uniform[15] ideations, such as the Brahmakāyika gods who came first into existence
3) There are beings with uniform bodies and different ideations, such as the Ābhāsvara gods
4) There are beings with uniform bodies and uniform ideations, such as the Subhakiṇha gods
5) There are beings which, by going completely beyond ideations of form, and the coming to an end of ideations of aversion, by not fixing their mind on different ideations, [thinking] 'space is infinite', reach the Stage of Infinity of Space (*ākāśānantyā-yatana*)
6) There are beings which, having completely gone beyond this Stage of Infinity of Space, [thinking] 'perception is infinite', reach the Stage of Infinity of Perception (*vijñānānantyāyatana*)
7) There are beings which, having completely gone beyond the Stage of Infinity of Perception, [thinking] 'there is nothing', reach the Stage of Nothingness (*ākiñcanyāyatana*).

Here the Stage of Infinity of Space, the Stage of Infinity of Perception and the Stage of Nothingness, occur together without the fourth, the Stage of Neither Ideation nor Non-Ideation (*naivasaṃjñānāsaṃjñāyatana*).

There is, however, an obvious reason why the Stage of Neither Ideation nor Non-Ideation is left out. This list enumerates Places of Perception. But perception (*vijñāna*) is always accompanied by ideation (*saṃjñā*), which is absent in the Stage of Neither Ideation nor Non-Ideation. This last stage, therefore, falls into another, higher category.

[80] The Buddhist canon also gives a list of nine Residences of Beings (*sattvāvāsa* / *sattāvāsa*; e.g., Daśo IX.3; Saṅg IX.2; DN III.263) which is the seven Places of Perception plus two items. Between 4) and 5) is added the Residence of Beings of those without ideations and feelings (*asaññino appaṭisaṃvedino*, in the Pāli version), or of those without ideations and discriminating ideations (*asaṃjñino 'pratisaṃjñinas*, in the Sanskrit version); and the Residence of Beings of those who have reached the Stage of Neither Ideation nor Non-Ideation (*naivasaṃjñānāsaṃjñā-*

15. MN I.169-70; MV I.7; MĀ[C] p. 777a-b; T. 1428, p. 787b.

yatana) is added at the end.

It appears from the above that the Stage of Nothingness (*ākiñcanyāyatana*) and the Stage of Neither Ideation nor Non-Ideation (*naivasaṃjñānāsaṃjñāyatana*) are the two final states of a row of graded exercises. By a process of increasing abstraction, in which the initial stages seem to be variable, the aspirant works himself up to a state where there is 'neither ideation nor non-ideation'. In the later stages of this process the mind is successively fixed on the notions "space is infinite", "perception is infinite" and "there is nothing". The Stage of Nothingness is the final state in which some kind of notion remains before the jump is made into (complete or almost complete) notionlessness, the real goal.

There is some independent evidence that the Stage of Nothingness and the Stage of Neither Ideation nor Non-Ideation were at one time aims in themselves.

The Buddha is said to have had two teachers before his enlightenment: Ārāḍa (P. Āḻāra) Kālāma and Udraka (P. Uddaka) the son of Rāma. From the former the Bodhisattva learned the Stage of Nothingness, from the latter the Stage of Neither Ideation nor Non-Ideation. No credence can be given to this story, for the following reasons, presented by Bareau (1963: 20 21).[16]

The episode of the Bodhisattva's training under Ārāḍa Kālāma and Udraka the son of Rāma is found in three versions in the older parts of the canon: in the *Majjhima Nikāya* of the Theravādins (thrice: in the *Ariyapariyesana Sutta,* nr. 26, MN I.163-67; *Mahāsaccaka Sutta,* nr. 36, MN I.240, Nālandā ed. I, p. 294-98; *Saṅgarāva Sutta,* nr. 100, MN II.212, Nālandā ed. II, p. 484-87); in the *Madhyamāgama* of the Sarvāstivādins (MĀ^{C} p. 776b5-777a4); in the *Vinaya* of the Dharmaguptakas (T. 1428, p. 780b7-c19). The names of Ārāḍa Kālāma and Udraka the son of Rāma occur again in the scriptures of these schools, where they relate how the Buddha, after his enlightenment, wonders to

16. [Discussions with Ghiorgo Zafiropulo – whose book *De la quête à l'annonce de l'éveil* is expected to come out soon (Innsbrucker Beiträge zur Kulturwissenschaft) – have now (1992) convinced me that Bareau's reasons may not be compelling. This does not, however, affect – or if it does, it strengthens – the following arguments.]

[81] whom he will preach his doctrine first. He thinks of Ārāḍa Kālāma and Udraka the son of Rāma, but learns that both have died recently. No word is said about the Buddha's relationship to these two people, nor indeed do we hear what these men had been or done. This would be hard to explain if the training of the Bodhisattva under them had been related at that time a few pages earlier as it is now. One suspects that the names of these two men originally occurred only where the Buddha thinks of possible persons with whom to start his missionary activity. In order to give some content to these mysterious names, the account of the Bodhisattva's training under teachers with these names was added. This supposition finds support in the fact that the *Vinaya* of the Mahīśāsakas relates the Buddha's doubt about whom to preach to first (T. 1421, p. 104a11-21; Bareau, 1963: 145-46) and mentions in this context the names of Ārāḍa Kālāma and Udraka the son of Rāma, but does not refer to the Bodhisattva's training under these two even though this *Vinaya* mentions a number of things about the Bodhisattva prior to his enlightenment (T. 1421, p. 101a10 - 102c14; tr. in Bareau, 1962).[17]

If this story does not reflect the historical truth, why was it invented? Part of the reason has been given above: the occurrence of the two names 'Ārāḍa Kālāma' and 'Udraka the son of Rāma' required an explanation which could be given in this manner. But clearly this does not explain why the story took exactly this shape. In its actual form the story serves the additional purpose of denouncing the Stage of Nothingness and the Stage of Neither Ideation nor Non-Ideation.

Let us note that in two of the three versions of this story (of the Theravādins and of the Sarvāstivādins) the Bodhisattva complains that these two stages do not lead to what he is looking for, an impossibility if, in the opinion of its author, they represented two steps which preceded the final steps of the way to enlightenment. If on the other hand, the criticism had been against, for instance, the eight Liberations (*vimokṣa*) – which have one more stage after the two stages mentioned in this story, viz. the Cessation of Ideations and Feelings, *saṃjñāvedayitanirodha* – the Bodhi-

---

17. Note further that the *Mahāparinirvāṇa Sūtra* mentions a Putkasa / Pukkusa who is supposed to be a follower of Ārāḍa Kālāma and visits the Buddha not long before the latter's death. See Bareau, 1970: 282-95, esp. p. 284; and § 7.1 above.

sattva should have been depicted as also practising this final stage and finding it worthless. Consequently it is only reasonable to assume that the account of the training under Ārāḍa Kālāma and Udraka the son of Rāma contains an implicit criticism of those who considered the Stage of Neither Ideation nor Non-Ideation the final aim of a course of training, immediately preceded presumably by the Stage of Nothingness.

The above observations have made it probable that in the early days of [82]
Buddhism the following list of meditational states existed (which may have been the end of a longer list of which the initial items were not strongly fixed):

a) the Stage of Infinity of Space (*ākāśānantyāyatana*);
b) the Stage of Infinity of Perception (*vijñānānantyāyatana*);
c) the Stage of Nothingness (*ākiñcanyāyatana*);
d) the Stage of Neither Ideation nor Non-Ideation (*naivasaṃjñānāsaṃjñāyatana*).

We know that this short list appears as a part of longer lists in the Buddhist canon and was therefore accepted in Buddhist circles. Interestingly enough, the evidence discussed above points to a time when this list was not accepted by at least some Buddhists.

The list agrees well with what we know of main stream meditation. There the aim is to stop mental activity. This can be compared with the Stage of Neither Ideation nor Non-Ideation studied above. It is striking that the Jaina scriptures describe reflection on infinity (*aṇaṃtavattiyā*, Skt. *anantavartitā* or *-vṛttitā*) as one of the reflections (*aṇuppehā*, Skt. *anuprekṣā*) underlying pure (*sukka*, Skt. *śukla*), i.e. the highest meditation (above, § 3.3). This corresponds with the Stage of Infinity of Space and the Stage of Infinity of Knowledge. A further point of resemblance is the fact that these four states of meditation, unlike the Four Dhyānas of Buddhism, are never described as pleasurable or blissful[18] (as already remarked by Schmidt (1953: 65)).

18. The only exception occurs in the *Cūḷasaññata Sutta* of the *Majjhima Nikāya*. However, the Chinese and Tibetan parallels leave out the sentences concerned. See note 10 above.

We hypothesize that the meditational states under discussion at present entered Buddhism from Jainistic or related circles.

7.2.2. How could these meditational practices find entrance into Buddhism? Where could they find a place side by side with the Four Dhyānas?

The Four Dhyānas can be briefly characterized as follows (cf. § 1.5 above):

- In the First Dhyāna there is deliberation (*vitarka*), thought (*vicāra*), joy (*prīti*) and bliss (*sukha*).
- In the Second Dhyāna deliberation and thought come to rest. Inner tranquillization (*adhyātmasamprasādana*), unification of the mind (*cetaso ekotībhāva*), concentration (*samādhi*), joy and bliss are present.

[83] - In the Third Dhyāna one is no longer attached to joy. Equanimity (*upekṣā*), mindfulness (*smṛti*), circumspection (*saṃprajanya*) and bliss are present.
- In the Fourth Dhyāna bliss and misery (*duḥkha*) are abandoned, as well as cheerfulness (*saumanasya*) and dejectedness (*daurmanasya*). Equanimity and mindfulness remain.

Clearly the Stage of Neither Ideation nor Non-Ideation can be compared with the Second Dhyāna, where deliberation and thought come to rest. Both states represent some kind of cessation of ordinary mental functioning. There is some evidence that an assimilation of this type was actually made at some time.

A Buddhist Sūtra (SN IV.297-300; SĀ^{C} p. 152b28 - 153a2) relates a discussion between Nigaṇṭha Nātaputta, i.e. the Jina, and the householder Citra / Citta. Citra is asked if he believes the recluse Gautama who says that there is a concentration free from deliberation and thought (*avitakko avicāro samādhi*), that there is cessation of deliberation and thought (*vitakkavicārāṇaṃ nirodho*). Initially Citra gives an ambiguous answer, but then turns out not to believe, but to know these things from his own experience which he obtained while practising the Four Dhyānas (Pāli) / the first two of the Four Dhyānas (Chinese). In this passage the leader of the Jainas is depicted as considering impossible the very aim of Jaina meditation. What is more, the Jaina road of meditation up to the cessation of all mental activity seems here to be identified with the first two of the Four Dhyānas of the Buddhists. Note that the word *nirodha* 'cessation' which is common in the main tradition of meditation, is used in the context of the Second Dhyāna, where normally 'coming to rest' (*vyupaśama / vūpasama*) is used.

Main stream meditation does not end with a mere cessation of all mental activity. In its highest stages there is a complete cessation of all activity whatever, particularly of breathing. If the cessation of mental activity was identified with the Second Dhyāna, one might expect that cessation of breathing in particular was assigned to a later Dhyāna, preferably the Fourth one. This is confirmed by the list of Successive Cessations (*anupubbanirodha;* DN III.266; 290; AN IV.409). It reads:

- For one who has reached the First Dhyāna the ideation of objects of sense (*kāma*) has ceased;
- for one who has reached the Second Dhyāna deliberation and thought (*vitakkavicāra*) have ceased; [84]
- for one who has reached the Third Dhyāna joy (*pīti*) has ceased;
- for one who has reached the Fourth Dhyāna *breathing out and breathing in* (*assāsapassāsa*) *have ceased*;
- for one who has reached the Stage of Infinity of Space the ideation of form has ceased;
- for one who has reached the Stage of Infinity of Perception the ideation of the Stage of Infinity of Space has ceased;
- for one who has reached the Stage of Nothingness the ideation of the Stage of Infinity of Perception has ceased;
- for one who has reached the Stage of Neither Ideation nor Non-Ideation the ideation of the Stage of Nothingness has ceased;
- for one who has reached the Cessation of Ideations and Feelings ideations and feelings have ceased.

We note the fourth item of this list, where the same terms are used as at MN I.242, where Jaina meditation is described (above, chapter I).

If it is true that the early Buddhists (or some of them) made attempts to assimilate the four stages under discussion to the Four Dhyānas, it cannot have escaped their attention that in the Second Dhyāna, where *vitarka* and *vicāra* come to rest, joy (*prīti*) and bliss (*sukha*) remain together with other feelings which do not disappear until the Third and Fourth Dhyānas. This would imply that after the Stage of Neither Ideation nor Non-Ideation another stage would be required where not only ideations (*saṃjñā*) but also feelings (*vedayita*) have stopped. Such a stage exists in the Cessation of Ideations and Feelings (*saṃjñāvedayitanirodha*) frequently met with in the texts.

The above assimilation of the four states and what follows them to the Four Dhyānas is clearly not very satisfactory. The differences between the four states and the Four Dhyānas are too great to allow of such an easy assimilation. No wonder that this assimilation was not accepted in the larger part of the Buddhist canon. The alternative, if one of the two groups was not to be discarded, was to place them one after the other. In the nine Successive States (*anupūrvavihāra* / *anupubbavihāra*)[19] we find the following order : first the Four Dhyānas, then the Stage of Infinity of
[85] Space, the Stage of Infinity of Knowledge, the Stage of Nothingness, the Stage of Neither Ideation nor Non-Ideation, and finally the Cessation of Ideations and Feelings.

The list obtained was justified with the help of the nine Successive Cessations (see above): in each next stage something more is stopped. The *Poṭṭhapāda Sutta* of the *Dīgha Nikāya* (nr. 9) contains a slightly different justification: the list[20] is presented as bringing about the successive cessation of several forms of ideation (DN I.182-84):

- In the First Dhyāna there is cessation of the ideation of objects of sense.
- In the Second Dhyāna there is cessation of the subtle and true ideation of the joy and bliss born from seclusion (*vivekajapītisukhasukhumasacca-saññā*).
- In the Third Dhyāna there is cessation of the subtle and true ideation of the joy and bliss born from concentration (*samādhijapītisukhasukhuma-*

19. See e.g. Daśo IX.8; Lamotte, 1970: 1308.
20. Properly speaking, a slightly different list. The final Cessation of Ideations and Feelings is lacking here, and the Stage of Neither Ideation nor Non-Ideation is designated differently. See the next note.

saccasaññā).

- In the Fourth Dhyāna there is cessation of the subtle and true ideation of indifference and bliss (*upekkhāsukhasukhumasaccasaññā*).
- In the Stage of Infinity of Space there is cessation of the ideation of form (*rūpasaññā*).
- In the Stage of Infinity of Perception there is cessation of the subtle and true ideation of the Stage of Infinity of Space (*ākāsānañcāyatana-sukhumasaccasaññā*).
- In the Stage of Nothingness there is cessation of the subtle and true ideation of the Stage of Infinity of Perception (*viññaṇānañcāyatana-sukhumasaccasaññā*).
- In the next and final state, simply described as Cessation (*nirodha*), there is cessation of all ideations.[21]

The Successive States became quite prominent in the Buddhist canon and are often said to lead to the vanishing of the Intoxicants (*āsrava / āsava*), i.e., final liberation (e.g., SN 16.9-11; AN 9.34; 35; MN I.159-60; 174-75; II.42-45; MĀ^c p. 701b12).

7.2.3. If it is true that the four states – from the Stage of Infinity of Space until the Stage of Neither Ideation nor Non-Ideation – were borrowed from main stream meditation in one form or another, we must assume that originally this list of graded exercises represented a road to liberation quite [86]
different from the authentic Buddhist one. Moreover, these states must then have been part of a scheme where liberation was not attained until the death of the body. Our idea that these states were borrowed from outside is therefore confirmed by the fact that several Buddhist schools were indeed of the opinion that an alternative road to liberation led through the Stage of Neither Ideation nor Non-Ideation; arhant-ship is here obtained at the end of one's final existence. These schools are the Vibhajyavādins, Mahīśāsakas, Theravādins[22] and the authors of the *Śāriputrābhidharma-*

21. This stage corresponds to the Stage of Neither Ideation nor Non-Ideation rather than to the Cessation of Ideations and Feelings, for, unlike the latter of these two, it does not stop feelings. There is at any rate nothing in the text to indicate this.
22. Bareau gives no reference for the Theravādins. Cf. Pp 13: *yassa puggalassa apubbaṃ acarimaṃ āsavapariyādānañ ca hoti jīvitapariyādānañ ca, ayaṃ vuccati*

śāstra[23] (Bareau, 1957: 248; 1955: 175, 184, 198, 262).

7.2.4. The above arguments make it likely that the four states discussed came into Buddhism from outside. The following, somewhat speculative considerations may support this.

Space (*ākāśa*) and perception (*vijñāna*) are the last two in the list of six *dhātus*, the earlier ones being earth, water, fire and wind (see, e.g., SN II.248) . This makes it tempting to think that these earlier *dhātus* could be added before the above four meditational states. Indeed, in AN V.324 and elsewhere[24] we find the following list of items which can, but should not be used as objects of meditation: (l) earth, (2) water, (3) fire, (4) wind,[25] (5) Stage of Infinity of Space, (6) Stage of Infinity of Perception, (7) Stage of Nothingness, (8) Stage of Neither Ideation nor Non-Ideation, (9) this world, (10) the world beyond, (11) whatever is seen, heard, thought, known, obtained, searched, pondered over by the mind.

If we leave out of consideration the last three items of this list, we arrive at something similar to what is described in a passage of the *Mokṣadharmaparvan*, viz. MBh 12.288.113-15. There we find a successive fixation of the mind (*dhāraṇā*) on earth, ether, water, fire, *ahaṃkāra*, *buddhi*, and *avyakta*[26] (cf. Bedekar, 1963b: 25-27; Frauwallner, 1953: 142-43; Hopkins, 1901: 351-52; Barnes, 1976: 66). Frauwallner (1953: 143) observed, no doubt correctly, that it was considered that the Yogin who practised these successive fixations was

---

puggalo samasīsī "The person in whose case no sooner does the termination of sinful tendencies take place than the life terminates. Such a person is said to be one who is 'equal-headed'."(tr. Law, 1924: 20).

23. Mahāsāṃghikas? See Lamotte, 1958: 208 n.24.
24. AN V.7-8; 318-20; 321-22; 353-58.
25. Note that these four (six in the case of MĀ[C]) elements are enumerated as objects of meditation in the *Smṛtyupasthāna Sūtra* (MN I.57-58; DN II.294; MĀ[C] p. 583b 17-23; EĀ[C] p. 568a23-b1). Schmithausen (1976: 252-53, n. 25) suggests that the four elements in this context are not original and derive from passages like MN I.185 f. and 421 f., where they occur in an analysis of *rūpa*.
26. The text announces seven fixations but appears to give eight. Are we to exclude *buddhi*, which has the suffix *-tas* that is so hard to explain in this context, or should we look upon *avyakta* as belonging to another category ?

able to go through the process of creation in reverse order.[27] It remains none the less possible that both these lists – the one of the *Mahābhārata* and the one of the *Aṅguttara Nikāya* – derive from a common ancestor. Their divergent developments may have been determined by ontological and other considerations.

7.3. This may be the place to say a few words about the four Brahmic States (*brahmavihāra*). As far as I know, the practice of these mental states is nowhere criticized in the Buddhist canon. Nor are these states immediately recognizable as belonging to main stream meditation. Indeed, it appears that they are not found in the old Hindu and Jaina scriptures.[28] Yet certain passages in the Buddhist canon show that they were known to and practised by non-Buddhists. [87]

The *Saṃyutta Nikāya* (SN V. 115f) and the *Saṃyukta Āgama* (SĀ^c p. 197 b15f.) contain the story of Buddhist monks who are embarrassed by heretical wanderers. These heretics claim that the teaching of the Buddha does not differ from their own : both teach the four Brahmic States.[29] In response to this allegation the Buddha is presented as saying that his followers practise the Brahmic States until their highest perfection, leading to purity in the case of benevolence (*maitrī* / *P. mettā*), to the Stage of Infinity of Space (*ākāśānantyāyatana* / *P. ākāsānañcāyatana*) for compassion (*karuṇā*), the Stage of Infinity of Perception (*vijñānānantyāyatana* / P. *viññāṇañcāyatana*) for joy (*muditā*), the Stage of Nothingness (*ākiñcanyāyatana* / *P. ākiñcaññāyatana*) for indifference (*upekṣā*).[30] All this merely confirms the main point: the Brahmic States were practised by non-Buddhists.

The *Paṭhamamettā Sutta* of the *Aṅguttara Nikāya* (AN II. 128f.) does not even try to show the difference between Buddhists and non-Buddhists in their practice of the Brahmic States. The only difference lies in the result. Both Buddhists and non-Buddhists attain to the state of certain gods

---

27. Recall Eliade's (1967: 107) remark that the Yogin aimed at the state which preceded creation, primordial unity.
28. They are referred to in Umāsvāti's *Tattvārthādhigama Sūtra* 7.6 (Jacobi, 1906: 523) but not in the Jaina canon (Schubring, 1935: 191).
29. The term *brahmavihāra* is not used here, but the four practices are described.
30. The Pāli text also brings in the Constituents of Enlightenment (*sambojjhaṅga*). These are absent from the Chinese.

as a result of these practices, and remain there for a long but finite period of time. After that the non-Buddhists go to hell, or become animals, or ghosts. The Buddhists, on the other hand, reach Nirvāṇa while in that divine state. We may conclude that at least for some time the Brahmic States were practised identically by Buddhists and certain non-Buddhists.

Some Sūtras indicate that their authors considered the Brahmic States older than and inferior to the practices taught by the Buddha. The *Makhādeva Sutta* (MN II.74-83; MĀ^{c} p. 511c-515b; EĀ^{c} p. 806c-810b) relates how king Makhādeva[31] and his successors abandon the world as soon as they get grey hair, and practise the Brahmic States.[32] The Buddha explains that he himself was Makhādeva in an earlier birth, but that Makhādeva's practices brought him not to the end, whereas the practices now taught by the Buddha lead to liberation (MĀ^{c} p. 515a23) and Nirvāṇa (MN II.82; EĀ^{c} p. 810b12).

[88] The Pāli version of the *Mahāgovinda Sutta* (DN II.220-52) indicates the same thing. Mahāgovinda practises the four Brahmic States and reaches the world of Brahman. The Buddha explains that he himself was Mahāgovinda, but that his practice was not satisfactory. Only the Noble Eightfold Path (*ariya aṭṭhaṅgika magga*) leads to enlightenment and Nirvāṇa (pp. 250-51). The fact that the Brahmic States are not clearly included in the Chinese (DĀ^{c} p. 30b-34b; T 8, p. 207c-210b) and Sanskrit (Mv III.197-224) versions of this story, makes it probable that they were inserted at a relatively late date, perhaps under the influence of the *Makhādeva Sutta*.

The assimilation of the Brahmic States to three of the four Stages discussed in § 7.2 may give us a clue regarding the origin of these practices. In both the Brahmic States and the four Stages we find a heavy emphasis on infinity. In the four Brahmic States the world is pervaded by the mind which is suffused with benevolence, compassion, joy and equanimity respectively. It seems reasonable to assume a historical connection with the reflection on infinity of the Jainas (see § 7.2.1 and

31. The Chinese (大天) presupposes rather 'Mahādeva'.

32. The Chinese versions have 梵行 which also translates *brahmacarya*. However, the specifications given in the *Ekottara Āgama* (p. 808b15-16; c11-12; 809a21; 810a13-14) leave no room for doubt.

§ 3.3, above).

7.4. We see that there is much reason to think that the influence from main stream meditation on Buddhist meditation was already widespread in canonical times. That this was solely due to the relatively small number of active Buddhists as compared with the much larger number of those who practised main stream meditation seems unlikely. Another factor must have been at work. Already early in the history of Buddhism there was uncertainty about the details of the practice taught by the Buddha. This explains why the Buddhist canon contains so many contradictions, some of which we have studied above. It also explains why very early disagreement arose about the nature of an *arhant* (see Bareau, 1957; La Vallée Poussin, 1937b). This uncertainty opened the door to foreign elements which could take the place of original but little understood elements. In this way outside influence could touch the very heart of the teaching of the Buddha. In this light we shall study some other questions.

Before we turn to these questions, let us see what remains that can be considered authentic Buddhist meditation in view of the conclusions of the present chapter. The Four Dhyānas and the subsequent destruction of the intoxicants survive the present analysis easily. I know of no indications that they too must be looked upon as due to outside influence. Moreover, [89] they occur very frequently in the canonical scriptures and already made the impression on other investigators of belonging to the oldest layers of the tradition.[33]

Closely connected with the Four Dhyānas is the practice of 'mindfulness' (*smṛti* / *sati*). Mindfulness is mentioned in the description of the Four Dhyānas, but is also independently described in the canon. It is possible that, originally, mindfulness merely concerned the body (Schmithausen, 1976: 253). It may have been borrowed from outside movements, because it appears to be known to Jainism (Schmithausen, 1976: 254). But this is no reason to doubt its role in original Buddhism, for mindfulness is nowhere criticized in the Buddhist canon, nor does it conflict with other practices accepted by the Buddhists.

---

33. See Frauwallner, 1953: 162 f.; Pande, 1974: 529-34; Schmithausen, 1978: 101; Griffiths, 1983: § 2; cf. Heiler, 1922: 45; Schmithausen, 1981: 218-19.

[93] VIII. Influence on Buddhist meditation (II).

8.1. In the preceding chapter we discussed the influence of main stream meditation on the techniques of Buddhist meditation. In the present chapter we shall examine the extent to which main stream ideas influenced the Buddhist conception of liberation and its commencement.

Recall that main stream asceticism led to liberation after death. Only where ascetic practices were wholly or partly replaced by insight, could the decisive transition take place in this life. Buddhism too promised liberation in this life (as will be shown in § 8.2). This leads us to expect two developments in Buddhism under outside influence: (i) liberation in Buddhism will tend to be postponed to the time after death (§ 8.3); (ii) liberating insight will tend to take an explicit form and a central position (§ 8.4).

8.2. Numerous canonical passages confirm that Buddhism preached liberation in this life, i.e., before death. The Buddha himself is said to have reached liberation at his moment of enlightenment, attaining Nirvāṇa and accomplishing his task at that time (see Bareau, 1963: 72-79). But with respect to others, or in general descriptions, the aim of the religious life is also said to be attained, or attainable, in this life (*dṛṣṭe dharme / diṭṭhe va dhamme*).[1] A special case is constituted by the oft-repeated formula: "Soon N. – having himself, in this very life, by means of his intuition witnessed that highest end of the religious life for which sons from good families completely go forth from their house to the state of houselessness – reached [that end] and remained there, and recognized: 'Birth is destroyed, the religious life has been lived, what had to be done has been done, there is no more of this state [of existence]'." (in Pāli : ... *na cirass' eva yass' atthāya kulaputtā sammad eva agārasmā anagāriyaṃ*

1. E.g. DN I.167f.; II.71; MN I.55, 71; SN II. 15, 46; AN I.50; cf. DĀ^{C} p. 34a24, p. 103c21; MĀ^{C} p. 596a24; SĀ^{C} p. 99a22, b7; EĀ^{C} p. 811b12; T. 1428, p. 788a4. See also Kumoi, 1969: 209.

pabbajanti, tad anuttaraṃ brahmacariyapariyosānaṃ diṭṭhe va dhamme sayaṃ abhiññā sacchikatvā upasampajja vihāsi 'khīṇā jāti, vusitaṃ brahmacariyaṃ, kataṃ karaṇīyaṃ, nāparaṃ itthattāyā' ti' abbhaññāsi.)[2]

The teaching of the Buddha is similarly characterized as 'belonging to this life' (*sāṃdṛṣṭika* / *sandiṭṭhika*) and 'inviting to come and see' (*ehipaśyika* / *ehipassika*).[3] The attribute *akālika*, which often occurs along with the preceding two, appears to mean 'not connected with death' (Bronkhorst,1985b) and draws attention to the this-worldly relevance of [94] the message of the Buddha as well. Sometimes these or similar attributes describe Nirvāṇa,[4] which is thus seen to be attainable in this life. Both Nirvāṇa and Arhant-ness (*arahatta*) are defined as 'destruction of desire, destruction of hatred, destruction of delusion' (*rāgakkhaya, dosakkhaya, mohakkhaya*) in SN IV.251-52, which indicates that the two are identical or, at any rate, related and therefore (also) part of this world.

8.3. The tendency to postpone liberation until after death becomes visible in those canonical passages which distinguish between Nirvāṇa – qualified in Sanskrit and Pāli as 'without a remainder of *upadhi* / *upādi*' (*anupadhiśeṣa* / *anupādisesa*) – and the 'highest and complete enlightenment' (*anuttara samyaksaṃbodhi* / *sammāsambodhi*).[5] The former occurs at death, the latter in life.

The *Nigrodhakappa Sutta* of the *Suttanipāta* (Sn 343-58) also assigns Nirvāṇa to the time after death. The prose introduction tells us that Nigrodhakappa is *aciraparinibbuta* "recently entered into Parinirvāṇa". The first verse states that he is dead (*kālam akāsi*). And Sn 354 (= Th 1274) asks: "Has he reached Nirvāṇa or is he with a remainder of *upādi* ? Let us hear if he was liberated." (*nibbāyi so ādu sa-upādiseso, yathā vimutto ahu taṃ suṇoma*).

Some passages, esp. in the *Mahāparinirvāṇa Sūtra,* speak about the

2. E.g. DN I.177; II.153; SN I.140, 161; AN II.249; III.70; Ud 23; Sn p. 16; p. 111-12; cf. MN I.172, 177; MPS p. 380-82; DĀ^{C} p. 104c12-14; p. 25b22-25; p. 39a2-9; SĀ^{C} p. 309a16-17; EĀ^{C} p. 612b24-26.
3. E.g. DN II.93, 217; MN I.37, 265; SN I.9, 220; AN I.149, 207; Mv III. 200.
4. AN I.158-59; IV.453-54; Ud 37.
5. E.g. DN II.108-09; III.135; AN II.120; IV.313; Ud 85; MPS p. 216-18; cf. DĀ^{C} p. 16a8-14; EĀ^{C} p. 753c23-26; T. 7, p. 192a1-5.

death of the Buddha as his 'Parinirvāṇa'.[6] (It is understandable that the opinion could arise that the term 'Parinirvāṇa' referred to the state after death of the Buddhist saint, 'Nirvāṇa' to the state while he was alive. This does not however appear to be correct. The canon also uses the term 'Parinirvāṇa' with reference to living men.[7] See Franke, 1913: 180n.; Thomas, 1947; Nyanatiloka, 1976: 160-61 (s.v. *parinibbāna*).)

The *Dhammasaṅgaṇi* (Dhs 1017-18) differentiates between Arhantness (*uparitthimaṃ arahattaphalaṃ*) and Nirvāṇa (*asaṅkhatā dhātu*), disagreeing with SN IV.251-52 discussed above. See C.A.F. Rhys Davids, 1900: 153-54, 342.

There is one canonical passage (It 38-39) where the conflict between Nirvāṇa in this life and Nirvāṇa after death is resolved by distinguishing two kinds of Nirvāṇa: with and without a remainder of *upādi* (Skt. *upadhi;* the terms used are *sa-upādisesa* and *anupādisesa*);[8] the former applies to Nirvāṇa in this life, the latter to Nirvāṇa after death. We saw that the distinction between Nirvāṇa without a remainder of *upādi* on the one
[95] hand, and enlightenment on the other, is more common in the canon. Introducing a 'Nirvāṇa with a remainder of *upādi*' was consequently a rather obvious thing to do. We do not, however, have to know the exact significance of *upādi*[9] in order to discover that the idea of a Nirvāṇa with a remainder of *upādi* does not agree with the use of the word elsewhere in the canon. An oft-recurring formula describes the two fruits of which certain advanced disciples will obtain either the one or the other: "perfect knowledge in this life, or – in case there is a remainder of *upādi* – the state of being a non-returner" (*diṭṭhe va dhamme aññā, sati vā upādisese*

6. E.g. DN I.204, II.140; SN V. 260-62; AN IV. 310-11; Ud 63-64; Th 1045; MPS p. 192; T. 5, p. 169a23; T. 6, p. 185b15; T. 7, p. 199b16-19; MĀ[C] p. 515b19.
7. E.g. DN III.55, 97; MN I.235; AN I. 204-05; II.167; Sn 359; SĀ[C] p. 57c8.
8. Note that the Chinese translations, where they translate these terms at all, often skip the word *upādi* in it: *sa-upādisesa* corresponds to 有餘, *anupādisesa* to 無餘. See e.g. DĀ[C] p. 16a13; MĀ[C] p. 584b17, 20, 23; p. 752c2; EĀ[C] p. 753c25.
9. For opinions, see Welbon, 1968: 208-20; Bhattacharya, 1968.

anāgāmitā).[10] Some other passages[11] use both the terms *anupādisesa* and *sa-upādisesa* with reference to living monks. In Sn 354 (= Th 1274) the Buddha is questioned about the fate of Nigrodhakappa who died: "Has he reached Nirvāṇa or is he with a remainder of *upādi* ?" (see above). We must conclude that the distinction between Nirvāṇa with and without a remainder of *upādi,* in spite of its later currency (see La Vallée Poussin, 1925: 171-77, 179-80), was initially no more than an attempt to find a middle course between the original idea of Nirvāṇa in this life and the later tendency to place Nirvāṇa after death.

Another solution of the problem of the two Nirvāṇas also came to be adopted. The highest stage of meditation – here *nirodhasamāpatti,* or *saṃjñāvedayitanirodha* – is said to be similar to Nirvāṇa, or touching it. (See La Vallée Poussin, 1937b: 213 f.; Schmithausen, 1981: 241, 219 n.67.) This opened the possibility for a Nirvāṇa which is really situated after death but can be anticipated in life.

8.4. The early Buddhists believed in liberation in this life. They must therefore have often been asked which is the insight by which one is liberated. For the main stream of meditation could only acknowledge liberation in life after one had acquired insight into the nature of the soul (above, ch. V). The Buddhists could not answer by saying that the soul is essentially not involved in action, as their opponents did. A firm tradition maintained that the Buddha did not want to talk about the soul, or even denied its existence.[12] Instead they adopted what they considered most essential to the Buddhist doctrine as liberating insight. We shall see that (1) this liberating insight varied along with what was considered most central to the teaching of the Buddha (§ 8.4.1); (2) insight and practice vied with each other, just as they did in main stream meditation (§ 8.4.2); (3) the Buddhist texts leave scope for the possibility that originally the liberating

---

10. DN II. 314-15; MN I.62, 63, 481; SN V.129, 181, 285, 314; AN III. 81-82, 143; It 39, 40, 41; Sn 140, 148; cf. MĀ[C] p. 584b16-24, p. 752c1-2.
11. AN IV. 75-78; 379-81.
12. It is possible that original Buddhism did not deny the existence of the soul (Frauwallner, 1953: 217-53; Schmithausen, 1969: 160-61; Bhattacharya, 1973; Pérez-Remón, 1980; Vetter, 1983). One reason why it did not want to talk about it may well be that conceptions of the soul were too closely connected with the methods of liberation described in Part II, above.

[96] insight was not described in any explicit form – they even support this to some extent (§ 8.4.3). These three points go a long way to show that the explicit descriptions of the content of liberating insight are not original to Buddhism, and were added under the influence of main stream meditation.

8.4.1. In order to show that liberating insight in Buddhism varied along with what was considered central to the teaching of the Buddha, it is enough to recall some articles by Lamotte (1977, 1980) and esp. Schmithausen (1981). I quote Schmithausen (1981: 211-12):

> The principle that Enlightenment and, analogously, Liberating Insight[13] are essentially characterized (and perhaps rendered effective) by the fact that ... their content must consist of, or at any rate contain, the most fundamental truth, can be observed to have been valid also in later periods, for we find that such concepts also were taken to be constitutive or essential to both as are expressive of what was, later on, regarded to be the most fundamental truth. E.g., in some obviously more or less later descriptions of Enlightenment or Liberating Insight, the Comprehension of the four Noble Truths is supplemented[14] or even supplanted[15] by the Comprehension of Origination-in-Dependence (*pratītyasamutpāda*) – in its two forms of *anuloma* and *pratiloma* corresponding to *samudaya*- and *nirodhasatya,* respectively[16] –, a fact which is easily understood if we bear in mind that, as an expression of the most fundamental soteriologically relevant truth, *pratītyasamutpāda* seems to have gradually superseded the four Noble Truths. In most of the Hīnayāna schools, however, it was in its turn later superseded by the doctrine of the non-existence of a substantial self or person ([*pudgala-*]*nairātmya*). Accordingly, it is not surprising

13. Schmithausen uses "the term 'Enlightenment' with exclusive reference to the (historical) Buddha, and the term 'Liberating Insight' either with special reference to his Disciples (*śrāvaka*), or in a comprehensive sense including both Enlightenment and the Liberating Insight of the Disciples" (1981: 199).
14. Schmithausen refers in a footnote to Waldschmidt, 1967: 410f.
15. Schmithausen refers to Nobel, 1955: 8 (translated p. 57-59) and texts like SN 12.65.
16. Schmithausen refers again to SN 12.65.

> to find this new fundamental truth, too, becoming the major content of Liberating Insight, which, e.g., according to one of three alternative explanations found in the *Śāriputrābhidharma*,[17] consists in a realization of all the four Noble Truths under the aspect if 'Lack of Self'.

Schmithausen (1981: 219 f.) further points at other forms which liberating insight has in the Buddhist canon:[18] "that the five Skandhas are impermanent, disagreeable, and neither the Self nor belonging to oneself";[19] "the contemplation of the arising and disappearance (*udayabbaya*) of the five Skandhas";[20] "the realization of the Skandhas as [97]
empty (*rittaka*), vain (*tucchaka*) and without any pith or substance (*asāraka*)".[21]

8.4.2. The competing roles of insight and practice already in canonical Buddhism have been pointed out by La Vallée Poussin in his article "Musīla et Nārada" (1937b; cf. Schmithausen, 1981: 214 f.; Griffiths, 1981). Musīla (in SN II. 115 f.) represents those who *know* and thereby reach the goal. Nārada is one of those who strive to reach the goal through direct experience. The canon also shows that attempts were made to remove the opposition between these two groups, e.g., in AN III.355 f. La Vallée Poussin further shows that all three schools – of knowledge, of direct experience, and of their combination – survive in later times. These are the same schools which we met in main stream meditation. La Vallée

17. At T. 1548, p. 595a3ff. Schmithausen further draws attention to Paṭis II.105: *katih'ākārehi cattāri saccāni ekapaṭivedhāni ? catūh'ākārehi ... : tathaṭṭhena, anattaṭṭhena, ...* ; Paṭis-a 594: *anattaṭṭhenā'ti: catunnaṃ saccānaṃ attavirahitattā* ... and explains that "in the latter passage, *sacca* has, of course, to be understood in a collective sense as denoting the totality of those *dharmas* the nature of which is Suffering, etc."
18. For later views see Schmithausen, 1981: 240f.
19. This is mentioned at Vin I. 13-14; MN I. 138-39; III. 19-20; 278-80; SN II. 124-25; III. 21-24; 195-98; 223; etc.; cf. further MN I. 500; III. 286-87; SN II. 244-52; etc. All these places have a formula in common which – as Schmithausen (1981: 219-20, n. 69) has rightly argued – contains traces to show that originally it belonged in another context, in the stereotyped detailed description of the Path of Liberation, as Schmithausen calls it.
20. AN II. 45.
21. SN III. 140-42.

Poussin rightly identifies the group represented by Musīla with *sāṃkhya*, the group of Nārada with *yoga*, as defined in the *Bhagavad Gītā*. We must look upon this parallelism as due to influence from main stream meditation on Buddhism. The explanations of the idea that liberation is obtained merely through insight given by La Vallée Poussin – that insight without meditation makes liberation accessible to more than just a few (1937b: 206) – and by Schmithausen – that there was an awareness of the difference of situation between the Buddha's Enlightenment and the Disciple's Liberating Insight, and that psychological plausibility was sought (1981: 222) – may add to our understanding, but only after we know that ideas of this type were already exerting an influence from the side of main stream meditation.

Those who emphasized practice did so usually in connection with the Cessation of [all] Ideation and Feelings (*saṃjñāvedayitanirodha* / *saññāvedayitanirodha*). What is particularly interesting is that in certain schools this state came to be looked upon as similar to Nirvāṇa, an anticipation in this life of Nirvāṇa; Nirvāṇa itself, and therefore liberation, was postponed until after death, just as was the case in main stream asceticism. See § 8.3, above.

8.4.3. In the stereotyped detailed description of the path of liberation which often recurs in the Buddhist canon (see Schmithausen, 1981: 203 f.) liberating insight takes place in the Fourth Dhyāna. It is described thus (e.g. MN I.23; cf. DN I. 83-84, 209; MN I. 183-84, 348; AN I. 165; II. 211; etc.):[22]

[98] Then, when my mind was thus concentrated, pure, cleansed, free from blemish, without stain, supple, ready, firm, immovable, I directed my mind to the knowledge of the destruction of the intoxicants. Then I recognized in accordance with reality 'this is suffering', I recognized in accordance with reality 'this is the origin

22. *so evaṃ samāhite citte parisuddhe pariyodāte anaṅgaṇe vigatūpakkilese mudubhūte kammaniye ṭhite ānejjappatte āsavānaṃ khayañāṇāya cittaṃ abhininnāmesiṃ / so idaṃ dukkhan ti yathābhūtaṃ abbhaññāsiṃ ayaṃ*

of suffering', I recognized in accordance with reality 'this is the cessation of suffering', I recognized in accordance with reality 'this is the path leading to the cessation of suffering'. I recognized in accordance with reality 'these are the intoxicants (*āsava*)', I recognized in accordance with reality 'this is the origin of the intoxicants', I recognized in accordance with reality 'this is the cessation of the intoxicants', I recognized in accordance with reality 'this is the path leading to the cessation of the intoxicants'. Then, when I knew and saw this, my mind was liberated from the intoxicant of desire, and from the intoxicant of existence, and from the intoxicant of ignorance. In [the mind thus] liberated the knowledge arose that it was liberated. I recognized: 'Birth is destroyed, the religious life has been lived, what had to be done has been done, there is no more of this state [of existence].'

In many passages this insight is preceded by two other insights, but those must be later additions (see below, § 9.2.7). Consequently we can concentrate on the present passage.

There can be no doubt that this passage does not represent the original account of enlightenment (so also Schmithausen, 1981: 205). The recognition of the intoxicants, their origin, cessation, and the path leading to their cessation is obviously modelled on the pattern of the recognition of suffering, its origin, cessation, and the path leading there. It is tempting to follow Bareau (1963:87) in thinking that the recognition of the intoxicants, their origin, etc., was added later to the text.[23] This would also solve problems relating to the origin of the intoxicants (Schmithausen, 1981: 205-06). Yet we may share Schmithausen's (1981: 206) misgivings about

---

dukkhasamudayo ti yathābhūtaṃ abbhaññāsiṃ, ayaṃ dukkhanirodho ti yathābhūtaṃ abbhaññāsiṃ, ayaṃ dukkhanirodhagāminī paṭipadā ti yāthabhūtaṃ abbhaññāsiṃ / ime āsavā ti yathābhūtaṃ abbhaññāsiṃ, ayaṃ āsavasamudayo ti yathābhūtaṃ abbhaññāsiṃ, ayaṃ āsavanirodho ti yathābhūtaṃ abbhaññāsiṃ, ayaṃ āsavanirodhagāminī paṭipadā ti yathābhūtaṃ abbhaññāsiṃ / tassa me evaṃ jānato evaṃ passato kāmāsavā pi cittaṃ vimuccittha, bhavāsavā pi cittaṃ vimuccittha, avijjāsavā pi cittaṃ vimuccittha / vimuttasmiṃ vimuttam iti ñāṇaṃ ahosi / khīṇā jāti, vusitaṃ brahmacariyaṃ, kataṃ karaṇīyaṃ, nāparaṃ itthattāyā 'ti abbhaññāsiṃ /

23. Some versions are without it; see Schmithausen, 1981: 205 n. 21.

dropping this part, for *āsava* "seems to be a key term of the whole passage".

The truth seems to be that the part on the recognition of the intoxicants, their origin, etc., is a bridge linking the recognition of the Four Noble Truths (suffering, its origin, etc.) with the destruction of the intoxicants. This bridge was necessary because destruction of the
[99] intoxicants is mentioned just before and after the Four Noble Truths. This bridge – regardless of the question whether it was added by the composer of this passage or later – therefore emphasizes the fact that the Four Noble Truths just do not fit here. They do not fit because the connection between their knowledge and the destruction of the intoxicants is not clear.

But the Four Noble Truths do not fit in this context for another far more serious reason. Recognition of the Four Noble Truths culminates in knowledge of the path leading to the cessation of suffering. This is useful knowledge for someone who is about to enter upon this path, but it is long overdue for someone at the end of the road. Knowledge of the path must and does precede a person commencing upon it. This also applies to the Buddha himself. In the passage which we studied above (§ 1.5, MN I. 246-47) we were told that the Bodhisattva remembered how once in his youth, he reached the First Dhyāna and wondered if this could be the road towards enlightenment. The text then continues: "following this memory I had this knowledge: 'This is really the road towards enlightenment'." In other words, also the Bodhisattva knew the path he was to traverse, and knowledge of the Four Noble Truths could not thereafter bring him anything new.

We observed that knowledge of the Four Noble Truths must come at the beginning of the path leading to 'the cessation of suffering'. We find this confirmed in many places in the Buddhist canon. The first sermon which the Buddha is supposed to have preached deals with them in many of its versions (Bareau, 1963: 172 f.; Feer, 1870; Waldschmidt, 1951: 96 f. (176 f.)). Here his listeners are obviously completely uninitiated in the Buddhist doctrine. Elsewhere the Four Noble Truths are often presented as the preaching of the Buddha in a nutshell, as in the following passage (SN V.438; similarly DN I.189; MN I.431; SN II.223; DĀC p.111a21-22; MĀC p.805c2-3):[24]

> What then, monks, have I taught ? 'This is suffering'; thus, monks, have I taught. 'This is the origin of suffering'; thus have I taught. 'This is the cessation of suffering'; thus have I taught. 'This is the path leading to the cessation of suffering'; thus have I taught.

Here too they constitute what an aspirant must know before he can actually go the path and become liberated.

The Four Noble Truths are specified at a number of places.[25] The [100]
specification shows what we knew already, viz., that the Four Noble Truths must be known before one can properly start out upon the path; the reason is that the Four Noble Truths specified contain a description of the path to be traversed. I translate the Pāli version:[26]

- This moreover, monks, is indeed the Noble Truth of suffering. Birth is suffering, union with what is not dear is suffering, separation from what is dear is suffering, that one does not get what one desires is suffering. In short, the five aggregates of grasping are suffering.
- This moreover, monks, is indeed the Noble Truth of the origin of suffering. It is the thirst which leads to renewed existence, is accompanied by enjoyment and passion, finding its delight here and there, viz., thirst for sensual pleasure, thirst for existence, thirst for non-existence.
- This moreover, monks, is indeed the Noble Truth of the cessation of

---

24. *kiñ ca, bhikkhave, mayā akkhātaṃ ? 'idaṃ dukkhaṃ' ti, bhikkhave, mayā akkhātaṃ, 'ayam dukkhasamudayo' ti mayā akkhātaṃ, 'ayaṃ dukkhanirodho' ti mayā akkhātaṃ, 'ayaṃ dukkhanirodhagāminī paṭipadā' ti mayā akkhātaṃ /*
25. Vin I. 10; SN V. 421-22; Mv III. 332; CPS p. 158-62; T. 1421, p. 104b29-c7; T. 1428, p. 788a16-29; cf. DN II. 305-14; MN I. 185-91; SN V. 425, 426; AN I. 176-77; MĀC p. 435c26-436a6, p. 464b27f.; T. 109, p. 503b21-c2.
26. *idaṃ kho pana, bhikkhave, dukkhaṃ ariyasaccaṃ / jāti pi dukkhā, jarā pi dukkhā, vyādhi pi dukkhā, maraṇaṃ pi dukkhaṃ, appiyehi sampayogo dukkho, piyehi vippayogo dukkho, yaṃ p'icchaṃ na labhati tam pi dukkhaṃ / saṃkhittena, pañc'upādānakkhandhāpi dukkhā / idaṃ kho pana, bhikkhave, dukkhasamudayaṃ ariyasaccaṃ / yā'yaṃ taṇhā ponobbhavikā nandirāgasahagatā tatratatrābhinandinī, seyyathī'dam: kāmataṇhā, bhavataṇhā, vibhavataṇhā / idaṃ kho pana,bhikkhave, dukkhanirodhaṃ ariyasaccaṃ / yo tassā yeva taṇhāya asesavirāga*

suffering. It is the complete detachment from and cessation of that same thirst, its rejection, renunciation, the liberation from it, the absence of attachment to it.

– This moreover, monks, is indeed the Noble Truth of the path leading to the cessation of suffering. It is the Noble Eightfold Road, viz., right view, right intention, right speech, right action, right livelihood, right exertion, right mindfulness, right concentration.

A number of versions of the account of the Buddha's first sermon[27] give evidence that the Buddhists themselves did not feel comfortable about recognizing the Four Noble Truths as liberating insight. They put into the mouth of the Buddha some remarks with respect to each of these, to the extent that the Noble Truth of suffering had to be fully known by him, then that it was actually fully known by him; the Noble Truth of the origin of suffering had to be abandoned, then was indeed abandoned; the Noble Truth of the cessation of suffering had to be seen with his own eyes, then it had indeed been seen with his own eyes; the Noble Truth of the path leading to the cessation of suffering had to be practised, then it had actually been practised by him. It is likely that these remarks are later additions to the text.[28] But it can be seen that they change the picture of the Buddha at his moment of enlightenment considerably. No longer does he simply know suffering, its origin, its cessation, and the path leading
[101] thereto. He now *knows* suffering, has *abandoned* the origin of suffering, has *seen with his own eyes* the cessation of suffering, and has completed *practising* the path leading to the cessation of suffering. The ill-fitting 'liberating insight' has in this was become something quite different from just an insight. The fact that the texts add that all this was clearly realized by the Buddha does not alter this at all.

---

nirodho, cāgo, paṭinissaggo, mutti, anālayo / idaṃ kho pana, bhikkhave, dukkha-nirodhagāminī paṭipadā ariyasaccaṃ / ayam eva ariyo aṭṭhaṅgiko maggo, seyyathī'dam: sammādiṭṭhi, sammāsaṅkappo, sammāvācā, sammākammanto, sammāājīvo, sammāvāyāmo, sammāsati, sammāsamādhi /

On the irregular gender of *-nirodhaṃ* and *-samudayaṃ*, see von Hinüber, 1976: 39 n. 28.

27. Vin I. 11; SN V. 422; CPS p. 146-48; T. 1421 p. 104c7-17; T. 1428 p. 788a16-b14; cf. SN V. 424-25, 436; Mv III. 332-33.
28. Feer, 1870: 429-35; Schmithausen, 1981: 203.

The different versions of the first sermon in Benares show another peculiarity, to which Bareau (1963: 178-81) has drawn attention. The versions which belong to Vinaya texts (Vin I. 10-11; Mv III.331f.; T.1421, p. 104b28-c17; T.1428, p. 788a14-b23) and the versions which have apparently been adjusted to or influenced by the Vinaya versions (SN V.421-23; CPS p. 142 f.; SĀ^C P 103c14f.; T.109; T.110) contain the part dealing with the Four Noble Truths; the versions which belong to Sūtra texts (MN I. 171-73; MĀ^C p 778a; EĀ^C p 593b24f.) do not. This seems to indicate that initially those Four Noble Truths were not part of the sermon in Benares, and consequently probably not as central to Buddhism as they came to be. We may surmise that the concise formulation of the teaching of the Buddha in the shape of the Four Noble Truths had not yet come into being, not necessarily that the contents of this teaching deviated from what they were meant to express.[29] If then the Four Noble Truths did not yet exist when the primitive version of what came to be known as the *Dharmacakrapravartana Sūtra* was composed, we can be sure that in that time they were not considered as constituting the insight which immediately preceded and brought about liberation. Let us be clear about it that we are not sure that the Four Noble Truths had not yet been formulated in earliest Buddhism. But the indications in that direction which we possess go a long way toward undermining the idea that these Four Noble Truths constituted liberating insight in earliest Buddhism.

If then, in all probability, neither the Four Noble Truths nor any of the other, later, specifications of liberating insight which we find in the Buddhist scriptures played this role in earliest Buddhism, how could they come to fill this place? One answer we know already: it is likely that the Buddhists were often asked what their liberating insight was like because they believed in liberation in this life. It may be, however, that another factor aided this development. The Buddhist texts often speak about 'insight' (*prajñā / paññā*) as something immediately preceding liberation[30] or characterize the teaching of the Buddha as especially

29. Note that *Dhammapada* 191 expresses the same truth in different words: *dukkhaṃ dukkhasamuppādaṃ, sukkhassa ca atikkamaṃ / ariyaṃ c'aṭṭhaṅgikaṃ maggaṃ, dukkhūpasamagāminaṃ //*. Cf. Feer, 1870: 418f.

30. See Schmithausen, 1981: 216, and note 33 below.

concerning *śīla* ('morality'), *samādhi* ('concentration') and *prajñā*
[102] ('insight'), to which sometimes *vimukti* ('liberation') is added.[31] This may have made it plausible to the Buddhists themselves that the Buddhist doctrine knew some 'liberating insight' as well which had to be specified. The choice fell on the Four Noble Truths and on the other contents which we have seen were subsequently given to this insight.

What I propose can be expressed more specifically. Perhaps the passages which now contain a description of 'liberating insight' as consisting in the Four Noble Truths etc., originally merely made a short reference to *prajñā*. Later tradition inserted the Four Noble Truths etc. in the place of *prajñā* wherever possible. Such a replacement was not however possible in the contexts where liberation comes about while there is Cessation of Ideations and Feelings (*saṃjñā-/saññāvedayita-nirodha*).[32] There is properly speaking no place for such an insight here because there are no ideations (see Schmithausen, 1981: 216-17; La Vallée Poussin, 1937 b: 220). The replacement was not made and the older short reference to *prajñā* – which originally belonged after the description of the Four Dhyānas – survived only here.

This proposal, though hypothetical, explains the facts which confront us in the extant canon. However, it raises another question. If *prajñā* was originally not intended to refer to the Four Noble Truths etc., what then was it ? And whatever it was, does not this term clearly point to some kind of liberating insight ?

The answer to these questions must be that *prajñā* referred to some unspecified and unspecifiable kind of insight. The reason to think so is as follows. If my reconstructions up to now are correct, *prajñā* became necessary at the stage where the aspirant had reached the Fourth Dhyāna. It is not in accordance with the line of approach adopted in this book to try and specify what kind of psychic state this fourth Dhyāna – or any of the

31. E.g. DN I. 206, II. 81, 91; AN II. 1-2, III. 15-16, IV. 105-06; It 51; Th 634; MPS p. 160, 228; DĀ[C] p. 12a20f., p. 13a3-4; MĀ[C] p. 486c23f.; T. 6 p. 178b5-6; T. 1421 p. 135b7.

32. Since Cessation of Ideations and Feelings appears to be a borrowed element in Buddhism (ch. VII, above), its mention in descriptions of liberation must be looked upon as a later adjustment of an earlier text. This explains the puzzling mention of insight (*prajñā*) in a state without ideations.

other Dhyānas – is. It will be agreed, to use very general terms, that it must be a state of consciousness different from what we call normal. After reaching the fourth Dhyāna the next step consists in the 'destruction of the intoxicants (*āsava*/*āsrava*)'. I have little doubt that this phrase 'destruction of the intoxicants' sounded almost as mysterious to the early listeners to the Buddha's words as it sounds to us, the reason being that it apparently refers to an inner-psychic process, the conditions for which are not fulfilled until the fourth Dhyāna has been reached. This means that the aspirant had to find his way to the most crucial and decisive steps of the process which he was undergoing while in a state of changed [103]
consciousness! One does not need to refer to psychiatric literature in order to know that many altered states of consciousness rather have the tendency to make a person lose his way. All this makes it plausible that the aspirant who had reached the fourth Dhyāna could do with, or rather could not do without, an insight into his psychic state and its possibilities. This, I propose, is *prajñā*.[33]

If this proposal is correct, it is not without consequences for the way the Buddha must have taught his advanced disciples. General statements – such as the Four Noble Truths etc. – would not be of help to them, but rather personal advice, adjusted to the needs of each person. It is therefore in direct support of the above proposal that the two main Sūtras which record the 'first sermon' of the Buddha without mentioning the Four Noble Truths, continue in a way which leaves no doubt regarding the personal nature of the Buddha's instruction (MN I. 173; similarly MĀ^{C} 778a3-5; cf. Bareau, 1963: 183f.):[34]

> I could indeed, monks, convince the monks belonging to the group of five. Monks, I instructed two monks, [while] three monks went

33. This seems confirmed by, or at any rate in agreement with, phrases like *āsavānaṃ khayo paññāya sacchikaraṇīyo* (DN III. 230; AN II. 183; cf. DĀ^{C} p. 51a12); *paññāya ca me / c'assa disvā āsavā parikkhayaṃ agamaṃsu / parikhīṇā honti* (e.g. MN I. 160, 175; AN IV. 448, 453; cf. MĀ^{C} p. 582a29; p. 701b12; see Schmithausen, 1981: 216 n.55); *paññāparibhāvitaṃ cittaṃ sammad eva āsavehi vimuccati* (e.g. DN II. 81, 91; cf. MPS p.160, 228; DĀ^{C} p. 12a21-23).
34. *asakkhiṃ kho ahaṃ bhikkhave pañcavaggiye bhikkhū saññāpetuṃ / dve pi sudaṃ*

> for alms. What the three monks who had gone for alms brought with them, we six lived on that. Monks, I instructed three monks, [while] two monks went for alms. What the two monks who had gone for alms brought with them, we six lived on that.[35]

I do not claim that this passage embodies a memory of an historical event. It does, however, appear to preserve the idea of how the early monks conceived what the Buddha's instruction had been like.

It is no doubt significant that the versions of the 'first sermon' which do mention the Four Noble Truths – the ones which occur in Vinaya texts or are influenced by them – do not contain the above episode (CPS p.142 f.; T. 1421, p. 104b-105a; SN V. 421-24) or preserve part of it in a context which completely changes the meaning of it (Vin. I.13; T. 1428, p. 789a). The five monks, moreover, become enlightened while the Buddha is still preaching. This shows that the accounts which include the Four Noble Truths had a completely different conception of the process of liberation than the one which includes the Four Dhyānas and the subsequent destruction of the intoxicants. This too supports our thesis that the Four Noble Truths were inserted later in the description of liberation by way of the Four Dhyānas and the destruction of the intoxicants. This modified description represents a hybrid of two views of the matter:
[104] according to one view an insight into the Four Noble Truths is sufficient for enlightenment; according to the other view liberation is rather attained by way of the Four Dhyānas and the destruction of the intoxicants. We cannot but be struck, once again, by the parallelism with main stream meditation, where we also find insight alone, practice alone, and the combination of both insight and practice as different ways to reach the goal. It is reasonable therefore to suspect influence from that side.

---

bhikkhave bhikkhū ovadāmi, tayo bhikkhū piṇḍāya caranti / yaṃ tayo bhikkhū piṇḍāya caritvā āharanti tena chabbaggo yāpema / tayo pi sudaṃ bhikkhave bhikkhū ovadāmi, dve bhikkhū piṇḍāya caranti / yaṃ dve bhikkhū piṇḍāya caritvā āharanti tena chabbaggo yāpema /

35. Note that according to the *Nidānakathā* (p. 82) four of the five monks are each instructed individually, while the remaining four go for alms. See Waldschmidt, 1951: 96 (176)

We can sum up the results of this section by stating that there is good reason to think that the Four Noble Truths did not constitute liberating insight in the earliest period of Buddhism. However, they were apparently considered to do so before any of the other 'liberating insights' which we find specified in the canon took their place. We must conclude that if the earliest Buddhist tradition acknowledged the existence of any liberating insight at all – and it possibly did – this insight remained unspecified. One of the main reasons why it came to be specified must have been that in main stream meditation liberation in life was always accompanied by an explicit 'liberating insight'.

[108] IX. The origin of Buddhist meditation.

9.1. We have seen that Buddhist meditation formed a tradition different from the meditation and ascetic practices found in Jainism and in many Hindu scriptures. There is little reason to doubt that this main stream of asceticism existed before the beginnings of Buddhism, i.e. before the historical Buddha. It is a far more interesting question, however, whether Buddhist meditation existed before the Buddha. This will be investigated in the present chapter.

9.2. Nothing like Buddhist meditation is, understandably, referred to in early Jaina literature. Vedic literature is for the most part silent about any form of meditation. Not until the oldest Upaniṣads do we find any references to it. The earliest sentence[1] that is of interest to us is *Bṛhadāraṇyaka Upaniṣad* (BĀU) 4.4.23: *tasmād evaṃvic chānto dānta uparatas titikṣuḥ samāhito*[2] *bhūtvātmany evātmānaṃ paśyati* "Therefore, knowing this, having become calm, subdued, quiet, patiently enduring, concentrated, one sees the soul in oneself."

It is most probable that this sentence refers to main stream meditation. However, its brevity and consequent lack of information leave this to some extent undecided. In order to invalidate the opinion that perhaps this sentence refers to an earlier form of meditation of the Buddhistic type, I shall try to show that this sentence is later than the beginnings of Buddhism, i.e., later than the Buddha. I shall present a number of

1. *Chāndogya Upaniṣad* 8.15 has ... *ātmani sarvendriyāṇi saṃpratiṣṭhāpy*[*a*] ... "having concentrated his senses upon the soul". This, if it refers to meditation at all, then clearly to that of the main stream. *Taittirīya Upaniṣad* 2.4 identifies a number of abstract things with the parts of a person. Here the phrase occurs: *yoga ātmā*. This is most naturally translated: "exertion is the body". There is no reason whatever, contextual or otherwise, to think that *yoga* here refers to anything like meditation. The word *yoga* is not attested in that sense until rather late; even the entry *yuja samādhau* in Pāṇini's Dhātupāṭha (IV.68) was added after Patañjali (Bronkhorst, 1983: § 1).
2. Thus the Kāṇva version. The Mādhyandina version has *śraddhāvittaḥ*.

arguments, of varying force, in support of this.[3]

9.2.1. My first argument is based on Horsch, 1966: 391f. I shall briefly and in a somewhat modified way restate Horsch's view.

Sūtra 4.3.105 of Pāṇini's *Aṣṭādhyāyī* reads: *purāṇaprokteṣu brāhmaṇakalpeṣu* [*tena proktam* 101, *ṇiniḥ* 103] "In the case of Brāhmaṇa and Kalpa works uttered by ancient [sages], [the *taddhita* suffix] *ṇini* is [semantically equivalent to][4] *tena proktam* ('uttered by him')." Kātyāyana restricts the scope of this sūtra in his first and only vārttika on it (vol.II, p.326, l.12-13): *purāṇaprokteṣu brāhmaṇakalpeṣu yājñavalkyādibhyaḥ pratiṣedhas tulyakālatvāt* "A prohibition [of P. 4.3.105:] *purāṇaprokteṣu brāhmaṇakalpeṣu* [must be stated] after *yājñavalkya* etc., because [they are] of the same time." Patañjali explains (l.14-16): *purāṇaprokteṣu brāhmaṇakalpeṣv ity atra yājñavalkyādibhyaḥ pratiṣedho vaktavyaḥ / yājñavalkāni brāhmaṇāni / saulabhānīti / kiṃ* [109]
kāraṇam / tulyakālatvāt / etāny api tulyakālānīti //. We learn from this that, according to Patañjali, the Brāhmaṇa works uttered by Yājñavalkya, rather than Yājñavalkya himself, are meant to be considered 'of the same time' in this vārttika.

The sense requires, in spite of Kaiyaṭa, that the Brāhmaṇa works uttered by Yājñavalkya are of the same time as Pāṇini. We do not have to take such a remark by Kātyāyana very literally. It is doubtful whether Kātyāyana was well informed about Pāṇini's time, for tradition had not even been able to preserve knowledge regarding certain essential features of the *Aṣṭādhyāyī* (see Kiparsky, 1980; Bronkhorst, 1980). We must rather understand from this vārttika that Kātyāyana was still aware of the recent origin of the 'Brāhmaṇa works uttered by Yājñavalkya'.

But Kātyāyana must also have been aware that these Brāhmaṇa works were ascribed to an ancient sage, for otherwise this vārttika would serve no purpose in the context of P. 4.3.105 which is about 'Brāhmaṇa and Kalpa works uttered by ancient sages'. What Kātyāyana must have had in view was a Brāhmaṇa work recently composed and ascribed to Yājña-

3. I am of course looking forward to the definitive study announced by M.Witzel (e.g. StII 13/14, 1987, p.407 n.96).
4. I translate as proposed by Wezler (1975: 5 etc.)

valkya, where in reality Yājñavalkya was an ancient sage who could not have composed this work.

This description fits BĀU 3-4 very well. Since Pāṇini does not use the term *Upaniṣad* in connection with Vedic literature, and divides Vedic literature in *mantra, brāhmaṇa* and *kalpa* (cf. Thieme, 1935: 67f.), his use of the word *brāhmaṇa* is wide and fit to cover the BĀU. This is all the more true since the BĀU is, indeed, the last part of the *Śatapatha Brāhmaṇa* (ŚB 14.4-9). Moreover, the subsections of the BĀU are called *brāhmaṇa* in their colophons. The reason that BĀU 3-4 must be meant by Kātyāyana, rather than any other text, is that only here Yājñavalkya is clearly the dominating person. Yājñavalkya is mentioned elsewhere, primarily in ŚB 1-4 and 11-13, further *Jaiminīya Brāhmaṇa* 1.19, 23; 2.76; *Śāṅkhāyana Āraṇyaka* 9.7 and 13.1, but nowhere as the sole dominating figure. Moreover, the BĀU is one of the youngest parts of the ŚB.

Horsch (1966: 396) further shows that the compilatory nature of the ŚB was still known to Patañjali[5] and the *Mahābhārata*.[6] This further corroborates that BĀU 3-4 is late.

The facts (i) that Pāṇini does not make an exception for the *yājñavalkāni brāhmaṇāni*, (ii) that Kātyāyana indicates that he considers these recent, and (iii) that Patañjali still knows the compilatory nature of the ŚB, allow of the conclusion that BĀU 3-4 is later than Pāṇini and but
[110] little earlier than Kātyāyana. Patañjali lived probably in the middle of the second century B.C. (Cardona, 1976: 263-66). If we assume that

---

5. Patañjali – in a verse on P. 4.2.60 – appears to have known a work named *Ṣaṣṭipatha*, which may have contained sixty of the present one hundred Adhyāyas of the ŚB. Weber (1850b: 185n.) assumed that these are the sixty Adhyāyas of the first nine books of the ŚB. But Minard (1968) argues for the sixty Adhyāyas contained in books I-V (35) and XI-XIII (25) of the Mādhyandina recension.

6. *Mahābhārata* 12.306.16 (where Yājñavalkya speaks) reads:
tataḥ śatapathaṃ kṛtsnaṃ sarahasyaṃ sasaṃgraham /
cakre sapariśeṣaṃ ca harṣeṇa parameṇa ha //
Here Yājñavalkya is said to have composed the whole of the ŚB. In BĀU 6.5.3 (*ādityānīmāni śuklāni yajūṃṣi vājasaneyena yājñavalkyenākhyāyante*), Yājñavalkya is said to have declared the sacrificial formulas of the Vājasaneyi school. Patañjali's *yājñavalkāni brāhmaṇāni* may therefore cover all the later portions of the ŚB, not just, but certainly including, BĀU 3-4. See Weber, 1850a: 57n.; Goldstücker, 1861: 146f.

Kātyāyana wrote a century earlier, BĀU 3-4 very well fits in the time after the death of the Buddha, even if we accept this to have taken place as late as 370 B.C. (Bechert, 1982).[7]

9.2.3. Further evidence regarding the late date of the BĀU, and of the later chapters of the ŚB as well, can be derived from a closer inspection of the figure of Yājñavalkya.

Pronouncements of Yājñavalkya occur repeatedly in ŚB 1-4. There is no reason to doubt that he was an authority on ritual, along with other ritualists. He appears again in ŚB 11-13, but often in a legendary context: a number of times he is depicted as debating with king Janaka of Videha. Moreover, since these parts of the ŚB are younger than its beginning (Eggeling, 1882: xxixf.; Weber, 1876: 130f.), we may assume that, at this time, Yājñavalkya had become a legendary person.[8] This is confirmed by the fact that later again (in the BĀU and the *Mahābhārata*) Yājñavalkya's fame had reached such proportions that he is said to have declared the sacrificial formulas (*yajus*) and composed the ŚB (see note 6). This [111]
development is parallel to the one of Śākalya, who, really being the maker of the Padapāṭha of the *Ṛgveda,* came to be considered the person who had 'seen' the Veda (see below).

The parallel development of Yājñavalkya and Śākalya is of special significance for the chronological problem we are investigating, as follows. At ŚB 2.5.1.2 Yājñavalkya's opinion is contrasted with that of the *ṛc*, and therefore of the Ṛgvedins. A way of visualizing this disagreement would be to describe a debate between Yājñavalkya and Śākalya. And indeed, we find such a debate described twice over, at ŚB 11.6.3 and BĀU 3.9.1-26. Both times the debate ends in the utter defeat and consequent death of Śākalya.[9] The important fact is that the disagreement between the followers of Yājñavalkya and the Ṛgvedins could not be

---

7. The section on Pāṇini's acquaintance with the Vedic Saṃhitās (§9.2.2.), which followed in the first edition of this book, has now been superseded by Bronkhorst, 1991.
8. This is more extensively established in Horsch, 1966: 380f.
9. The Ṛgvedins perhaps took revenge by not mentioning Yājñavalkya in their *Kauṣītaki Upaniṣad,* in spite of mentioning Uddālaka Āruṇi and Śvetaketu who occur in the BĀU (Esnoul, 1968: 280).

visualized in this way until after Śākalya had become the most important representative of the *Ṛgveda,* rather than merely the representative of one of its versions and the maker of its Padapāṭha.

What we know about the development of the legend of Śākalya can be summarized as follows : Pāṇini's *Aṣṭādhyāyī* and Yāska's *Nirukta* know him as an early grammarian and as the maker of the Padapāṭha of the *Ṛgveda*. In Patañjali's *Mahābhāṣya* he has become the redactor of the *Ṛgveda Saṃhitā* (Bronkhorst, 1981: 142-43, 147), and apparently the most important representative of the *Ṛgveda*. In the *Anuvākānukramaṇī* Śākalya is even said to have seen the Veda (Bronkhorst, 1982b: §4). The legend of the debate between Yājñavalkya and Śākalya seems to fit best at a time closer to Patañjali than to Pāṇini, i.e., closer to 150 B.C. than to 350 B.C.[10]

9.2.4. We turn to a question which is directly related to our chronological observations. The ŚB, including the BĀU, is one of the late Vedic texts which preserve Vedic accents. Both were composed in a time when Vedic accents were still in use. Also the language described by Pāṇini contains Vedic accents as an integral part. If then the origin of Buddhism is earlier than (portions of) the BĀU, can it be that the earliest layers of Buddhist literature contain indications that Vedic accent was still used ?

An affirmative answer to this question has been given by Lévi (1915, esp. p. 426-47), in a study where he shows, on the basis of Vinaya texts of a variety of schools,[11] that in an early period the tendency existed to use
[112] Sanskrit *with Vedic accent* in the recitation of Buddhist texts. Lévi thinks that this accent could not have been transposed mechanically from the sacred texts of the Veda onto the sacred texts of Buddhism and concludes (1915: 447): "Les premier essais de littérature canonique iraient donc rejoindre l'époque des derniers textes accentués du canon védique: le Brāhmaṇa, l'Āraṇyaka des Taittirīya et le Śatapatha Brāhmaṇa."

---

10. This is the date which best seems to fit the evidence studied by Hinüber, 1989: 34-35.

11. The most important passages have again been discussed by Brough (1980), who gives references to the Taishō edition for the Chinese passages (p. 37), and refutes Norman's (1971: 329-31; cf. 1980: 61-63) alternative interpretation of a Pāli passage. Also see Lin Li-kouang, 1949: 216f; Demiéville, 1929; Lamotte, 1958: 610f.; De Jong, 1982: 215.

Lévi argues his case on the basis of texts taken from the Vinaya work *Skandhaka*. This allows us – with Frauwallner (1956b: 62-63) – to be more precise about the period when Vedic accents were still in use. The *Skandhaka* was composed, according to Frauwallner (1956b: 67), shortly before or after the second council, which is at least 40 years after the demise of the Buddha (Bechert, 1982: 36). Parts of the BĀU may therefore be as late as this period. The fact that the *bhāṣika* accent used in the ŚB is later than the accent system described by Pāṇini (Kiparsky, 1982: 74) agrees well with the above results.

9.2.5. Perhaps conclusions can be drawn from the fact that BĀU 2.1[12] features a Kṣatriya named 'Ajātaśatru'. Ajātaśatru is approached by Dṛptabālāki Gārgya, who proposes to tell about Brahman. Ajātaśatru offers thousand (cows) in response, and compares himself to Janaka, the former king of Videha. Apparently also Ajātaśatru was a king. Our text describes him as *kāśya,* which can be taken to mean that he ruled over Kāśī.

The name[13] Ajātaśatru occurs nowhere in Vedic literature except here in the BĀU and in the parallel version in *Kauṣītaki Upaniṣad* 4. It is, however, well-known from Buddhist literature. Ajātaśatru (Pāli 'Ajātasattu') is there described as the son of king Bimbisāra, from whom he seized the throne eight years before the death of the Buddha (Malalasekera, 1937-38: I: 31-35, s.v. Ajātasattu).

A serious difficulty is that the Buddhist texts depict Ajātaśatru as king of Magadha, not Kāśī. He is not, to be sure, entirely without connection with Kāśī. He is said to have fought battles in Kāśī against king Prasenajit [113]
(Pasenadi) of Kosala and to have come in the possession of a village in Kāśī (Malalasekera, 1937-38: I: 33). Ajātaśatru later reputedly battled and defeated king Ceṭaka of Vaiśālī, who was joined, among others, by the *gaṇarājas* of Kāśī (Lamotte, 1958: 100-01).

The discussion between Gārgya and Ajātaśatru in the BĀU (and in

12. Almost the same episode, with the same actors (Bālāki for Dṛptabālāki), is found at *Kauṣītaki Upaniṣad* 4 (= *Śāṅkhāyana Āraṇyaka* 6).
13. The *word ajātaśatru* 'whose enemies are unborn, having no enemies' occurs in several Vedic Saṃhitās, but not as a name.

the *Kauṣītaki Up.*) is clearly legendary. This means that if there ever was a king Ajātaśatru of Kāśī, he must have lived a considerable time before this discussion was laid down, long enough, perhaps, to make a confusion between Kāśī and Magadha possible. If, further, this Ajātaśatru is identical with the king who ruled over Magadha during the last years of the Buddha's life,[14] we can be sure that this part of the BĀU was composed a considerable time after the Buddha.

9.2.6. BĀU 2.4 and BĀU 4.5 give two versions of a discussion between Yājñavalkya and one of his wives, Maitreyī. The former version appears to be the older one. Hanefeld (1976: 71-115) has argued that two independent texts underlie it, one (BĀU 2.4.5-6, 12 [*na pretya*] - 14) dealing with the *ātman*, the other (BĀU 2.4.7-12 [*vinaśyati*]) dealing with *mahad bhūtam*. This latter concept has a universal-cosmic aspect, in that *mahad bhūtam* is said to be the origin of all literary texts (BĀU 2.4.10). At the same time it has an individual aspect, viz. *vijñāna* 'discerning knowledge': BĀU 2.4.12 describes the *mahad bhūtam* as a mass of discerning knowledge (*vijñānaghana*). The 'Great Being' (*mahad bhūtam*) apparently unites a universal-cosmic and an individual aspect.

But classical Sāṃkhya unites these two aspects in its *mahān / buddhi* as well, whereas the Sāṃkhya texts in the *Mahābhārata* do not, or hardly, do so (Frauwallner, 1925: 200f. (76f.)). Hanefeld (1976: 114-15) raises the question as to whether or not the older Upaniṣads in their present form must be dated much later than has generally been supposed.

9.2.7. We come to an important point. Buddhism presupposes a belief in transmigration determined by one's preceding (mental or physical) behaviour or state.[15] The BĀU, on the other hand, presents such a belief as something new. At BĀU 3.2.13 Yājñavalkya takes Jāratkārava Ārtabhāga apart to inform him, in secret, about *karman*. "What they said was *karma* (action). What they praised was *karma*. Verily, one becomes

---

14. This point of view was accepted by Hoernle (1907: 106) and, it seems, by Lassen (Weber, 1850b: 213).

15. See Schmithausen (1986: 205), who points out that craving (*tṛṣṇā*) etc., rather than *karman*, is said to be responsible for suffering and rebirth in numerous canonical texts.

good by good action, bad by bad action." (tr. Hume, 1931: 110). Similar remarks occur at BĀU 4.4.5. A more primitive idea seems to prevail at [114] BĀU 6.2.16. Does this not show that the BĀU represents an earlier phase in the development of these ideas, and that it is consequently older than the beginning of Buddhism ?

Not necessarily. The BĀU originated in surroundings quite different from those of early Buddhism. The former was part of an esoteric movement confined to Brahmins who dwelt in villages; the latter centred in the cities (cf. Horsch, 1966: 400). What is more, Jainism, as much as Buddhism, presupposes a belief in transmigration determined by one's preceding behaviour or state (cf. Malvania, 1981).[16] But Jainism may have existed, in the form preached by Pārśva (Pkt. Pāsa), as many as 250 years before Mahāvīra (Schubring, 1935: 24f.), which is certainly earlier than the BĀU. Therefore it is not possible to see in the passages on transmigration in the BĀU evidence that this Upaniṣad preceded the Buddha. Rather, they may have been attempts to sanctify a belief which was anyhow irresistibly gaining adherents among the Brahmins.

There is some reason to think that the early Buddhists were confronted with people who did not believe in transmigration of the kind described:

The majority of versions of the long account of the enlightenment of the Buddha describe three insights:[17] memory of earlier lives; knowledge of the births and deaths of beings; knowledge regarding the destruction of the intoxicants. Only the third insight has an obvious connection with liberation, which consists in the destruction of the intoxicants. The first two insights make the impression of having been added to the text which underlay these versions, and which was therefore without these first two insights.

---

16. Jaini (1980: 225-29) thinks that certain 'inconsistencies' of the Jaina doctrine may point to an earlier linear-evolutionary scheme similar to that of the Ājīvikas, and asks (p. 227-28): "Is it possible that, for the Jainas, the doctrine of karma represents a relatively late (albeit prehistorical) accretion, a set of ideas imposed upon [that linear-evolutionary scheme]?" Even if this is indeed the case, we must date this 'accretion' well before Mahāvīra.

17. MN I. 22-23, 117, 247-49; EĀ[c] p. 666b22-c20; T. 1421, p. 102c18-20; T. 1428 p. 781b5-c11. These passages have been translated and discussed by Bareau (1963: 75f.), whom I mainly follow.

And indeed, one version of the long account of the Buddha's liberation survives in which only the knowledge regarding the destruction of the intoxicants precedes final liberation: a Sūtra of the Sarvāstivādins (MĀ^C p. 589c14-23). A closer study of all these parallel versions – undertaken by Bareau (1963: 81f.) – confirms that the long account of the Buddha's liberation originally made no mention of his earlier lives and of the knowledge of the births and deaths of beings.

Schmithausen (1981: 221-22, n. 75) comes to the same conclusion, also basing himself on texts which describe the way to salvation for others than the Buddha. The *Madhyama Āgama* (T. 26), Schmithausen observes, seems to have fewer accounts *with* memory of earlier lives and knowledge
[115] of the births and deaths of beings, than *without*. Schmithausen further points at the difference in tense in the description of this memory and of the knowledge of the birth and death of beings (present tense), and everywhere else in the account (aorists).

Why then were these first two insights added? The reason must be sought in the circumstance that what the Buddha realized in his moment of liberation cannot but be the most essential in Buddhism (see § 8.4, above). The memory of earlier lives and the knowledge of the births and deaths of beings may therefore have been added in order to press a point which was considered essential to the teaching of the Buddha. There can be no doubt that this point is the belief in transmigration determined by one's earlier behaviour or state.

The faculty to remember former lives is not, in most of Buddhist literature, confined to Buddhist sages (Demiéville, 1928). This seems to indicate that soon belief in transmigration had become common to Buddhists and all those they were confronted with. But in such a time the addition of the memory of former lives and of the knowledge of the births and deaths of beings to the account of the Buddha's liberating insight would be inexplicable. We must rather assume that this addition took place when such a belief had not yet become common to all.[18] Among those who were not yet fully convinced we may have to count the Brahmins.

---

18. At least twice the Jaina canon mentions the memory of former lives, but not together with the knowledge of the births and deaths of beings. It seems less concerned with establishing the correctness of rebirth. See *Samavāya* 10.2, and Tatia and Kumar, 1980: 37, 39.

These had to wait until new 'old' scriptures like the BĀU gave them free way to accept this belief.

In this connection it must be pointed out that the Buddhist canon knows a few characters who deny transmigration and the moral efficacy of acts. One is Pāyāsi, appearing in the *Pāyāsi Sutta* (DN II. 316f.; cf. DĀ^{C} p. 42bf.). Then there are some of the six heretic teachers, in particular Ajita Keśakambalin and Pūraṇa Kāśyapa (Malalasekara, 1937-38: I: 37; Basham, 1951: 10-26; Vogel, 1970: 20-21). It is, however, unlikely, at least in the case of Pāyāsi, that we must see in his opinion a leftover from early times. Pāyāsi's opinion is described as very exceptional, not held by anyone known to his opponent Kumāra Kassapa. Further, in the Jaina version of the story of Pāyāsi – there Paesi – in the *Rāyapaseṇaijja,* the second Uvaṅga of the Jaina canon, this opinion is not ascribed to Paesi; see Leumann, 1885b: 467-539.

9.2.8. A possible counterargument against some of the preceding arguments will be that the language of the BĀU still contains Vedic features, and must therefore be older than classical Sanskrit, older also than the grammar of classical Sanskrit which is Pāṇini's *Aṣṭādhyāyī*. This [116]
counterargument can be answered by pointing out that there is reason to believe that Vedic and classical Sanskrit were used for some time side by side. Since this point has been discussed elsewhere (Bronkhorst, 1982c), I need not dwell upon it here.

9.3. The preceding observations have made it clear that no traces of a pre-Buddhistic form of 'Buddhist meditation' survive in the non-Buddhist literature of India. What do the Buddhist scriptures say in this regard ?

9.3.1. We have become acquainted with a number of descriptions of non-Buddhist religious practices in the Buddhist canon in the course of this book. None of them ascribe to outsiders what we have come to regard as authentic Buddhist meditation.

In this connection it deserves notice that the ideas in the canon usually ascribed to the 'six heretics' contain nothing regarding meditation (see Basham, 1951: 10-26; Vogel, 1970).[19]

---

19. The opinions ascribed to these heretics may have been put together on the basis of different sources; see Basham, 1951: 25, 218-19; Norman, 1976a: 120-21.

The Buddhist canon tells us that the Buddha learned the Stage of Nothingness and the Stage of Neither Ideation nor Non-Ideation from two teachers, Ārāḍa Kālāma and Udraka the son of Rāma. Since the two stages which they allegedly taught him are not part of authentic Buddhist meditation (see ch. VII, above), we cannot draw any conclusions regarding pre-Buddhistic 'Buddhist meditation' from this account.

9.3.2. If then the Buddhist scriptures contain no reliable information that the Buddha got his meditational techniques from someone else, they contain some very clear passages that claim that the Buddha discovered these techniques himself.

First among these is the passage in which the Buddha to be remembers how he reached the First Dhyāna while still a child (§ 1.5, above). On the basis of this memory he is then said to have discovered the path leading to liberation.

Second come the passages where the Buddha is said to have made his discoveries 'among the things (*dharma*) which had not been heard of before'.[20] The phrase *pubbe ananussutesu dhammesu cakkhuṃ udapādi, ñāṇaṃ udapādi, paññā udapādi, vijjā udapādi, āloko udapādi* and its equivalents in other languages occur in many different contexts.[21] In the
[117] 'first sermon' it applies to the Four Noble Truths and consequently to the path of liberation discovered by the Buddha. Since this appears to be the oldest context to which the phrase applies, we must again conclude that the path taught by the Buddha, including his method of meditation, was considered a new discovery by his early followers.

9.4. We can sum up our findings regarding the origin of Buddhist meditation as follows. None of the early scriptures of India, whether Buddhist or non-Buddhist, contain any indication that the Buddhist form

---

20. *pūrvam ananuśruteṣu dharmeṣu / pubbe ananussutesu dhammesu*. See CPS p. 144-48; Mv III. 332-33; Vin I.11; SN II. 10-11, 105; IV. 233-34; V. 178-79; 258, 422; AN III.9; cf. SĀ^{C} p. 103c-104a; T. 1428, p. 788 a-b. T. 1421, p. 104c7 etc. interprets, no doubt incorrectly, 'things (*dharma*) which had not before been heard of *by me*'.
21. It is a 'pericope'. For an explanation and application of this useful concept see Griffiths, 1983.

of meditation existed prior to the beginnings of Buddhism. Some passages in the Buddhist canon, on the other hand, describe the Buddha as an innovator, also where the technique of meditation is concerned.

There seems little reason to doubt that Buddhist meditation was introduced by the founder of Buddhism, i.e., by the historical Buddha.

[120] X. Pratyekabuddhas, the Sutta Nipāta, and the early Saṅgha.

10.1. The previous chapter has made it clear that the early Buddhist tradition supports the view that the method of salvation preached by the Buddha was new and unknown before him. Unfortunately this point of view was not retained in the Buddhist tradition. On the one hand the historical Buddha came to be looked upon as one in a chain of Buddhas. On the other hand, a second category of Buddhas came to be accepted – the Pratyekabuddhas (P. Paccekabuddha) – who obtained enlightenment without the help of a Buddha (Samyaksaṃbuddha, P. Sammāsambuddha, contrasted with Pratyekabuddha), and did not preach the doctrine; they were supposed to have lived in periods not covered by the preaching of a Samyaksaṃbuddha, i.e., before Śākyamuni.

The acceptance of Pratyekabuddhas conflicts with our assumptions in a way which demands attention. The Pāli canon, it is believed, preserves utterances of Pratyekabuddhas in the *Khaggavisāṇa Sutta* of the *Sutta Nipāta*. This belief has essentially been accepted in a recent study by Wiltshire (1990),[1] who further argues that the Pratyekabuddha tradition in Buddhism preserves the memory of the time before Śākyamuni.

There is no doubt that the *Khaggavisāṇa Sutta* is old. It is commented upon in the canonical *Culla Niddesa*. At the same time, it contains an unmistakable reference to the Fourth Dhyāna in Sn 67.[2] Does this mean that the four Dhyānas were already known before Śākyamuni ?

---

1. Wiltshire (1990:17) takes care to state that he regards the Gāthās of the *Khaggavisāṇa Sutta* "as shedding light *conceptually* on [Pratyekabuddhas]".
2. *vipiṭṭhikatvāna sukhaṃ dukhañ ca*
pubbe va ca somanadomanassaṃ
laddhān 'upekhaṃ samathaṃ visuddhaṃ
eko care khaggavisāṇakappo
"Turning one's back on bliss and pain,
and earlier already on cheerfulness and dejection.
Obtaining pure indifference and calm,
one should walk alone like the horn of a rhinoceros."
Compare this with the description of the Fourth Dhyāna in § 1.5, above.

The answer to this question must be negative. There is no evidence that the *Khaggavisāṇa Sutta* is pre-Śākyamuni. Rather, this Sūtra contains a clear indication that it is later than 'our' Buddha: it refers to him. Sn 54cd reads:[3] "Observing the word of Ādiccabandhu, one should walk alone like the horn of a rhinoceros." Ādiccabandhu 'kinsman of the Ādicca family' (Fausböll, 1881: 8) is "[a]n often-used epithet of the Buddha" (Malalasekara, 1937-38: I: 245). In Sn 423 – to take but one example – the Buddha specifies the family to which he belonged as follows:[4] "Ādiccas by lineage, Sākiyas by birth; from that family I have wandered forth, oh king, not longing for sensual pleasures." The *Khaggavisāṇa Sutta* must therefore have been composed after, or at the earliest during the preaching of the Buddha.

How then could it be thought of as being composed by Pratyeka-buddhas ? The commentators obviously invented this explanation in order to be able to keep the Sutta without having to draw the consequences.[5] We [121]
must conclude that here again we have no reason to think that the Four Dhyānas existed before Śākyamuni.

10.2. Why were the later Buddhists hesitant to accept the *Khaggavisāṇa Sutta* as part of the post-Śākyamuni tradition ? The answer is not difficult. The *Khaggavisāṇa Sutta* celebrates the lonely wanderer. The later Buddhist monk, on the other hand, was part of a community of monks, and lived as a rule in a monastery. Solitary life was no longer common.

But the *Khaggavisāṇa Sutta* constitutes evidence that in the early days of Buddhism monks did often live alone. Other parts of the canon confirm this. The solitary life is often praised in the *Sutta Nipāta, Dhammapada, Thera Gāthā,* and elsewhere.[6] Life in monasteries seems to be still rather

---

3. *ādiccabandhussa vaco nisamma*
eko care khaggavisāṇakappo.
4. *ādiccā nāma gottena, sākiyā nāma jātiyā*
tamhā kulā pabbajito 'mhi rāja na kāme abhipatthayaṃ
5. Pj II. 104, Ap-a 181, Nidd II. 103.
6. Cf. Nakamura, 1979: 574-75. Przyluski (1926: 292) surmises that solitary ascetics primarily joined Buddhism in western regions, whereas in the east groups of monks travelled with a teacher. He derives support from the 12th Khandhaka of the *Cullavagga* (Vin II. 299) where *āraññakas* are found to be numerous in the west, no mention of them being made in the east, at the time of the Second Council.

uncommon in the time the Vinaya work called *Skandhaka* was composed (Frauwallner, 1956b: 121), i.e., at least forty years after the death of the Buddha (p. 117 above). This same work prescribed that "the monk should ... live under trees" (Frauwallner, 1956b: 74). Life in monasteries probably developed out of the habit to spend the rainy season at one place (Olivelle, 1974; Dutt, 1962: 53f.). Before this took place, and perhaps also to some extent simultaneously with it, followers of the Buddha led a wandering and often solitary life.

Works like the *Sutta Nipāta, Dhammapada* and *Thera Gāthā* derived wholly or in part from these early wanderers. This is confirmed by the fact that these works or parts of them are known to be among the oldest portions of the Buddhist canon.[7] The language of parts of the *Sutta Nipāta* is archaic (Fausböll, 1881: xi-xii). The *Aṭṭhaka Vagga, Pārāyaṇa* and *Khaggavisāṇa Sutta* – all part of the *Sutta Nipāta* – are commented upon in the *Niddesa*, itself considered a canonical work. The *Arthavargīyāṇi Sūtrāṇi* (= *Aṭṭhaka Vagga*) are referred to in all the versions corresponding to the original *Skandhaka* (Frauwallner, 1956b: 149; Lévi, 1915: 401-17; Bapat, 1951: Intr. p. 1-2). Other early enumerations often include *Pārāyaṇa, Satyadṛśa* (*Satyadṛṣṭa*), *Munigāthā, Śailagāthā*, probably all of them corresponding to parts of the *Sutta Nipāta*; and *Dharmapada, Thera* (*Sthavira*) *Gāthā*[8] (Lamotte, 1956: 258-61; 1957: 346-47).

10.3. If then the *Sutta Nipāta* and other collections of verses arose in circles where solitary wandering was held in high esteem, one might expect that these works in particular are likely to show traces of outside influence. Wanderers are more exposed to such influence than monks who reside in monasteries among their likes.

[122] Many of the verses in these works are such that they would be acceptable to Buddhists and non-Buddhists alike. They cannot help us to find outside influence. Some verses of the *Sutta Nipāta* however do show such influence:

---

7. Bechert (1961: 43f.) argues for a long and complicated history of the origin of the *Thera* and *Therī Gāthā*.
8. On the correspondence of *Thera* and *Sthavira Gāthā* see Bechert, 1961: 10-12.

The *Dvayatānupassanā Sutta* (Sn 724-65) enumerates a number of items – many of them also occur in the Pratītyasamutpāda – which cause suffering. Three of them are: *ārambha* 'effort', *āhāra* 'food', *iñjita* 'movement' (Sn 744-51). These three, like the other ones, have to be suppressed in order to prevent further suffering. Suppression of effort, food and movement sounds much like the asceticism we encountered in Jainism and Hinduism; the use of *ārambha* as a synonym of *karman* is familiar from the Jaina texts we studied in chapter III, above. Asceticism (*tapas*) is often approvingly referred to (Sn 77; 267; 284; 292; 655). Sleep is disapproved of (Sn 926).[9]

The presence of borrowed elements in the *Sutta Nipāta* and other collections of verses may be part of the reason why the canonicity of these works – though old – remained uncertain (Lamotte, 1956; 1957).

---

9. Main stream asceticism includes restriction of breathing, as we know. This is possibly meant in Sn 1090-91, where a question and answer regarding the one without desire, thirst and doubt is translated as follows by Fausböll (1881: 202-03): "Is he without breathing or is he breathing ... ? ... He is without breathing, he is not breathing ..." (*nirāsaso so uda āsasāno ... nirāsaso so na so āsasāno ...*). This translation can be defended by deriving *-āsasa* and *āsasāna* from *ā-śvas*. However, most scholars take the sense of these verses differently, either by accepting a v.l. (*nirāsayo; āsamāna*) or by interpreting the words in another way (see CPD s.v. *-āsasa, āsasāna*).

Dixit (1978: 86-92) argues that "there are Suttanipāta passages which throw interesting light on certain technical concepts of Jainism, concepts which obviously are not current among Buddhists" (p. 87). He concludes that "the presumption is strengthened that the two traditions were particularly close kins in the beginning" (p. 92). The *Sutta Nipāta* does not share many lines with the oldest books of the Jainas (Bollée, 1980).

[124]

Conclusion

XI. The position and character of early Buddhist meditation.

11.1. The results of this study can be briefly restated as follows : in the ancient Indian religious movements other than Buddhism there was a tradition of asceticism and meditation which can be described and understood as direct and consistent answers to the belief that action leads to misery and rebirth. In this tradition some attempted to abstain from action, literally, while others tried to obtain an insight that their real self, their soul, never partakes of any action anyhow. Combinations of these two answers were also formed.

The Buddhist scriptures criticize this tradition repeatedly. Yet practices and ideas connected with this tradition appear to have made their way into the Buddhist community. Some of these practices and ideas even came to occupy rather central positions in the Buddhist tradition. Practices of this kind include the Eight Liberations, or at any rate the last five steps of them, which also occur in other contexts in the Buddhist canon; and the Brahmic States. Among the ideas which influenced Buddhism, the gradual postponement of liberation to the time after death, and the prominence of an explicit liberating insight must be mentioned.

11.2. We have come as far as philology could take us, it seems. For a further understanding of Buddhist meditation, philology will probably not be of much help. An altogether different approach may be required to proceed further. Such a different approach does not fall within the scope of the present book. I may return to it in another study.

Abbreviations

AMg.	Ardha Māgadhī
AN	Aṅguttara Nikāya (PTS ed.)
Ap-a	Apadāna-aṭṭhakathā (PTS ed.)
ĀpDhS	Āpastambīya Dharma Sūtra
Āv.	Āvassaya Sutta
Āyār.	Āyāraṃga Sutta
BĀU	Bṛhadāraṇyaka Upaniṣad
BhG	Bhagavad Gītā
CPD	Critical Pāli Dictionary
CPS	Catuṣpariṣatsūtra
DĀ^{c}	Dīrghāgama (T. 1)
Daśo	Daśottara Sūtra (= Mittal, 1957, and Schlingloff, 1962)
Dhs	Dhammasaṅgaṇi
DN	Dīgha Nikāya (PTS ed.)
EĀ^{c}	Ekottara Āgama (T. 125)
HYPr	Haṭha Yoga Pradīpikā of Svātmārāma
It	Itivuttaka (PTS ed.)
KU	Kaṭha Upaniṣad
MĀ^{c}	Madhyamāgama (T. 26)
MBh	Mahābhārata
MN	Majjhima Nikāya (PTS ed.)
MPS	Mahāparinirvāṇasūtra (ed. Waldschmidt)
MU	Maitrāyaṇīya Upaniṣad
MuktU	Muktikā Upaniṣad
Mv	Mahāvastu
Nidd I	Mahā-niddesa (PTS ed.)

Nidd II	Culla-niddesa (PTS ed.)
P.	Pāli
Paṭis	Paṭisambhidā-magga (PTS ed.)
Paṭis-a	Saddhammapakāsinī (Ct. on Paṭis), Bangkok 1922
Pj II	Sutta-nipāta-aṭṭhakathā, Paramattha-jotikā II (PTS ed.)
Pkt.	Prakrit
Pp	Puggala-paññatti (PTS ed.)
PTS	Pāli Text Society
SĀ[c]	Saṃyuktāgama (T. 99)
Sang	Sangīti Sūtra (= Stache-Rosen, 1968)
ŚB	Śatapatha-Brāhmaṇa (Mādhyandina version)
SN	Saṃyutta Nikāya
Sn	Sutta-nipāta (PTS ed.)
Sp	Samanta-pāsādikā, ct. on Vin (PTS ed.)
Sūy.	Sūyagaḍaṃga Sutta
T.	Taishō edition of the Tripiṭaka in Chinese
Th	Thera-gāthā (PTS ed.)
Ṭhāṇ.	Ṭhāṇaṃga Sutta
Ud	Udāna (PTS ed.)
Uttar.	Uttarajjhayaṇa
Uvav.	Uvavāiya
Vin	Vinaya-piṭaka I-V (PTS ed.)
Vism	Visuddhi-magga (PTS ed.)
Viy.	Viyāhapaṇṇatti Sutta
VS	Vaiśeṣika Sūtra of Kaṇāda
YS	Yoga Sūtra

Primary Sources

Abhinavagupta, *Tantrāloka*. Vol. III. Edited by Pandit Madhusūdan Kaul. Bombay: Tatva-Vivechaka Press. 1921. (Kashmir Series of Texts and Studies, No. XXX.)

Agniveśa, *Caraka Saṃhitā*. Edited, with the commentary Āyurvedadīpikā of Cakrapāṇidatta, by Vaidya Jādavaji Trikamji Āchārya. Bombay: Nirṇaya Sāgar Press. 1941.

Annapūrṇa Upaniṣad = Shastri, 1970: 493-509.

Āpastambīya Dharma Sūtra. Edited by George Bühler. Third Edition. Poona: Bhandarkar Oriental Research Institute. 1932. (Bombay Sanskrit Series Nos. XLIV and L.)

Aśvaghoṣa, *Buddhacarita*. Edited by E. H. Johnston. Calcutta: Baptist Mission Press. 1935.

Āvassaya Sutta. Edited by Muni Shri Puṇyavijayaji and Pt. Amritlāl Mohanlāl Bhojak. Bombay: Shri Mahāvīra Jaina Vidyālaya. 1977. (Jaina-Āgama-Series No. 15, pp. 331-58.)

Āyāraṃga Sutta / Ācārāṅga Sūtra. 1. Edited by Muni Jambūvijaya. Bombay: Shrī Mahāvīra Jaina Vidyālaya. 1976. (Jaina-Āgama-Series No. 2(I).) 2. See Schubring, 1910.

Bṛhadāraṇyaka Upaniṣad = Limaye-Vadekar, 1958: 174-282.

Catuṣpariṣatsūtra. Herausgegeben und bearbeitet von Ernst Waldschmidt. Teil II-III: Textbearbeitung. Berlin: Akademieverlag. 1957-62. (Abhandlungen der Deutschen Akademie der Wissenschaften zu Berlin, Klasse für Sprachen, Literatur und Kunst, Jahrgang 1956, Nr. 1 - Jahrgang 1960, Nr.l.)

Chāndogya Upaniṣad = Limaye-Vadekar, 1958: 68-173.

Gautama, *Nyāya Sūtra*. Edited, with Vātsyāyana's Bhāṣya and Viśvanātha's Vṛtti, by Digambara Nāgeśa Jośī. Poona: Ānanda Āśrama. 1922. (Ānandāśramasaṃskṛtagranthāvali, 91).

Gheraṇḍa Saṃhitā. Edited and translated by Rai Bahadur Srisa Chandra Vasu. Delhi: Sri Satguru Publications. 1981.

Ṭhāṇaṃga Sutta. 1. Edited by Muni Jambūvijaya. Bombay: Shrī Mahāvīra Jaina Vidyālaya. 1985 (Jaina-Āgama-Series No. 3, pp. 1-322). 2. Edited by Muni Nathamal. Ladnun: Jain Viswa Bhārati. V.S. 2031 (Anga Suttāni I, pp. 489-823).

Triśikhibrāhmaṇa Upaniṣad = Sastri, 1920: 116-51.

Uttarajjhayaṇa. Edited by Muni Shri Puṇyavijayaji and Pt. Amritlāl Mohanlāl Bhojak. Bombay: Shri Mahāvīra Jaina Vidyālaya. 1977. (Jaina-Āgama-Series no. 15, pp. 85-329.)

Umāsvāti, *Tattvārthādhigama Sūtra*. See Jacobi, 1906.

Uvavāiya = Das Aupapātika Sūtra, erstes Upānga der Jaina. I. Theil. Einleitung, Text und Glossar. Von Ernst Leumann. Leipzig, 1883. Genehmigter Nachdruck, Kraus reprint Ltd., Nendeln, Liechtenstein, 1966. (Abhandlungen für die Kunde des Morgenlandes, VIII. Band, No. 2.)

Vasubandhu, *Abhidharmakośabhāṣya*. Edited by P. Pradhan. Revised second edition with introduction and indices etc., by Aruna Haldar. Patna: K.P. Jayaswal Research Institute. 1975.

Viṣṇusmṛti. Edited, with the commentary Keśavavaijayantī of Nandapaṇḍita, by Pandit V. Krishnamacharya, Part II. Madras: Adyar Library and Research Centre. 1964.

Viyāhapaṇṇatti Sutta / Bhagavaī. 1. Edited by Pt. Bechardas J. Doshi, assisted by Pt. Amritlal Mohanlal Bhojak. Bombay: Shri Mahāvīra Jaina Vidyālaya. Part II. 1978. (Jaina-Āgama-Series No. 4 (Part 2).) 2. Edited by Muni Nathamal. Ladnun: Jain Viswa Bhārati. (Anga Suttāni II.)

Yājñavalkyasmṛti. Edited, with the commentary Bālakrīḍā of Viśvarūpācārya, by T. Gaṇapati Sastrī. Part II: Prāyaścittādhyāya. Trivandrum: Government Press. 1924.

Yoga Bhāṣya. In: Pātañjalayogadarśanam. Vācaspatimiśraviracita-Tattvavaiśāradī-Vijñānabhikṣukṛta-Yogavārttikavibhūṣita-Vyāsabhāṣyasametam. Edited by Nārāyaṇa Miśra. Vārāṇasī: Bhāratīya Vidyā Prakāśana. 1971.

Yogakuṇḍalī Upaniṣad = Sastri, 1920: 307-36.

Yogaśikhā Upaniṣad = Sastri, 1920: 390-463

Yoga Sūtra. See *Yoga Bhāṣya*.

Modern Authors

Alsdorf, Ludwig: 1951, "Pañcatantra-Miszellen." ZDMG 100 (1950), 356-61. Reprinted: *Kleine Schriften.* Wiesbaden: Franz Steiner. 1974. Pp. 586-91.

Alsdorf, Ludwig: 1965, *Les études jaina* : État présent et tâches futures. Paris: Collège de France.

Alsdorf, Ludwig: 1966, *The Āryā Stanzas of the Uttarajjhāyā.* Contributions to the text history and interpretation of a canonical Jaina text. Wiesbaden: Franz Steiner. (Akademie der Wissenschaften und der Literatur, Abhandlungen der Geistes- und Sozialwissenschaftlichen Klasse, Jahrgang 1966, Nr. 2.)

Alsdorf, Ludwig: 1967, *Die Āryā-Strophen des Pāli-Kanons metrisch hergestellt und textgeschichtlich untersucht.* Akademie der Wissenschaften und der Literatur, Abh. d. Geistes- und Sozialw. Kl., Jahrgang 1967, Nr. 4.

Alsdorf, Ludwig: 1969, "Verkannte Mahāvastu-Strophen". WZKS 12-13 (1968-69; Festschrift Erich Frauwallner), 13-22. Reprinted: *Kleine Schriften,* pp. 370-79.

Bapat, P. V.: 1937, "Dhutangas (or the ascetic practices of purification in Buddhism)." IHQ 13, 44-51.

Bapat, P. V.: 1951, *The Arthapada Sutra.* Santiniketan: Visva-Bharati. (Visva-Bharati Studies 13.)

Bapat, P. V.: 1964, *Vimuktimārga: Dhutaguṇa-Nirdeśa.* A Tibetan text critically edited and translated into English. London: Asia Publishing House.

Bareau, André: 1955, *Les sectes bouddhiques du Petit Vehicule.* Paris: École Française d'Extrême-Orient. (Publications de l'École Française d'Extrême-Orient, Volume XXXVIII.)

Bareau, André: 1957, "Les controverses relatives à la nature de l'Arhant dans le Bouddhisme ancien." IIJ 1, 241-50.

Bareau, André: 1962, "La légende de la jeunesse du Buddha dans les Vinayapiṭaka anciens." Oriens Extremus 9, 6-33.

Bareau, André: 1963, *Recherches sur la biographie du Buddha dans les Sūtrapiṭaka et les Vinayapiṭaka anciens* : De la quête de l'éveil à la conversion de Maudgalyāyana. Paris: École Française d'Extrême-Orient. (Publications de l'École Française d'Extrême-Orient, Volume LIII.)

Bareau, André: 1970-71, *Recherches sur la biographie du Buddha dans les Sūtrapiṭaka et les Vinayapiṭaka anciens* : II. Les derniers mois, le parinirvāṇa et les funérailles. Tome I-II. Paris: École Française d'Extrême-Orient. (Publications de l'École Française d'Extrême-Orient, Volume LXXVII.)

Bareau, André: 1980, "The place of the Buddha Gautama in the Buddhist religion during the reign of Aśoka." Buddhist Studies in Honour of Walpola Rahula. London: Gordon Fraser; in collaboration with Vimamsa, Sri Lanka. Pp. 1-9.

Barnes, Michael Anthony: 1976, *The Buddhist Way of Deliverance* : A Comparison between the Pāli Canon and the Yoga-praxis of the Great Epic. Unpublished thesis. Oxford University.

Barua, Benimadhab: 1934, *Barhut*. Book I. Stone as a Storyteller. Calcutta: Indian Research Institute. (Indian Research Institute Publications, Fine Arts Series - No. 1.)

Basham, A. L.: 1951, *History and Doctrines of the Ājīvikas* : A Vanished Indian Religion. Delhi: Motilal Banarsidass. 1981.

Basham A. L.: 1982, "Asoka and Buddhism – a reexamination." Journal of the International Association of Buddhist Studies 5, 131-43.

Bechert, Heinz: 1961, *Bruchstücke buddhistischer Verssammlungen aus zentralasiatischen Sanskrithandschriften*. 1. Die Anavataptagāthā und die Sthaviragāthā. Berlin: Akademie-Verlag. (Deutsche Akademie der Wissenschaften zu Berlin, Institut für Orientforschung, Veröffentlichungen Nr. 51.)

Bechert, Heinz: 1974, "Buddhismus." Taschenlexikon für Religion und Theologie. Göttingen. Pp. 130-46.

Bechert, Heinz: 1982, "The date of the Buddha reconsidered." Indologica Taurinensia 10, 29-36.

Bedekar, V. M.: 1963a, "The Dhyānayoga in the Mahābhārata." BhV 20-21 (1960-61; Munshi Indological Felicitation Volume), 116-25.

Bedekar, V. M.: 1963b, "'Dhāraṇā' and 'Codanā' (Yogic terms) in the Mokṣadharmaparvan of the Mahābhārata in their relationship with the Yogasūtras." BhV 22 (1962), 25-32.

Bernard, Theos: 1950, *Haṭha Yoga*. The report of a personal experience. London: Rider. 1967.

Bhaskar, Bhagchandra Jain: 1972, *Jainism in Buddhist Literature*. Nagpur: Alok Prakashan.

Bhattacharya, Kamaleswar: 1968, "upadhi-, upādi-, et upādāna- dans le canon bouddhique pāli." Mélanges d'Indianisme (à la mémoire de Louis Renou). Paris: E. de Boccard. Pp 81-95. (Publications de l'Institut de Civilisation Indienne, Serie In-8° , Fascicule 28.)

Bhattacharya, Kamaleswar: 1973, *L'Ātman-Brahman dans le Bouddhisme ancien*. Paris: École Française d'Extrême-Orient. (Publications de l'École Française d'Extrême-Orient, Volume XC)

Bollée, Willem B.: 1971, "Anmerkungen zum buddhistischen Häretikerbild." ZDMG 121, 70-92.

Bollée, Willem B.: 1974, "Buddhists and Buddhism in the earlier literature of the Śvetāmbara Jains." Buddhist Studies in Honour of I. B. Horner. Dordrecht-Boston: D. Reidel. Pp. 27-39.

Bollée, Willem B.: 1977, *Studien zum Sūyagaḍa*. Teil I. Wiesbaden: Franz Steiner. (Schriftenreihe des Südasien-Instituts der Universität Heidelberg, Band 24.)

Bollée, Willem B.: 1980, *The Pādas of the Suttanipāta with Parallels from the Āyāraṅga, Sūyagaḍa, Uttarajjhāyā, Dasaveyāliya and Isibhāsiyāiṃ*. Reinbek: Inge Wezler. (Studien zur Indologie und Iranistik, Monographie 7).

Bronkhorst, Johannes: 1980, "Asiddha in the Aṣṭādhyāyī: a misunderstanding among the traditional commentators ?" JIP 8, 69-85.

Bronkhorst, Johannes: 1981, "The orthoepic diaskeuasis of the Ṛgveda and the date of Pāṇini." IIJ 23, 83-95.

Bronkhorst, Johannes: 1982b, "The Ṛgveda-Prātiśākhya and its Śākhā." StII 8/9, 77-95.

Bronkhorst, Johannes: 1982c, "The variationist Pāṇini and Vedic: a review article." IIJ 24, 273-82.

Bronkhorst, Johannes: 1983, "On the history of Pāṇinian grammar in the early centuries following Patañjali." JIP 11, 357-412.

Bronkhorst, Johannes: 1985a, "Patañjali and the Yoga sūtras." StII 10 (1984), 191-212.

Bronkhorst, Johannes: 1985b, "Akālika in the Buddhist canon." StII 10 (1984), 187-190.

Bronkhorst, Johannes: 1986, *Tradition and Argument in Classical Indian Linguistics*: the Bahiraṅga-Paribhāṣā in the Paribhāṣenduśekhara. Dordrecht: Reidel.

Bronkhorst, Johannes: 1991, "Pāṇini and the Veda reconsidered". *Pāṇinian Studies*. Professor S. D. Joshi Felicitation Volume. Ed. by Madhav M. Deshpande and Saroja Bhate. University of Michigan: Center for South and Southeast Asian Studies. Number 37. Pp. 75-121.

Brough, John: 1980, "Sakāya Niruttiyā: Cauld kale het". Die Sprache der ältesten Buddhistischen Überlieferung / The Language of the Earliest Buddhist Tradition. (Symposien zur Buddhismusforschung, II.) Edited by Heinz Bechert. Göttingen: Vandenhoeck & Ruprecht. Pp. 35-42.

Bruhn, Klaus: 1981, "Āvaśyaka studies I." Studien zum Jainismus und Buddhismus. Gedenkschrift für Ludwig Alsdorf. Wiesbaden: Franz Steiner. (Alt- und Neu-Indische Studien, 23.) Pp. 11-49.

Bühler, Georg: 1879. *The Sacred Laws of the Āryas*. Part I. Āpastamba and Gautama. Oxford: Clarendon Press.

Caillat, Colette: 1977, "Fasting unto death according to Āyāraṅga-Sutta and to some Paiṇṇayas." Mahāvīra and his Teachings. Edited by A. N. Upadhye et al. Bombay: Bhagavān Mahāvīra 2500th Nirvāṇa Mahotsava Samiti. Pp. 113-17.

Cardona, George: 1976, *Pāṇini: A Survey of Research*. The Hague-Paris: Mouton.

Collins, Steven: 1987, Review of the *The Two Traditions...* JRAS, 1987, 373-75.

Critical Pāli Dictionary. Begun by V. Trenckner. Copenhagen: Munksgaard. 1924f.

Dantinne, Jean : 1991, *Les qualités de l'ascète* (*Dhutaguṇa*). Étude sémantique et doctrinale. Bruxelles: Thanh-Long.

De Jong, J. W.: 1982, Review of *Die Sprache der ältesten buddhistischen Überlieferung* edited by Heinz Bechert (1980), IIJ 24, 215-18.

Demiéville, Paul: 1928, "Sur la mémoire des existences antérieures." BEFEO 27 (1927), 283-98.

Demiéville, Paul: 1929, "Bombai: la psalmodie en Inde." Hōbōgirin, fasc. I, pp. 93-95.

Dixit, K. K.: 1978, *Early Jainism*. Ahmedabad: L.D. Institute of Indology. (L.D. Series 64).

Dutoit, Julius: 1905, *Die duṣkaracaryā des Bodhisattva in der buddhistischen Tradition*. Strassburg: Karl J. Trübner.

Dutt, Sukumar: 1962, *Buddhist Monks and Monasteries of India*. Their history and their contribution to Indian culture. London: George Allen and Unwin.

Edgerton, Franklin: 1924, "The meaning of Sāṅkhya and Yoga." American Journal of Philology 45, 1-46.

Eggeling, Julius (tr.): 1882, *The Śatapatha-Brāhmaṇa according to the Text of the Mādhyandina School*. Part I. Delhi: Motilal Banarsidass. 1966.

Eimer, Helmut: 1976, *Skizzen des Erlösungsweges in buddhistischen Begriffreihen*. Bonn: Religionswissenschaftliches Seminar der Universität Bonn. (Arbeitsmaterialien zur Religionsgeschichte, 1.)

Eliade, Mircea: 1967, *Le Yoga : immortalité et liberté*. Paris: Petite Bibliothèque Payot.

Esnoul, Anne-Marie: 1968, "Notes sur quatre Upaniṣad." Mélanges d'Indianisme (à la mémoire de Louis Renou). Paris: E. de Boccard. Pp. 279-88. (Publications de l'Institut de Civilisation Indienne, Serie In-8°, Fascicule 28.)

Fausböll, V. (tr.): 1881, *The Sutta-Nipāta*. Delhi-Patna-Varanasi: Motilal Banarsidass. 1973. (Sacred Books of the East, Vol. X, Part II.)

Feer, M.: 1870, "Études bouddhiques: les quatre vérités et la prédication de Bénarès. (Dharma-cakra-pravartanam)." JA Sixième Série, Tome XV, 345-472.

Franke, R. Otto: 1913, *Dīghanikāya*. Das Buch der langen Texte des buddhistischen Kanons in Auswahl übersetzt. Göttingen: Vandenhoeck & Ruprecht.

Franke, R. Otto: 1917, "Die Buddhalehre in ihrer erreichbar-ältesten Gestalt (im Dīghanikāya)". ZDMG 71, 50-98.

Frauwallner, Erich: 1925, "Untersuchungen zum Mokṣadharma: die sāṃkhyistischen Texte." WZKM 32, 179-206. Reprinted: *Kleine Schriften*. Wiesbaden: Franz Steiner. 1982. (Glasenapp-Stiftung, Band 22.) Pp. 55-82.

Frauwallner, Erich: 1953, *Geschichte der indischen Philosophie*. I. Band. Salzburg: Otto Müller.

Frauwallner, Erich: 1956a, *Geschichte der indischen Philosophie*. II. Band. Salzburg: Otto Müller. (Reihe Wort und Antwort, Band 6/II.)

Frauwallner, Erich, 1956b, *The Earliest Vinaya and the Beginnings of Buddhist Literature*. Roma: Is.M.E.O. (Serie Orientale Roma, VIII.)

Frauwallner, Erich: 1971, "Abhidharma-Studien." III. Der Abhisamayavādaḥ (p. 69-102). IV. Der Abhidharma der anderen Schulen (p. 103-21). WZKS 15, 69-121.

Gethin, R. M. L. : 1992, *The Buddhist Path to Awakening*. A study of the Bodhi-Pakkhiyā Dhammā. Leiden: E. J. Brill. (Brill's Indological Library, 7.)

Gombrich, Richard F.: 1988, *Theravāda Buddhism*. A social history from ancient Benares to modern Colombo. London and New York: Routledge & Kegan Paul.

Gombrich, Richard: 1990, "Recovering the Buddha's message." = Ruegg and Schmithausen, 1990: 5-23.

Griffiths, Paul: 1981, "Concentration or insight: the problematic of Theravāda Buddhist meditation-theory." *The Journal of the American Academy of Religion* 49, 605-24.

Griffiths, Paul: 1983, "Buddhist jhāna: a form-critical study." *Religion* 13, 55-68.

Gusdorf, Georges: 1988, *Les origines de l'herméneutique*. Paris: Payot.

Halbfass, Wilhelm: 1980, "Karma, apūrva, and 'natural' causes: observations on the growth and limits of the theory of saṃsāra." *Karma and Rebirth in Classical Indian Traditions*. Edited by Wendy Doniger O'Flaherty. Berkeley - Los Angeles - London: University of California Press. Pp. 268-302.

Hanefeld, Erhardt: 1976, *Philosophische Haupttexte der älteren Upaniṣaden*. Wiesbaden: Otto Harrassowitz. (Freiburger Beiträge zur Indologie, Band 9.)

Harvey, Peter: 1990, *An Introduction to Buddhism*. Teachings, history and practices. Cambridge University Press.

Heiler, Friedrich: 1922, *Die buddhistische Versenkung*. 2. vermehrte und verbesserte Auflage. München: Ernst Reinhardt.

Hinüber, Oskar von: 1968, *Studien zur Kasussyntax des Pāli, besonders des Vinaya-Piṭaka*. München: J. Kitzinger.

Hinüber, Oskar von: 1976, "Sprachliche Beobachtungen zum Aufbau des Pāli-Kanons." StII 2, 27-40.

Hinüber, Oskar von: 1989, *Der Beginn der Schrift und frühe Schriftlichkeit in Indien*. Stuttgart : Franz Steiner.

Hinüber, Oskar von: 1991, "Linguistic considerations on the date of the Buddha." In: *The Dating of the Historical Buddha / Die Datierung des historischen Buddha*. Part 1. Ed. by Heinz Bechert. Gottingen: Vandenhoeck & Ruprecht. (Symposien zur Buddhismusforschung, IV, 1) Pp. 183-193.

Hoernle, A. F. Rudolf: 1907, *Studies in the Medicine of Ancient India*. Part I. Osteology or the Bones of the Human Body. Oxford: Clarendon Press.

Hohenberger, A.: 1960, *Rāmānuja: Ein Philosoph indischer Gottesmystik*. Bonn: Selbstverlag des Orientalischen Seminars der Universität Bonn. (Bonner Orientalische Studien, Neue Serie, Band 10.)

Hopkins, E. Washburn: 1901, "Yoga-technique in the Great Epic." JAOS 22, 333-79.

Horner, Isaline Blew: 1936, *The Early Buddhist Theory of Man Perfected*. A study of the arahan concept and of the implications of the aim to perfection in religious life. Amsterdam: Philo Press. 1975.

Horsch, Paul: 1964, "Buddhas erste Meditation." AS 17, 100-54.

Horsch, Paul: 1966, *Die vedische Gāthā und Śloka-Literatur*. Bern: Francke.

Hume, Robert Ernest (tr.): 1931, *The Thirteen Principal Upanishads*. Second edition, revised. Oxford University Press. 1975.

Jacobi, Hermann: 1880: "On Mahāvīra and his predecessors." IA 9, 158-63.

Jacobi, Hermann (tr.): 1884, *Jaina Sūtras*. Part I. The Ācārāṅga Sūtra; the Kalpa Sūtra. Delhi-Patna-Varanasi: Motilal Banarsidass. 1980. (Sacred Books of the East, vol. XXII.)

Jacobi, Hermann (tr.): 1895, *Jaina Sūtras*. Part II. The Uttarādhyayana Sūtra; the Sūtrakṛtāṅga Sūtra. 2nd reprint. Delhi-Patna-Varanasi: Motilal Banarsidass. 1968. (Sacred Books of the East, Vol. XLV.)

Jacobi, Hermann: 1906, "Eine Jaina-Dogmatik: Umāsvāti's Tattvārthādhigama Sūtra übersetzt und erlautert." ZDMG 60, 287-325 and 512-51.

Jaini, Padmanabh S.: 1979, *The Jaina Path of Purification*. Berkeley-Los Angeles-London: University of California Press.

Jaini, Padmanabh S.: 1980, "Karma and the problem of rebirth in Jainism." *Karma and Rebirth in Classical Indian Traditions*. Edited by Wendy Doniger O'Flaherty. Berkeley-Los Angeles-London: University of California Press. Pp. 217-38.

Jha, V. N.: 1979, Review of Nyāyokti-Kośa by Chhabinath Mishra, Ajanta Publications, Delhi, 1978: ABORI 60, 274-76.

Johansson, Rune E. A.: 1979, *The Dynamic Psychology of Early Buddhism*. London-Malmö: Curzon Press. New Delhi – Calcutta-Bombay: Oxford and IBH.

Kamptz, Kurt von: 1929, *Über die vom Sterbefasten handelnden älteren Paiṇṇa des Jaina-Kanons*. Dissertation Hamburg.

Karunaratne, W. S.: 1976, "The effortless way to Nirvāṇa." Malalasekera Commemoration Volume. Edited by O. H. de A. Wijesekera. Colombo. Pp. 180-86.

Keith, A. Berriedale: 1923. *Buddhist Philosophy in India and Ceylon*. Varanasi: Chowkhamba Sanskrit Series Office. 1963. (Chowkhamba Sanskrit Studies, Vol. XXVI.)

Kiparsky, Paul: 1980, *Pāṇini as a Variationist*. Edited by S. D. Joshi. Pune: Centre of Advanced Study in Sanskrit, University of Poona. (Pubications of the Centre of Advanced Study in Sanskrit, Class B, No. 6.)

Kiparsky, Paul: 1982, *Some Theoretical Problems in Pāṇini's Grammar*. Poona: Bhandarkar Oriental Research Institute. (Post-graduate and Research Department Series No. 16.)

Klimkeit, Hans-Joachim: 1990, *Der Buddha*. Leben und Lehre. Stuttgart - Berlin - Koln: Kohlhammer. (Urban-Taschenbucher, 438.)

Koelman, Gaspar M.: 1970, *Pātañjala Yoga* : From Related Ego to Absolute Self. Poona: Papal Athenaeum.

Kumoi, Shozen: 1969, "Der Nirvāṇa-Begriff in den kanonischen Texten des Frühbuddhismus." WZKS 12/13 (Festschrift für Erich Frauwallner), 205-13.

Lamotte, Etienne: 1956, "Problèmes concernant les textes canoniques 'mineurs'." JA 244, 249-64.

Lamotte, Etienne: 1957, "Khuddakanikāya and Kṣudrakapiṭaka." EW 7, 341-48.

Lamotte, Etienne, 1958, *Histoire du Bouddhisme indien*. Des origines à l'ère Śaka. Louvain: Université de Louvain, Institut Orientaliste. Réimpr. 1967.

Lamotte, Etienne: 1967, "Un Sūtra composite de l'Ekottarāgama." BSOAS 30, 105-16.

Lamotte, Etienne: 1970, *Le Traité de la Grande Vertu de Sagesse*. Tome III. Louvain: Institut Orientaliste, Université de Louvain. (Publications de l'Institut Orientaliste de Louvain, 2.)

Lamotte, Etienne: 1977, "Die bedingte Entstehung und die höchste Erleuchtung." Beiträge zur Indienforschung (Festschrift Ernst Waldschmidt). Berlin: Museum für Indische Kunst. Pp. 279-98.

Lamotte, Etienne: 1980, "Conditioned Co-production and Supreme Enlightenment." Buddhist Studies in Honour of Walpola Rahula. London: Gordon Fraser. Pp. 118-32.

La Vallée Poussin, Louis de: 1923-31, *L'Abhidharmakośa de Vasubandhu*. Paris: Paul Geuthner.

La Vallée Poussin, Louis de: 1925, *Nirvāṇa*. Paris: Gabriel Beauchesne. (Études sur l'Histoire des Religions, 4)

La Vallée Poussin, Louis de: 1937a, "Le Bouddhisme et le Yoga de Patañjali." Mélanges chinois et bouddhiques 5, 223-42.

La Vallée Poussin, Louis de: 1937b, "Musīla et Nārada." Mélanges chinois et bouddhiques 5, 189-222.

La Vallée Poussin, Louis de: 1937c, "Documents d'Abhidharma: Les deux, les quatre, les trois vérités." Mélanges chinois et bouddhiques 5, 159-87.

Law, Bimala Churn (tr.): 1924, *Designation of Human Types* (Puggala-Paññatti). London: Pāli Text Society. (Translation Series, No. 12.)

Leumann, E.: 1885a, "Die alten Berichte von den Schismen der Jaina." IS 17, 91-135.

Leumann, E.: 1885b, "Beziehungen der Jaina-Literatur zu andern Literaturkreisen Indiens." *Actes du Sixième Congrès International des Orientalistes tenu en 1883 à Leyde*. Troisième Partie, Section 2: Aryenne. Leyde: E. J. Brill. Pp. 467-564.

Lévi, Sylvain: 1915, "Sur la récitation primitive des textes bouddhiques." JA Onzième Série, Tome V, pp. 401-47.

Lévi, Sylvain (ed. and tr.): 1932, *Mahākarmavibhaṅga et Karmavibhaṅgopadeśa*. Paris: Librairie Ernest Leroux.

Limaye, V. P., and Vadekar, R. D. (ed.): 1958, *Eighteen Principal Upaniṣads*, Vol. I. Upaniṣadic Text with Parallels from Vedic Literature, Exegetical and Grammatical Notes. Poona: Vaidika Saṃśodhana Maṇḍala.

Lin Li-kouang: 1949, *L'Aide-Mémoire de la Vraie Loi* (*Saddharma-Smṛtyupasthāna-Sūtra*). Recherches sur un Sūtra développé du Petit Vehicule. Paris: Librairie d'Amérique et d'Orient.

Lüders, Heinrich: 1941, *Bhārhut und die buddhistische Literatur*. Leipzig: F. A. Brockhaus. (Abhandlungen für die Kunde des Morgenlandes XXVI, 3.)

Malalasekera, G. P.: 1937-38, *Dictionary of Pāli Proper Names*. 2 Vol. London: Pāli Text Society. 1974.

Malvania, Dalsukh D.: 1981, "Beginnings of Jaina philosophy in the Ācāraṅga." Studien zum Jainismus und Buddhismus. Gedenkschrift für Ludwig Alsdorf. Wiesbaden: Franz Steiner. (Alt- und Neu-Indische Studien, 23.) Pp. 151-53.

Mehta, Mohanlal, and Chandra, K. Rishabh: 1970-72, *Āgamic Index*. Vol I. Prakrit Proper Names. Parts I-II. Edited by Dalsukh Malvania. Ahmedabad: L. D. Institute of Indology. (Lalbhai Dalpatbhai Series, No. 28, 37.)

Minard, Armand: 1968, "Sur les divisions du Śatapatha-Brāhmaṇa." Mélanges d'Indianisme (à la mémoire de Louis Renou). Paris: E. de Boccard. Pp. 523-28. (Publications de l'Institut de Civilisation Indienne, Série In-8°, Fasc. 28.)

Mishra, Umesha: 1936, *Conception of Matter according to Nyāya-Vaiśeṣika*. Allahabad.

Mukherjee, Biswadeb: 1966, *Die Überlieferung von Devadatta, dem Widersacher des Buddha, in den kanonischen Schriften*. München: J. Kitzinger. (Münchener Studien zur Sprachwissenschaft, Beiheft I.)

Nakamura, Hajime: 1979, "Aspects of original Buddhism." *Ludwik Sternbach Felicitation Volume*. Part I. Lucknow: Akhila Bharatiya Sanskrit Parishad. Pp. 573-78.

Nobel, Johannes: 1955, *Udrāyaṇa, König von Roruka. Eine buddhistische Erzählung*. Erster Teil: Tibetischer Text, deutsche Übersetzung und Anmerkungen. Wiesbaden: Otto Harrassowitz.

Norman, K. R.: 1971, "Middle Indo-Aryan studies VIII." JOIB 20, 329-36.

Norman, K. R.: 1976, "The labialisation of vowels in Middle Indo-Aryan." StII 2, 41-58.

Norman, K. R.: 1976a, "Pāli and the language of the heretics." Acta Orientalia 37, 117-26.

Norman, K. R.: 1980, "The dialects in which the Buddha preached." *Die Sprache der ältesten buddhistischen Überlieferung*. Edited by Heinz Bechert. Göttingen: Vandenhoeck & Ruprecht. Pp. 61-77.

Nowotny, Fausta: 1976, *Das Gorakṣaśataka*. Köln: Karl A. Nowotny. (Dokumente der Geistesgeschichte 3.)

Nyanatiloka: 1976, *Buddhistisches Wörterbuch.* Konstanz: Christiani. (Buddhistische Handbibliothek, 3.)

Oberhammer, Gerhard: 1984, *Wahrheit und Transzendenz*: Ein Beitrag zur Spiritualität des Nyāya. Wien : Verlag der Österreichischen Akademie der Wissenschaften.

Oldenberg, Hermann: 1915, *Die Lehre der Upanishaden und die Anfänge des Buddhismus*. Göttingen : Vandenhoeck & Ruprecht.

Olivelle, Patrick: 1974, *The Origin and the Early Development of Buddhist Monachism.* Colombo: M. D. Gunasena & Co.

Pande, Govind Chandra: 1974, *Studies in the Origins of Buddhism.* Second Revised Edition. Delhi: Motilal Banarsidass.

Pandey, Kant Chandra: 1963, *Abhinavagupta: A Historical and Philosophical Study.* Second edition, revised and enlarged. Varanasi: Chowkhamba Sanskrit Series Office. (Chowkhamba Sanskrit Studies, Vol. I.)

Pensa, Corrado: 1973, "Observations and references for the study of ṣaḍaṅgayoga . " *Yoga Quarterly Review* 4, 9-24.

Pérez-Remón, Joaquín: 1980, *Self and Non-Self in Early Buddhism.* The Hague-Paris-New York: Mouton. (Religion and Reason, 22.)

Pischel, R.: 1900, *A Grammar of the Prākrit Languages.* Translated from German by Subhadra Jhā. Second Revised Edition. Delhi-Varanasi-Patna: Motilal Banarsidass. 1981.

Potter, Karl H. (ed.): 1977, *Encyclopedia of Indian Philosophies.* Vol. II. Indian Metaphysics and Epistemology. The tradition of Nyāya-Vaiśeṣika up to Gaṅgeśa. Delhi-Varanasi-Patna: Motilal Banarsidass.

Przyluski, Jean: 1926, *Le concile de Rājagṛha.* Introduction à l'histoire des canons et des sectes bouddhiques. Paris: Paul Geuthner. (Buddhica, première série: mémoires – tome II.)

Rhys Davids, Caroline A. F. (tr.): 1900, *A Buddhist Manual of Psychological Ethics entitled Dhamma-Saṅgaṇi.* London: Pāli Text Society. 1974. (Pāli Text Society Translation Series No. 41.)

Rhys Davids, T. W. and C. A. F.: 1921, *Dialogues of the Buddha.* Translated from the Pali of the Dīgha Nikāya. Part III. London: Humphrey Milford, Oxford University Press. (Sacred Books of the Buddhists, Vol. IV).

Rowland, Benjamin: 1967, *The Art and Architecture of India: Buddhist / Hindu / Jain*. Third revised edition. Penguin Books. (The Pelican History of Art.)

Ruegg, David Seyfort: 1989, *Buddha-nature, Mind and the Problem of Gradualism in a Comparative Perspective*. On the transmission and reception of Buddhism in India and Tibet. London: School of Oriental and African Studies. (Jordan Lectures 1987)

Ruegg, David Seyfort, and Schmithausen, Lambert (ed.)(1990): *Earliest Buddhism and Madhyamaka*. Leiden: Brill. (Panels of the VIIth World Sanskrit Conference, vol. II.)

Sastri, A. Mahadeva (ed.): 1920, *The Yoga Upaniṣads with the Commentary of Śri Upaniṣad-Brahmayogin*. Madras: The Adyar Library and Research Centre. 1968 .

Schmidt, Kurt: 1953, *Leer ist die Welt*. Buddhistische Studien. Konstanz: Christiani.

Schmithausen, Lambert: 1969, "Ich und Erlösung im Buddhismus." ZMR 53, 157-70 .

Schmithausen, Lambert, 1976, "Die vier Konzentrationen der Aufmerksamkeit." ZMR 60, 241-66 .

Schmithausen, Lambert, 1978, "Zur Struktur der erlösenden Erfahrung im indischen Buddhismus." In : Gerhard Oberhammer (ed.): Transzendenzerfahrung, Volzugshorizont des Heils. Wien, 1978. Pp. 97-119.

Schmithausen, Lambert: 1981, "On some aspects of descriptions or theories of 'Liberating Insight' and 'Enlightenment' in Early Buddhism." *Studien zum Jainismus und Buddhismus*. Gedenkschrift für Ludwig Alsdorf. Wiesbaden: Franz Steiner. Pp. 199-250.

Schmithausen, Lambert: 1986, "Critical response." In : *Karma and Rebirth : post-classical developments*. Edited by Ronald W. Neufeldt. State University of New York Press. Pp. 203-230.

Schmithausen, Lambert: 1990, "Preface" = Ruegg and Schmithausen, 1990: 1-4.

Schneider, Ulrich: 1980, *Einführung in den Buddhismus*. Darmstadt: Wissenschaftliche Buchgesellschaft.

Schubring, Walther: 1910, *Ācārāṅga-Sūtra* : Erster Śrutaskandha. Text, Analyse und Glossar. Leipzig: F. A. Brockhaus.

Schubring, Walther: 1926, *Worte Mahāvīras*. Kritische Übersetzungen aus dem Kanon der Jaina. Göttingen: Vandenhoeck & Ruprecht.

Schubring, Walther: 1935, *Die Lehre der Jainas*. Berlin und Leipzig: Walter de Gruyter u. Co. (Grundriß der Indo-Arischen Philologie und Altertumskunde, III. Band, 7. Heft.)

Schumann, Hans Wolfgang: 1957, *Bedeutung und Bedeutungsentwicklung des Terminus Saṃkhāra im frühen Buddhismus*. Dissertation Bonn.

Senart, Emile: 1900, "Bouddhisme et Yoga." RHR 42, 345-64.

Shastri, J. L. (ed.): 1970, *Upaniṣat-Saṃgrahaḥ*. Containing 188 Upaniṣads. Reprinted 1980. Delhi-Varanasi-Patna: Motilal Banarsidass.

Sprockhoff, Joachim Friedrich: 1962, "Die Vorbereitung der Vorstellung der Erlösung bei Lebzeiten in den Upaniṣads." WZKS 6, 151-78.

Sprockhoff, Joachim Friedrich: 1963, "Die Idee der Jīvanmukti in den späten Upaniṣads." WZKS 7, 190-208.

Sprockhoff, Joachim Friedrich: 1964, "Der Weg zur Erlösung bei Lebzeiten, ihr Wesen und ihr Wert, nach dem Jīvanmuktiviveka des Vidyāraṇya." WZKS 8, 224-62.

Sprockhoff, Joachim Friedrich: 1976, *Saṃnyāsa: Quellenstudien zur Askese im Hinduismus*. I. Untersuchungen über die Saṃnyāsa-Upaniṣads. Wiesbaden: Franz Steiner. (Abhandlungen für die Kunde des Morgenlandes, XLII, 1.)

Sprockhoff, Joachim Friedrich: 1981, "Āraṇyaka und Vānaprastha in der vedischen Literatur." WZKS 25, 19-90.

Strong, D. M. (tr.): 1902, *The Udāna or the Solemn Utterances of the Buddha*. London: Luzac & Co.

Tatia, Nathmal: date unknown, "The interaction of Jainism and Buddhism and its impact on the history of Buddhist monasticism." *Studies in History of Buddhism*. Edited by A. K. Narain. Pp. 321-38.

Tatia, Nathmal, and Kumar, Muni Mahendra: 1980, "Cittasamāhiṭṭhānas or the ten stages of the concentrated mind." *Aspects of Jaina Monasticism* = Tulasī-Prajñā (The Journal of the Jain Vishva Bharati) 6 (English Section), 36-40. (*Aspects of Jaina Monasticism* has been published as a separate book as well, by Today and Tomorrow's Printers and Publishers, New Delhi, 1981.)

Thieme, Paul: 1935, *Pāṇini and the Veda*. Studies in the early history of linguistic science in India. Allahabad: Globe Press.

Thomas, E. J.: 1947, "Nirvāṇa and parinirvāṇa." *India Antiqua* (presented to Jean Philippe Vogel). Leyden: E. J. Brill. Pp 294-95.

Van Buitenen, J. A. B.: 1962, *The Maitrāyaṇīya Upaniṣad*. A critical essay, with text, translation and commentary. 's-Gravenhage: Mouton.

Verclas, Katrin: 1978, *Die Āvaśyaka-Erzählungen über die Upasargas des Mahāvīra im vergleich mit den Versuchungen des Bodhisattva in der buddhistischen Literatur*. Dissertation Hamburg.

Vetter, Tilmann: 1983, Review of Pérez-Remón, 1980. WZKS 27, 211-15.

Vetter, Tilmann: 1988, *The Ideas and Meditative Practices of Early Buddhism*. Leiden : E. J. Brill.

Vogel, Claus: 1970, *The Teachings of the Six Heretics*. Wiesbaden: Franz Steiner. (Abhandlungen für die Kunde des Morgenlandes, XXXIX. Band.)

Waldschmidt, Ernst: 1951, "Vergleichende Analyse des Catuṣpariṣatsūtra." *Festschrift Walther Schubring*. Hamburg. Pp 84-122. Reprinted: Von Ceylon bis Turfan. (Festgabe Ernst Waldschmidt). Göttingen: Vandenhoeck & Ruprecht. 1967. Pp. 164-202.

Waldschmidt, Ernst: 1967, *Von Ceylon bis Turfan*. Festgabe zum 70. Geburtstag. Göttingen: Vandenhoeck & Ruprecht.

Weber, Albrecht: 1850a: "Über die Literatur des Sāmaveda." IS 1, 25-67.

Weber, Albrecht: 1850b, "Zwei Sagen aus dem Çatapatha-Brāhmaṇa über Einwanderung und Verbreitung der Ārier in Indien, nebst einer geographisch-geschichtlichen Skizze aus dem Weissen Yajus." IS 1, 161-232.

Weber, Albrecht: 1876, *Akademische Vorlesungen über indische Literaturgeschichte*. Zweite, vermehrte, Auflage. Berlin: Harrwitz u. Gossmann.

Welbon, G. R.: 1968, *The Buddhist Nirvāṇa and its Western Interpreters*. Chicago.

Wezler, Albrecht: 1975, *Bestimmung und Angabe der Funktion von Sekundärsuffixen durch Pāṇini*. Wiesbaden: Franz Steiner.

Wezler, Albrecht: 1978, *Die wahren 'Speiseresteesser'* (*Skt. vighasāśin*). Beiträge zur Kenntnis der indischen Kultur- und Religionsgeschichte I. Wiesbaden: Franz Steiner. (Akademie der Wissenschaften und der Literatur : Abhandlungen der Geistes- und Sozialwissenschaftlichen Klasse, Jahrgang 1978, Nr. 5.)

Wezler, Albrecht: 1982, "Remarks on the definition of 'yoga' in the Vaiśeṣikasūtra." *Indological and Buddhist Studies. Festschrift J. W. de Jong*. Canberra: Faculty of Asian Studies. Pp. 643-86.

Wiltshire, Martin G. : 1990, *Ascetic Figures before and in Early Buddhism*. Berlin - New York : Mouton de Gruyter.

Winternitz, Moriz: 1920, *Geschichte der indischen Literatur*. Band 2. Die buddhistische Literatur und die heiligen Texte der Jainas. Stuttgart: K. F. Köhler. 1968.

Woods, James Haughton (tr.): 1914, *The Yoga-system of Patañjali*. Third Edition. Delhi-Varanasi-Patna: Motilal Banarsidass. 1966.

Woodward, F. L. (tr.): 1936, *The Book of the Gradual Sayings* (*Aṅguttara-Nikāya*), vol. V. London: Luzac and Co. 1955. (PTS Translation Series, No. 27.)

Index

Ājīvikas	9, 16
ākāśānantyāyatana / ākāsānañcāyatana	80, 82-84, 87, 89, 91-93
ākiñcanyāyatana / ākiñcaññāyatana	81-85, 87, 89, 91-93, 122
anupubbanirodha	89-91
anupūrvavihāra / anupubbavihāra	90-91
Ārāḍa / Āḷāra Kālāma	17, 18, 75, 79, 85-86, 122
arhant / arahant	5, 9-10, 12, 15, 91, 95, 97
ārūpya / arūpa	83
asceticism	10, 16, 20, 22, 27, 30, 36n.13, 42, 51-52, 56-60, 65-66, 78, 96, 102, 112, 127, 128
Bhārhut	19
Bodhisattva	1, 15, 17, 19, 20, 22, 85-87, 104
brahmavihāra	93-94, 128
Bṛhadāraṇyaka Upaniṣad, date of	112f.
Devadatta	78
dhutaṅgas	79
Digambaras	11
enlightenment	9, 15, 19-20, 23, 43, 85, 94, 96-98, 100, 102-104, 106, 110, 119, 124
fasting	1-22, 30, 32-37, 45-46, 50-53, 58, 64, 76
First Dhyāna	22, 70-71, 74, 88-90, 104, 122
Four Dhyānas	23-24, 30, 42, 70, 74, 77, 87-90, 95, 108, 110, 124-125
Four Noble Truths	100-101, 104-111, 122

insight	54f., 71-75, 99-103, 106-111, 128
Jaina practices	9, 15-17, 22-23, 26-30, 31f., 79 n.2, 88-89, 94-95, 112, 127
Jātakas	19
jñānayoga	55
karmayoga	54, 55, 59 n.16
Kātyāyana	113-115
liberation	35-37, 54-57, 59, 61-64, 74 n.7, 77, 91, 96-102, 106-111, 120-122, 128
main stream	53, 68, 71, 76-77, 78-80, 87-89, 91, 93, 95, 96, 99-102, 110-111, 112, 127 n.9
maṅgura	8, 10-11, 15
meditation without breath	1-5, 9, 11, 13-15, 17-18, 20-21, 30
naivasaṃjñānāsaṃjñāyatana / nevasaññānāsaññāyatana	81-92, 122
Nigaṇṭha	16-18, 26-29, 88
nirodhasamāpatti	99
nirvāṇa	24 n.36, 68, 70, 97-99, 102
non-activity	26-30, 31-40, 43-44, 45-53, 54-55, 57, 59, 63, 67, 68 72-73, 79, 87-89, 99, 127, 128
Nyāya-Vaiśeṣika	61-63
Original Mahāsaccaka Sūtra	18, 22-24, 48-49, 53, 79
Pāṇini	112 n.1, 113-114, 116-117, 121
parinirvāṇa	97-98
Patañjali, grammarian	112 n.1, 113-114, 116
restraint of breath	1f., 30, 47, 49-50, 52, 65-67, 76, 80 n.4, 89, 127 n.9
Śākalya	115-116
saṃjñā- / saññāvedayitanirodha	81, 86, 89-90, 99, 102, 108

sāṃkhya	55, 57, 63, 102, 118
saṃskāra / saṃkhāra	72-73, 75-76
sattvāvāsa / sattāvāsa	84
Skandhaka	20 n.26
smṛti / sati	74 n.7, 75, 88, 95
soul, nature of	54-59, 61-64, 71, 77, 99, 112, 118, 128
standing erect	26, 29-31, 34
śukladhyāna / sukkajjhāṇa	37-42, 44, 87
tarka	47-48
transmigration	118-121
Udraka / Uddaka the son of Rāma	17-18, 75, 85-87, 122
Vaiśeṣika	61-64
vāsanā	75-77
Vedānta	57
vijñānānantyā- / viññāṇañcāyatana	81, 83-84, 87, 91, 93
vijñānasthiti / viññāṇaṭṭhiti	83-84
vimokṣa / vimokkha	80, 86, 128
Vrātyas	10 n.8
Yājñavalkya	113, 114-116, 118
yoga	46-47, 49, 55, 60, 64-66, 68-74, 76-77, 102, 112 n.1